Anatomy of a Patent Case

Second Edition

Intellectual Property Titles from Bloomberg BNA

Anatomy of a Patent Case by American College of Trial Lawyers

Biotechnology and the Federal Circuit by Kenneth J. Burchfiel

Constructing and Deconstructing Patents by Irah H. Donner

Copyright Law Deskbook by Robert W. Clarida

Drafting Patent License Agreements by Brian G. Brunsvold, D. Patrick O'Reilley, and D. Brian Kacedon

Drafting Patents for Litigation and Licensing Bradley C. Wright, *Editor-in-Chief*

Electronic and Software Patents: Law and Practice Steven W. Lundberg, Stephen C. Durant, and Ann M. McCrackin, *Editors-in-Chief* and ALPIA

Harmon on Patents: Black-Letter Law and Commentary by Robert L. Harmon

Intellectual Property Law in Cyberspace by G. Peter Albert, Jr. and AIPLA

Intellectual Property, Software, and Information Licensing: Law and Practice by Xuan-Thao N. Nguyen, Robert W. Gomulkiewicz, and Danielle Conway

Intellectual Property Taxation: Transaction and Litigation Issues by Jeffrey A. Maine and Xuan-Thao N. Nguyen

Intellectual Property Technology Transfer Aline C. Flower, *Editor-in-Chief*

International Patent Litigation: A Country-by-Country Analysis Edited by Michael N. Meller and William O. Hennessey

Patents and the Federal Circuit by Robert L. Harmon, Cynthia A. Homan, and Charles M. McMahon

Patent Law and Practice by Herbert F. Schwartz and Robert J. Goldman

Patent Infringement Remedies by Lawrence M. Sung

Patent Litigation Strategies Handbook Barry L. Grossman and Gary M. Hoffman, *Editors-in-Chief*

Patent Prosecution: Law, Practice, and Procedure by Irah H. Donner

Patent, Trademark, and Copyright Laws Edited by Jeffrey M. Samuels

Pharmaceutical Patent Law by John R. Thomas

Post-Grant Patent Practice by Nancy J. Linck, Bruce H. Stoner, Lee E. Barrett, and Carol A. Spiegel

Products Comparison Manual for Trademark Users by Francis M. Pinckney and David R. Higgins

Trademark Dilution: Federal, State, and International Law by David S. Welkowitz

Trademark Infringement Remedies Brian E. Banner, *Editor-in-Chief*

Trademark Litigation Practice by David S. Fleming and John T. Gabrielides

Anatomy of a Patent Case

Second Edition

prepared by the

Complex Litigation Committee
of the
American College of Trial Lawyers

Bloomberg
BNA

Bloomberg BNA, Arlington, VA

American College of Trial Lawyers
19900 McArthur Boulevard, Suite 530
Irvine, California 92612
Telephone: (949) 752-1801
Facsimile: (949)752-1674
E-mail: nationaloffice@actl.com
Website: www:actl.com

Library of Congress Cataloging-in-Publication Data

Anatomy of a patent case / Henry B. Gutman, Editor-in-Chief.
p. cm.
Previous ed. prepared by American College of Trial Lawyers. Complex Litigation Committee.
Includes bibliographical reference and index.
ISBN 978-1-61746-180-4
1. Patent suits--United States. 2. Patent laws and legislation--United States. 3. Trial practice--United States. I. Gutman, Henry B.
KF3155.A96 2012
346.7304'86--dc23

2012022749

Published by Bloomberg BNA
1801 S. Bell Street, Arlington, VA 22202
bna.com/bnabooks

ISBN 978-1-61746-180-4
Printed in the United States of America

Board of Contributors

Editors-in-Chief

HENRY B. GUTMAN
Simpson Thacher & Bartlett LLP
New York, New York

JOHN L. COOPER
Farella Braun + Martel, LLP
San Francisco, California

GEORGE F. PAPPAS
Covington & Burling, LLP
Washington, D.C.

Contributing Authors

GEORGE E. BOWLES *Locke Lord LLP* *Dallas, Texas*	HENRY B. GUTMAN *Simpson Thacher & Bartlett LLP* *New York, New York*
CHRISTINE W.S. BYRD *Irell & Manella, LLP* *Los Angeles, California*	ROY W. HARDIN *Locke Lord LLP* *Dallas, Texas*
JOSEPH A. CALVARUSO *Orrick, Herrington & Sutcliffe, LLP* *New York, New York*	HON. ROGER T. HUGHES *Justice of the Federal Court of Canada* *Ottawa, Ontario*
STEVEN CHERNY *Kirkland & Ellis, LLP* *New York, New York*	NOAH LEIBOWITZ *Simpson Thacher & Bartlett LLP* *New York, New York*

Morgan Chu *Irell & Manella, LLP* *Los Angeles, California*	Robert Long *Covington & Burling LLP* *Washington, D.C.*
John L. Cooper *Farella Braun + Martel, LLP* *San Francisco, California*	Brandy R. McMillion *Perkins Coie LLP* *Chicago, Illinois*
Ronald E. Dimock *Dimock Stratton LLP* *Toronto, Ontario, Canada*	George F. Pappas *Covington & Burling, LLP* *Washington, D.C.*
Ford F. Farabow, Jr. *Finnegan, Henderson, Farabow, Garrett & Dunner, LLP* *Washington, D.C.*	Nancy L. Schroeder *WilmerHale LLP* *New York, New York*
Alexander C.D. Giza *Irell & Manella LLP* *Los Angeles, California*	Michael O. Warnecke *Perkins Coie, LLP* *Chicago, Illinois*
Lawrence B. Goodwin *Kasowitz Benson Torres & Friedman LLP* *New York, New York*	Kenneth S. Weitzman *Weitzman Law Offices, LLC* *Roseland, New Jersey*
Michael Graif *Curtis, Mallet-Prevost, Colt & Mosle, LLP* *New York, New York*	Daiske Yoshida *Latham & Watkins, LLP* *Tokyo, Japan*
Robert J. Gunther, Jr. *WilmerHale LLP* *New York, New York*	

Judicial Board of Review

Circuit Courts of Appeals

Federal District Courts

Preface to the Second Edition

When George Pappas and his co-editors, John Cooper and Morgan Chu, and a collection of talented contributing authors, created the original edition of this work in 2009, the idea was to write a simple handbook of patent litigation: a short and concise guide that both practitioners and the judiciary would find useful and easily accessible, as they wrestled with the issues and problems that are unique to patent cases. Consistent with that goal, the editors assumed that the reader would already have a basic familiarity with the Federal Rules of Civil Procedure and Evidence and the case law interpreting both. The editors worked hard to strip from the draft any generalized discussion of procedural or evidentiary issues that was not focused on what makes patent litigation different.

Their efforts met with great success. The first edition, published jointly by BNA and the Federal Judicial Center, which distributed copies to all United States District Judges, became a best seller. Not only did the work, in fact, provide the concise and usable guide the editors intended, but patent litigators were understandably anxious to own the same book that the judges who try patent cases turn to for guidance.

Much has happened in the world of patent litigation since the original publication. Numerous important new patent decisions have come from the Supreme Court and the Court of Appeals for the Federal Circuit and, after decades of debate, Congress enacted and the President signed into law the America Invents Act, the first major revision of patent law since 1952. These developments led the Complex Litigation Committee of the American College of Trial Lawyers to conclude that it was time for a Second Edition of the book.

In creating the Second Edition, our objective has been to adhere to the premise of the original edition, while updating the existing chapters to address important new cases and adding three new chapters concerning:

(i) the America Invents Act,
(ii) special Considerations in Hatch-Waxman Litigation (an important and growing area in patent litigation), and
(iii) the Use of Special Masters in Patent Cases. We have done our best to keep the text short and simple and to focus on those things that distinguish patent litigation from other forms of civil litigation. We hope that the judges who decide patent cases and the lawyers who practice before them will continue to find this a useful guide to the unique issues that arise in patent litigation.

The Second Edition is the product of the substantial efforts of a talented team of contributing authors and editors, particularly those authors of chapters of the original edition who graciously agreed to update their work. These include George Bowles, Lawrence Goodwin, Robert Gunther, Roy Hardin, Michael Warnecke, as well as Ronald Dimock, who updated the chapter on Canadian law. Special thanks are due to John Cooper and Noah Leibowitz, who authored the new chapters written expressly for this Second Edition. George Pappas and John Cooper not only updated their own prior work, but continued to perform admirably as editors—making sure that we all adhered to the mission and met the high standards set by the original edition. None of this would have been possible without the hard work of this exceptional group of patent litigators.

We would also like to extend our gratitude to the Federal Judicial Center and, in particular, to Judge Jeremy Fogel, for reviewing and commenting on our draft. And thanks to all the fine judges, serving on our Judicial Board of Review, who have inspired and helped guide this effort from the beginning.

Of course, this project depended upon the continued support and encouragement of the American College of Trial Lawyers, under the leadership of Presidents Gregory P. Joseph, Thomas H. Tongue and Chilton Davis Varner. All of us involved in working on this book understood that the effort was born of the College's commitment to promoting excellence in the trial bar. It was an honor to be part of such a distinguished team.

HENRY B. GUTMAN
Chair, Complex Litigation Committee
American College of Trial Lawyers

October 2012

Preface

Conflicts over intellectual property, and specifically over patents, have assumed a pivotal role in the world economy. Fred Warshofsky, in his 1994 book *The Patent Wars*, wrote:

> In the war for global economic dominance, the fiercest battles today are over intellectual property. Where nations once fought for control of trade routes and raw materials, they now fight for exclusive rights to ideas, innovations, and inventions. The battlefields in this bloodless war are the world's courts, where billions of dollars are won and lost each year through patent litigation. Beyond licensing fees and individual companies' rights to manufacture specific products, what is at stake is the ultimate control of key high-tech industries such as biotechnology, electronics, and communications.

Legislation proposing significant patent law reform was considered by the Congress in the last few years for the first time since 1952, the last time significant changes were enacted to the patent statute.

Judgments and settlements in favor of patent holders routinely amount to millions of dollars and recently have even reached the one billion dollar mark. Injunctions are often sought, and sometimes these injunctions command wide public attention, as evidenced by the 2003 Research in Motion (RIM) litigation where the patent holder prevailed and Blackberry users faced the real possibility that an injunction would be entered that would have disrupted the continued use of those devices.

Against this background, the Complex Litigation Committee of the American College of Trial Lawyers (ACTL) was charged in 2005 with drafting a manual detailing a patent case for the purpose of informing judges and lawyers not familiar with patent litigation of commonly used practices in this area of the law. Our intention was to prepare a concise, narrative summary of the steps required to bring a patent case to trial and of the key elements of such litigation.

This idea originated with a suggestion by ACTL Judicial Fellow the Honorable Garr M. (Mike) King and was endorsed by former ACTL President David W. Scott and the Regents of the College. The Committee formed a Working Group consisting of members of the Complex Litigation Committee, other members of the College, and other experienced patent practitioners. Working Group members reviewed the many published treatises on patent litigation and determined that none addressed the issues in the form of a concise guide to patent litigation for trial judges and lawyers. The object of this manual is to offer suggestions as to how judges and lawyers may deal with some of the procedural problems presented in patent litigation. We hope that this manual will add to the resources currently available.

The Committee would like to acknowledge the efforts of the following members of the Working Group who contributed to this project: George E. Bowles, Christine W.S. Byrd, Joseph A. Calvaruso, Steven Cherny, Morgan Chu, John L. Cooper, Ford F. Farabow, Jr., Lawrence B. Goodwin, Michael Graif, Robert J. Gunther, Jr., Roy W. Hardin, George F. Pappas, Michael O. Warnecke, and Ken S. Weitzman. The Editorial Committee, chaired by George F. Pappas and ably assisted by John L. Cooper and Morgan Chu, blended the several chapters into a condensed text.

The Committee owes special thanks to the following judges who reviewed our draft outline and provided meaningful suggestions: District Judges William H. Alsup, P. Kevin Castel, David J. Folsom, Garr M. (Mike) King, Kathleen M. O'Malley, James L. Robart, Fern M. Smith, Sam Sparks, Thomas John Ward, and Ronald M. Whyte, Third Circuit Judge Kent A. Jordan, Federal Circuit Chief Judge Paul R. Michel, and Federal Circuit Senior Judge S. Jay Plager.

The project would have been impossible without the assistance and support of several past Presidents of the College, including David W. Scott, James W. Morris III, Michael A. Cooper, David J. Beck, and Mikel L. Stout, and current President John J. (Jack) Dalton.

The American College of Trial Lawyers' Statement of Purpose is included below.

JOHN NYHAN
Chair

GEORGE F. PAPPAS
Vice Chair
Complex Litigation Committee
American College of Trial Lawyers

American College of Trial Lawyers' Statement of Purpose

The American College of Trial Lawyers, founded in 1950, is composed of the best of the trial bar from the United States and Canada. Fellowship in the College is extended by invitation only, after careful investigation, to those experienced trial lawyers who have mastered the art of advocacy and those whose professional careers have been marked by the highest standards of ethical conduct, professionalism, civility, and collegiality. Lawyers must have a minimum of 15 years' experience before they can be considered for Fellowship. Membership in the College cannot exceed one percent of the total lawyer population of any state or province. Fellows are carefully selected from among those who represent plaintiffs and those who represent defendants in civil cases; those who prosecute and those who defend persons accused of crime. The College is thus able to speak with a balanced voice on important issues affecting the administration of justice. The College strives to improve and elevate the standards of trial practice, the administration of justice and the ethics of the trial profession.

Summary Table of Contents

Detailed Table of Contents

1

The Pizza Box Case: Anatomy of a Case for Patent Novices*

I. Introduction

This chapter describes a hypothetical case for judges and lawyers who are new to patent litigation. The case is hypothetical, but the patent is real. There are differences and similarities between a patent case and other civil suits in federal court. The focus here will be on the important differences.

*Morgan Chu, Irell & Manella LLP, Los Angeles, California.

II. The Patent

In this case, Carmela Vitale owns a patent. Vitale's patent is entitled "Package Saver." The patent is short, a total of three pages. The patent tries to solve a problem for pizza delivery boxes: The top cover of a pizza box sags into the hot cheese. The invention is a small plastic device that sits on top of the pizza and holds up the box cover so that it will not sag. Figures 1 and 2 from the patent show this best. The annotations for each number in the figures are added, but they come from the body of the patent.

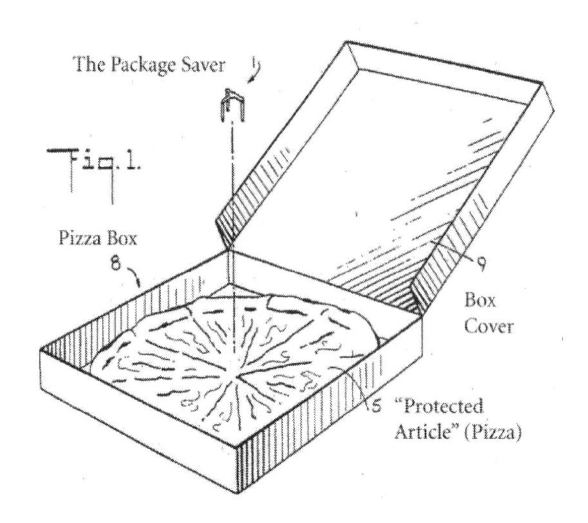

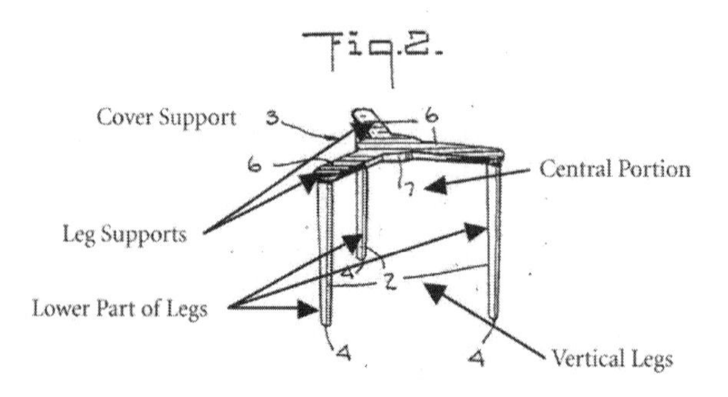

A. *Patent Terms*

The Vitale patent is reproduced at the end of this chapter (Section H). The first page of a patent has some basic information. The Vitale patent application was filed February 10, 1983. On many patents, there is also a statement of earlier filing dates for related applications. The earliest filing date is often the date claimed by the inventor as his or her "priority date." The priority date is used to decide what articles, patents, and devices known to the public can be used as prior art to determine whether the patent is new and nonobvious over the prior art.

Vitale's patent was issued February 12, 1985, two years after the application. This is not unusual. Most patent applications take two or more years before they are issued.

The Vitale patent number is 4,498,586. This means it is the 4,498,586th patent issued in the United States since the first head of the patent office, Thomas Jefferson, issued the first U.S. patent. As a matter of convenience, people dealing with patents often use the last three digits of the patent number to refer to a specific patent, so people commonly refer to the Vitale patent as the '586 patent.

The "claims," which appear at the end of a patent, define the invention. Claims are granted by the U.S. Patent Office. Claims are similar to the metes and bounds that define real property. A patent is property; it is a deed for an idea.

Before the claims, the phrase "I claim" or "we claim" usually appears. The Vitale patent states:

> Having thus described my invention, I claim:
>
> 1. in combination a package having a flexible cover, a food article packaged therein and spaced downwardly from the cover, a unitary molded plastic package saving device for positioning between the cover and the article for supporting the package cover thereby preventing damage to the packaged food article by the cover, said device comprising the combination of *three or more spaced legs, each leg having one relatively flat end* adapted for engaging the packaged article and having its opposite end attached to a device cover portion."

Claims have "limitations" or "elements." For example, two of the limitations (italicized above) in claim 1 are "three or more spaced legs" and "each leg having one relatively flat end."

The patent is infringed only if all of the limitations are met. For example, if someone has a device that has a pedestal (one leg) or two legs, but everything else is the same as claimed in the patent, then there is no literal infringement because the claim requires "three or more spaced legs." As another example, if "each leg" does not have "one relatively flat end," then there would be no literal infringement.

Suppose there are three spaced legs, two of them have "relatively flat ends," but one of them has a rounded end. Does it infringe? Literally, no.

An equitable doctrine developed to take account of these situations. Where there is no literal infringement, there can be infringement under the "doctrine of equivalents" if the difference between the claims and the allegedly infringing device are "insubstantial." There is a huge body of law on this question, and applying it to a particular situation can be difficult.

Generally, juries are asked to decide both whether there is literal infringement and whether there is infringement under the doctrine of equivalents.

Claim 1 is an "independent claim," which means it stands on its own. In contrast, claims 2, 3, and 4 of the Vitale patent are "dependent claims." Dependent claims always refer to another claim. In this case, the dependent claims all refer to claim 1. This means that all of the limitations of claim 1 are included in each dependent claim. The dependent claims add at least one additional limitation. Dependent claims are always narrower than the independent claims on which they "depend."

Claims are read in light of a patent's "specification." The specification includes all of the text and figures that come before the claims. Sometimes the specification defines claim terms, but usually it just describes the invention and one or more "preferred embodiments." A preferred embodiment does not limit the scope of the claims. Instead, it is merely one example of how to "practice," or use, the invention.

The "prosecution history" is the official written record before the patent office. This includes the patent application, the response of the patent office, which is usually called an "office action," and the ensuing back-and-forth between the applicant and the patent office. The prosecution history is also called the "file wrapper."

A patent's specification and its prosecution history are considered "intrinsic evidence" and are the primary sources for interpreting the scope of a patent's claims. There is a rough analogy to contracts, where the language of the contract is considered to be intrinsic evidence.

"Extrinsic evidence" for patents is everything else that might be used to interpret the patent. This includes dictionaries, inventor testimony, expert testimony, articles, and other patents. In the contract analogy, extrinsic evidence includes the negotiating history leading up to the signing of the contract and the conduct of the parties afterward.

In interpreting disputed claim terms in a patent, much more weight is given to intrinsic evidence in comparison to extrinsic evidence, though all forms of evidence may be considered. The evidence may be considered in any order the court deems appropriate.

B. Pleadings and Motions

As with many suits, patent cases often involve early motions to dismiss for failure to state a cause of action, for lack of jurisdiction, or for improper venue. Some special rules apply to patent cases, but the basic principles are the same or nearly the same as those in other cases.

In our hypothetical case, Vitale sues PizzaBoxCo in the District of Venus. The next day, PizzaBoxCo files a declaratory relief action in the District of Mars, asking for a declaration that the '586 patent is invalid and not infringed. This battle over forums is common because some district courts are viewed as being patent friendly or unfriendly. The District of Mars transfers the case to Venus, applying its circuit's first-to-file rule.

C. Patent Reexamination

After a patent has been issued, it may be reexamined by the U.S. Patent Office. The Patent Office usually decides to conduct the reexamination in response to a petition from the patent owner, the defendant in patent litigation, or anyone else, although in a very small number of cases, the patent office decides on its own—without a petition from anyone—to reexamine a patent. The entire reexamination process usually takes at least one to two years, but there is large variation among reexamined patents. At the end of the process, claims may be canceled, allowed without any amendment, or allowed with specific amendments.

PizzaBoxCo files a petition for reexamination of the patent. The petition is granted. That means the patent office decided formally to reexamine the validity of the patent. PizzaBoxCo then moves to stay the litigation pending the outcome of the patent office's reexamination.

PizzaBoxCo's motion argues that the litigation should be stayed pending reexamination because the court should not expend its resources and those of the parties when claims of Vitale's patent may change. In other words, why should the court conduct litigation that involves a moving target? Vitale opposes the motion, arguing that the reexamination is a delaying tactic and statistics show a very high percentage of patents emerge from reexaminations without meaningful changes.

Courts have discretion to grant or deny the requested stay. Each case is fact-specific, but statistically, stays are often granted.

The Venus court denies PizzaBoxCo's motion. The court expresses a concern that granting the motion would prematurely end our hypothetical tale.

D. Discovery

Some districts have enacted specific rules for patent cases, and the Federal Circuit Advisory Council has promulgated a Model Order to address electronic discovery issues.[1] The rules usually require the patent owner to identify with specificity the infringing products and the claims that are infringed, and to state how each product infringes each claim. The rules also require "claim charts." A claim chart sets forth each limitation in a claim and charts the limitation against the components of the allegedly infringing product. The alleged infringer then must state in writing all bases on which the patent is alleged to be invalid, including the specific identification of invalidating prior art.

The parties continue to exchange in writing their positions on infringement and validity. They will also identify any claim terms they believe should be defined by the court and describe their differing views on how those claim terms should be interpreted.

Most districts have not enacted specific patent rules. Many individual judges have developed their own scheduling orders, often based on the local patent rules of other districts.

---

[1] *See infra* Chapter 7.

Here, Vitale and PizzaBoxCo jointly propose a specific schedule to exchange positions on:

- infringement;
- validity; and
- claim terms to be construed by the court.

The court adopts the proposal at its initial scheduling conference. The parties then begin to exchange positions, and they later employ the normal discovery devices of serving interrogatories and taking corporate, fact, and expert depositions.

E. Claim Construction

"Claim construction" is unique for patent cases. The Supreme Court required judges to decide the meaning of disputed claim terms in its *Markman*[2] decision.[3] Oral argument for claim construction is often called a *Markman* hearing. There is an analogy to statutes, albeit a somewhat imperfect one. When the meaning of a statute is disputed, judges are required to decide on the proper interpretation; it cannot be left to a jury. Usually there are many claim terms in dispute. Some judges have tried to limit the number of claim terms for interpretation. In *Vitale v. PizzaBoxCo,* there is a dispute over the meaning of only one claim limitation.

Vitale sued PizzaBoxCo because it sells pizza boxes with a plastic device that is used for holding up the top of the box cover. The parties stipulated to a description of the allegedly infringing device:

From the top plan view, the legs are attached, in pairs, to the ends of two U-shaped or semi-circle pieces. Each piece is molded. The two U-shaped pieces are fused together. The "accused" device looks like:

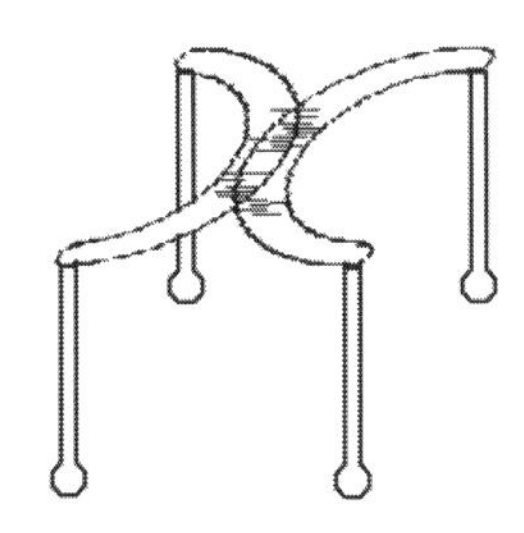

[2]Markman v. Westview Instrs., Inc., 517 U.S. 370 (1996).

[3]*See infra* Chapter 9.

The court required the parties to state the disputed claim term and their competing claim constructions in a chart, which was filed with the court.

Vitale v. PizzaBoxCo Joint Claim Construction Chart		
Claim 1		
Disputed Claim Term	Plaintiff Vitale's Construction	Defendant PizzaBox-Co's Construction
"a *unitary molded* plastic package-saving device"	1. No construction is necessary. 2. If the court decides a construction is necessary, then a "unitary molded" device "is a device that consists of a part or parts that were formed from a mold, and it functions as a unit or single piece."	A "unitary molded" device is a device formed whole from a single mold only.

1. Plaintiff Vitale's Claim Construction Arguments

Vitale argues that the first step in claim construction is to determine whether anything in the intrinsic record (the patent specification or the prosecution history) limits "unitary" or "molded." Vitale's principal argument is that words in the claim should be given their ordinary meaning unless the inventor clearly sets forth an explicit definition of a claim term different from its ordinary meaning or uses words representing a clear disavowal of claim scope. Vitale states that nothing in the intrinsic evidence favors a restrictive interpretation.

Since the word "unitary" is not a term of art in the "science" of pizza box construction, Vitale points to a common definition.

unitary
u·ni·tar·y (yōō¢nĭ-tĕr¢ē) *adj.* 1. of or relating to a unit. 2. having the nature of a unit; whole. 3. based on or characterized by one or more units.
Source: The American Heritage® Dictionary of the English Language: Fourth Edition

Dictionaries are not primary sources for defining claim terms, but Vitale argues that this supports the ordinary meaning of "unitary," which means one part. Vitale's claim construction argument is summarized by some of the PowerPoint slides, reproduced below, used during the claim construction hearing.

"Unitary" Means One Part

- where the part was always a single piece, "from scratch"

OR

- where the part was once more than one part, but is now permanently connected together (fused) into a single part that cannot be separated without breaking

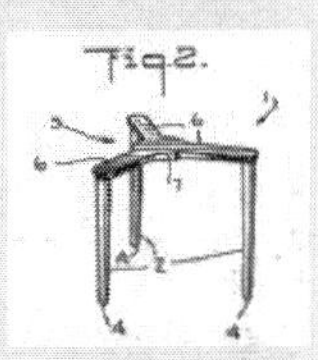

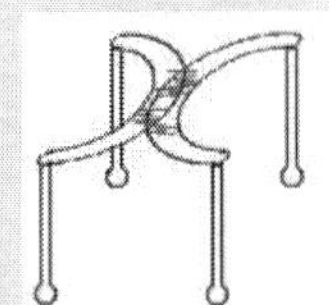

Nothing in the intrinsic record limits "unitary" to top example.

Moore, Gan & Chew LLP

Molded

- Dictionary definition: Made from a mold — a hollow form or matrix for shaping a fluid or plastic substance.

mold[1] (mōld) *n.* **1.** A hollow form or matrix for shaping a fluid or plastic substance. **2.** A frame or model around or on which something is formed or shaped. **3.** Something that is made in or shaped on a mold.

Source: American Heritage College Dictionary

Moore, Gan & Chew LLP

"Unitary Molded . . . Device"

- Must have a device that is both "unitary" and "molded."
- Ordinary meaning — a device that consists of a part or parts that were formed from a mold, and it functions as a unit or single piece.

Moore, Gan & Chew LLP

Defendant's Argument: Device Must Be Molded from a Single Piece

- Defendant argues the patent says "the saver is *preferably molded* as a unitary device."
- But it is <u>impermissible</u> to import limitations from the *preferred* embodiment into the claims.

Moore, Gan & Chew LLP

There Is No Support for Defendant's Interpretation that "Molded Device" Is Device That Is Only Molded

- Defendant claims that because its accused device is molded and then fused, it is no longer "molded."
- No support for "molded" meaning "only molded."
- Goes against tenet of patent law — cannot escape infringement by adding extra features or steps.

Moore, Gan & Chew LLP

Prosecution History Disavowals Must Be "Clear and Unmistakable"

- Defendant also tries to use prosecution history to change plain meaning of claim.
- But in order for statements in prosecution history to be limiting, must be "clear and unmistakable" disavowing actions or statements.

Omega Eng'g, Inc. v. Raytek Corp., 334 F.3d 1314, 1325–26 (Fed. Cir. 2003).

Moore, Gan & Chew LLP

No Reason to Deviate from Ordinary Meaning

- Defendant's definition restricts claim to a device formed whole and only from a single mold.
- BUT: There is no "whole/only/single" restriction by inventor that is a "clear and unmistakable disavowal."

Moore, Gan & Chew LLP

Prosecution History Does Not Limit "Unitary Molded Device"

- Defendant argues: Claims were originally not limited to a "unitary molded device" and limitation added in response to prior art patent (Bonekamp).
- Defendant's arguments distort the official record.

Moore, Gan & Chew LLP

Vitale '586 Patent vs. Bonekamp — "Differs in Concept"

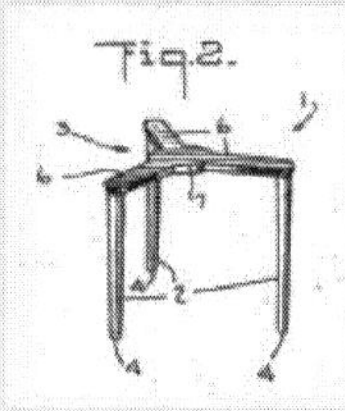

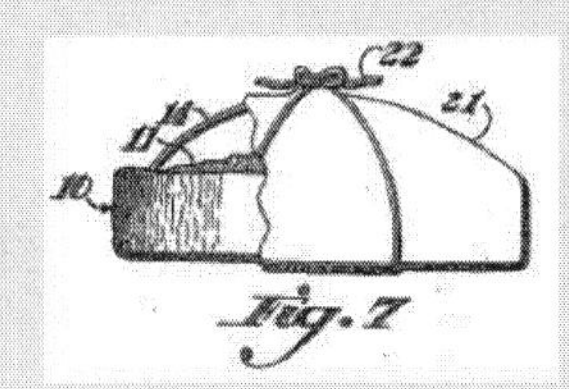

Vitale

- One flat cover piece — no circular dome
- Legs extending

Bonekamp

- Circular dome that used separate pieces
- No legs extending

Moore, Gan & Chew LLP

Prosecution History — Discussion of Bonekamp

- Original claim 3: "Unitary molded device." Claim rejected at first because of Bonekamp.
- Inventor argued that Bonekamp "*differs significantly from that of applicant in concept and in product engagement* and most likely in difficulty of manufacture and access . . . structure is remote."
- This is hardly a clear and unmistakable surrender of a unitary molded device that is a single piece from two molded parts fused together.

Moore, Gan & Chew LLP

Distinguishing Bonekamp Had Little, If Anything, To Do with One-Piece Molding

- Mention of manufacturing costs or difficulty is not a "manifest exclusion or restriction" or a "clear and unmistakable" disavowal.

  See, e.g., Sunrace Roots Enter. Co. v. SRAM Corp., 336 F.3d 1298, 1334–37 (Fed. Cir. 2003) (finding recitation of goals to not be limitation of patent claims).

Moore, Gan & Chew LLP

Conclusion: Proper Construction of "Unitary Molded Device"

- Term should get *ordinary meaning*:

  "One device made from molds":
  (a) "unitary" is one device;
  (b) "molded" means the device is made from molds.

Moore, Gan & Chew LLP

2. Defendant PizzaBoxCo's Argument

PizzaBoxCo argues it relies on intrinsic evidence that should be given controlling weight, in contrast to extrinsic dictionary definitions. Nevertheless, dictionary definitions support its position. PizzaBoxCo states that the ordinary meaning of "unitary" should be applied to the phrase "unitary molded . . . device" to require the device to be formed whole from one mold.

PizzaBoxCo contends that something is not "molded" if it is "molded and then fused together with something else"—a molded article does not require further assembly steps.

PizzaBoxCo also used a PowerPoint presentation at the claim construction hearing.

Specification Supports Defendant's Construction

- Specification shows "unitary molded . . . device" means a device formed as a single unit.
- "In order to provide a lightweight and inexpensive device for the purposes discussed above, the saver is preferably *molded as a unitary device. . . .*"

  '586 Patent 2:10–13.

Old, Coll, Edge & Try LLP

Specification Only Discloses a Device Made from a Single Mold

- No suggestion that two or more molds can be used.
- "Unitary molded" does not refer to two molds.
- No suggesting of "fusing" different molded parts.

Old, Coll, Edge & Try LLP

Prosecution History Supports Defendant's Construction

- Original claims 1 and 2 did not have a "unitary" or "molded" limitation. They broadly claimed "a package saving device."
- Original claims 1 and 2 were rejected for obviousness.
- The applicant canceled original claims 1 and 2.
- The only independent claim remaining contains the limitation in original claim 3 ("unitary molded plastic . . . device"), which describes the preferred embodiment.

Old, Coll, Edge & Try LLP

Bonekamp Prior Art Distinguished

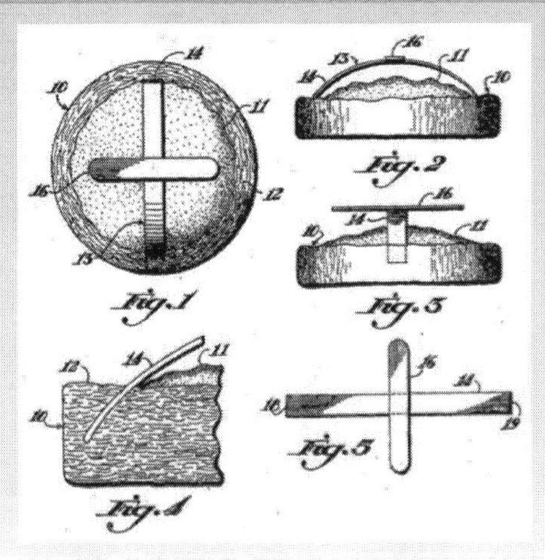

Old, Coll, Edge & Try LLP

"Unitary Molded Plastic" Distinguishes Bonekamp Prior Art

- "[The Bonekamp device] *differs significantly* from that of applicant in concept and in product engagement and most likely *in difficulty of manufacture and access.*"

  Applicant's Remarks, Feb. 16, 1984, p. 3.

Old, Coll, Edge & Try LLP

Bonekamp Distinguished: Attaching Two Pieces Together Is Not "Unitary"

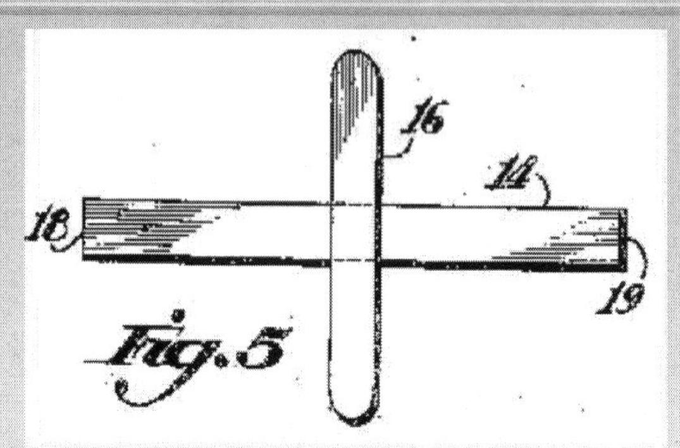

- Device was "two strips of cardboard . . . or the like which are attached together at their central points."
  Bonekamp '629 Patent 2:10–12.

Old, Coll, Edge & Try LLP

A Device Like This Is Not "Molded" or "Unitary"

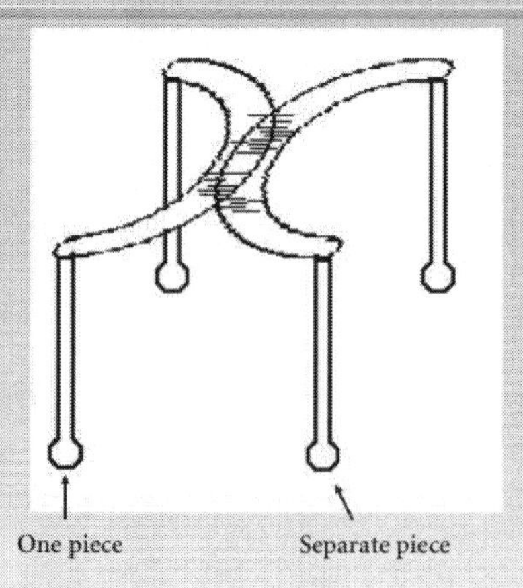

No single molding process makes the device.

Old, Coll, Edge & Try LLP

Conclusion

- "Unitary molded" device is a device formed whole from a single mold only.
- This is supported by intrinsic evidence from:
  - specification
  - prosecution history

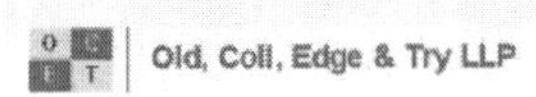

The court adopts Vitale's proposed construction and rules that a "unitary molded . . . device" must be "one device made from molds."

F. Summary Judgment Motions

Vitale moves for summary judgment that PizzaBoxCo infringes because it sells pizza boxes with a unit that is a plastic molded device. PizzaBoxCo cross-moves for summary judgment of noninfringement because the device it sells is made from two components that are fused together. PizzaBoxCo also moves for further claim construction to clarify that the entire device must be made from one mold.

The court declines to do further claim construction and denies the cross-motions for summary judgment.[4]

---

[4]For a detailed review of summary judgment motions, see *infra* Chapter 10.

G. Trial

The case goes to trial. PizzaBoxCo's main defenses are non-infringement and inequitable conduct. The inequitable conduct defense is based on the allegation that Vitale's attorneys intentionally withheld material prior art from the Patent Office when the office was considering the original patent application.

Vitale moves to sever the inequitable conduct defense for a bench trial to be held at the conclusion of the jury trial in the event that liability is found. The motion is granted.

The jury finds in favor of Vitale and awards damages equal to 5 percent of PizzaBoxCo's revenues on sales of the plastic device. No additional royalties are awarded for the sales of pizza boxes, even though they were always sold by PizzaBoxCo with the plastic device.

At the bench trial, the court concludes there was no inequitable conduct.

Vitale moves for a permanent injunction and, in the alternative, for a 5 percent compulsory license fee to be paid pending appeal. Before the motion is decided—after an extensive mediation before retired Judge Armtwister—the case settles.

Both sides declare victory.

H. Reproduction of Vitale Patent

United States Patent [19]
Vitale

[11] **Patent Number:** **4,498,586**
[45] **Date of Patent:** **Feb. 12, 1985**

[54] **PACKAGE SAVER**

[76] Inventor: **Carmela Vitale,** 1076 Carll Straight Path, Dix Hills, N.Y. 11746

[21] Appl. No.: **465,642**

[22] Filed: **Feb. 10, 1983**

[51] **Int. Cl.**[3] **B65D 85/72**
[52] **U.S. Cl.** **206/525;** 426/124; 426/128; 206/45.32; 206/541
[58] **Field of Search** 206/525, 527, 45.32, 206/541, 551; 229/36, 33; 426/128, 124; 215/231; 248/346

[56] **References Cited**

U.S. PATENT DOCUMENTS

1,357,155 10/1920 Dinkins 215/231
2,452,629 11/1948 Bonekamp 426/128
2,928,537 3/1960 Stagner 426/124
3,180,739 4/1965 Stoker 426/124

Primary Examiner—William T. Dixson, Jr.
Attorney, Agent, or Firm—Stoll, Wilkie, Previto & Hoffman

[57] **ABSTRACT**

A temperature resistant molded plastic device is described for use in boxes or packages such as pizza boxes where there is a tendency of large cover portions to sag downwardly to damage the soft pizza or other packaged products. In use, the saver is positioned near the center of the package to support the box cover for protecting the contents.

4 Claims, 4 Drawing Figures

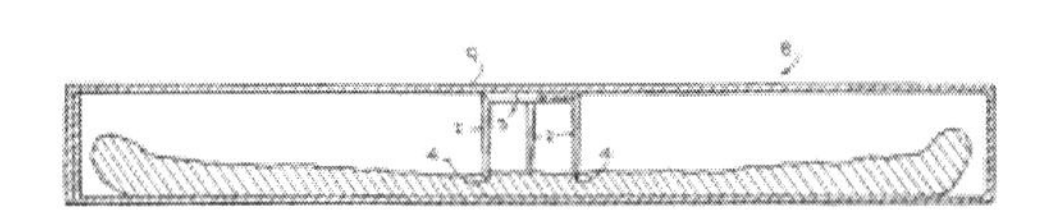

U.S. Patent **Feb. 12, 1985** **4,498,586**

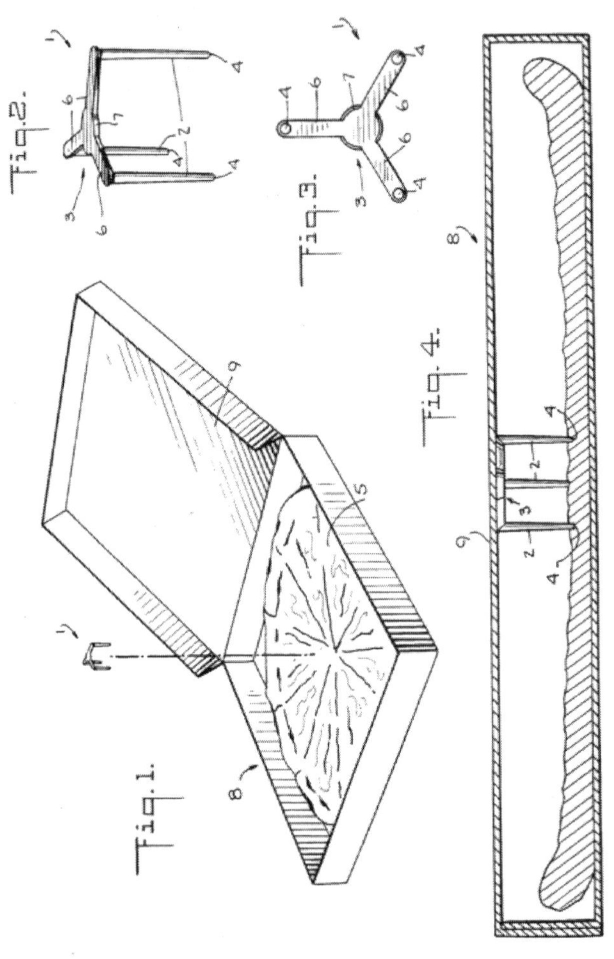

4,498,586

1

PACKAGE SAVER

BACKGROUND OF THE INVENTION

The present invention relates to a package saver or device for improving the packaging of soft products which may be damaged in boxes or cartons with relatively large sagging covers.

More particularly, the invention relates to such a package saver which is molded from plastic to have minimal size, weight, and cost and which is suitable for supporting large carton covers such as those used for pizza pies. The molded plastic saver is positioned centrally of the completed pie or other product to support the cover during storage and delivery.

The package saver is useful in connection with the delivery of products which require a package, but whose cost necessarily requires a relatively inexpensive and disposable box or carton. Cartons of this type, and particularly those used to deliver pizza pies or large cakes or pies, comprise boxes with relatively large covers formed of inexpensive board material.

Due to the quality of the board and their large size, there is a tendency of the covers to sag or to be easily depressed at their center portions so that they may damage or mark the pies or cakes during storage or delivery.

Accordingly, an object of the present invention is to provide an easily manufactured, relatively inexpensive, lightweight article which is placed on the pie or cake within the package to support the central portion of the package cover during delivery.

Another object of the present invention is to provide an improved means for protecting articles such as pizza and other pies or cakes from damage during delivery in boxes.

Another object of the present invention is to provide an inexpensive device for protecting pizza and other pies or cakes during delivery.

Other and further objects of the present invention will become apparent upon an understanding of the illustrative embodiments about to be described, or will be indicated in the appended claims, and various advantages not referred to herein will occur to one skilled in the art upon employment of the invention in practice.

BRIEF DESCRIPTION OF THE DRAWINGS

A preferred embodiment of the invention has been chosen for purposes of illustration and description and is shown in the accompanying drawings, forming a part of the specification, wherein:

FIG. 1 is a perspective view illustrating the package saver being used with a typical pizza pie delivery box.

2

FIG. 2 is a perspective view of a package saver in accordance with the invention.

FIG. 3 is a top plan view of the package saver of FIG. 2.

FIG. 4 is a vertical sectional view of a typical pizza box with the package or pizza saver in position.

DESCRIPTION OF THE PREFERRED EMBODIMENT

In order to provide a lightweight and inexpensive device for the purpose discussed above, the saver is preferably molded as a unitary device from one of the plastics which is heat resistant such as the thermo set plastics and which will resist temperatures of as high as about 500° F.

In its preferred form, as illustrated, the saver **1** has spaced vertical legs **2** connected to a cover support **3**. The lower portions of the legs **4** have a minimal cross section to minimize any marking of to the protected article **5** and they are also made thin for minimizing the volume of plastic required. The cover support **3** of the saver **1** also preferably has a minimum volume by consisting of a spoke-like arrangement of radially oriented leg supports **6** molded to extend from a central portion **7**.

This construction of portion support **3** provides a suitable broad and stable support for box **8** cover **9** which is of minimal volume and thus has minimal cost. A disposable saver **1** is provided which may be used in the boxes or cartons without damage to the packaged pizza pie or other product.

As various changes may be made in the form, construction and arrangement of the invention and without departing from the spirit and scope of the invention, and without sacrificing any of its advantages, it is to be understood that all matters herein is to be interpreted as illustrative and not in a limiting sense.

Having thus described my invention, I claim:

1. In combination a package having a flexible cover, a food article packaged therein and spaced downwardly from the cover, a unitary molded plastic package saving device for positioning between the cover and the article for supporting the package cover thereby preventing damage to the packaged food article by the cover, said device comprising the combination of three or more spaced legs, each leg having one relatively flat end adapted for engaging the packaged article and having its opposite end attached to a device cover portion.

2. The combination as claimed in claim 1 in which said device cover portion comprises a number of flat cover sections radiating from a common flat central portion.

3. The combination as claimed in claim 1 wherein said device is formed of heat resistant plastic.

4. The combination as claimed in claim 1 wherein said device is formed of thermo-setting plastic.

* * * * *

2

The America Invents Act and its Impact on Patent Litigation*

---

*John L. Cooper, FACTL, Farella, Braun + Martel, LLP, San Francisco, California, with the assistance of Alex Reese.

I. Introduction

On September 16, 2011, President Obama signed into law the Leahy-Smith America Invents Act ("AIA"). The Act makes substantial changes to patent prosecution at the Patent and Trademark Office (PTO) and patent litigation in federal courts.

This chapter addresses how the AIA's most significant changes to patent law will affect litigation in federal courts. Because different provisions in the AIA take effect on different dates and apply to different patents, the chapter concludes with a chart detailing the effective dates and scopes of various provisions in the AIA.

II. New Proceedings at the PTO and their Effect on Civil Actions

Perhaps the broadest change in the AIA is that it creates three entirely new kinds of proceedings at the Patent and Trademark Office (PTO): (1) Post-Grant Review, (2) Inter Partes Review, and (3) Supplemental Examination. Both Post-Grant Review and Inter Partes Review proceedings will take place before a new hearing board at the PTO called the Patent Trial and Appeal Board (PTAB) in which panels of three Administrative Patent Judges (similar to ALJs) will adjudicate disputes. The new procedures will affect civil litigation through automatic stays, estoppel, and more.

A. *Post-Grant Review*

The new Post-Grant Review proceeding allows third parties to challenge a patent within nine months after it is issued by the PTO. The PTO will begin hearing Post-Grant Review proceedings only for business method patents and patents involved in interference proceedings on September 16, 2012; the proceeding will become available for all patents on March 16, 2013.

Stays: There is no automatic stay of pending civil proceedings when a petitioner files for Post-Grant Review. However, the PTAB must issue decisions within one year, and some commentators have speculated that courts will be more willing to grant stays considering this condensed timeline.

Estoppel: If the PTAB issues a final written decision in any Post-Grant Review, that decision will have estoppel effects on the litigants in later civil proceedings. Specifically, new 35 U.S.C. §325(e)(2) provides that any litigant in federal court or before the International Trade Commission may not argue that a patent or claim is invalid on "any ground" that "the petitioner raised or reasonably could have raised" during a Post-Grant Review that resulted in a final written decision. Estoppel extends to the petitioner in the proceeding, his privy, and the "real party in interest."

B. Inter Partes Review

The new Inter Partes Review procedure will replace the existing Inter Partes Reexam process discussed in Chapter 1.C beginning on September 16, 2012. In these hearings, petitioners may challenge the validity of a patent or claim at any time after the nine-month window for Post Grant Review has expired.

Stays: Once a petitioner files for Inter Partes Review, any subsequent civil action filed by the petitioner is automatically stayed under the new Section 315(a)(2). The stay remains in effect until the patent owner moves the court to lift the stay or files a civil action or counterclaim alleging infringement. The stay also will terminate if the petitioner moves to dismiss the action. Like Post-Grant Review, the AIA states that the PTAB should conclude an Inter Partes Review procedure within one year after the petition for review is filed. Therefore, when the automatic stay does not apply, judges may consider this condensed timeline in evaluating motions to stay.

Estoppel: The estoppel provision is the same as that discussed for Post-Grant Review: a litigant, his privy or the real party in interest is estopped from raising any ground for invalidity that he raised or reasonably could have raised during a prior Inter Partes Review proceeding. Note however that the grounds on which a petitioner may initiate an Inter Partes Review are fairly narrow. The new 35 U.S.C. §311(b) states that an Inter Partes Review petitioner may challenge a patent's validity only under Sections 102 and 103, and "only on the basis of prior art consisting of patents or printed publications." Therefore, even though the estoppel provision is the same for Post-Grant Review as for Inter Partes Review, the effective scope of estoppel is narrower for Inter Partes Review because the grounds for a challenge in that procedure are narrower.

C. Supplemental Examination

The AIA creates yet a third new procedure at the PTO: Supplemental Examination. Unlike Post-Grant Review and Inter Partes Review, the patent owner himself initiates Supplemental Examination. This new procedure has little effect on the conduct of civil cases except for its impact on inequitable conduct, a defense to infringement allegations. Supplemental Examination is therefore discussed more in depth in the section addressing defenses below.

III. The (Modified) First to File Rule

One of the AIA's primary goals was to bring U.S. patent practice more in line with patent laws worldwide. Perhaps the AIA's largest step in this direction is to abolish the U.S.'s unique "first to invent" rule. Since the first patent act, the U.S. has granted patents to the first person to invent, not necessarily the first to file for a patent. The AIA ends this approach and puts in its place a modified first to file regime that more closely resembles the patent rules in other countries.

Under the new first to file rule, patents will normally be granted to the first inventor to file for a patent, who may or may not be the first person to conceive of the invention. The only exception is the so-called one year grace period. Under the new Section 102(2)(b), if the inventor discloses the invention to the public but files for a patent within one year of that disclosure, he is still entitled to the patent. In other words, making the public disclosure gives the inventor a one year grace period during which time no one else could successfully file for a patent on the same invention because the inventor's disclosure would be considered prior art. But the inventor may still successfully file for a patent within the one-year limit.

The practical effect of the new first to file rule for patent litigation is that it will eliminate the practice of "swearing behind references" in which litigants attempt to prove an invention date earlier than the date they filed for a patent. Under the new first to file rule, courts no longer need consider issues such as conception and reduction to practice in determining the date of an invention. The invention date will now be the same as the filing date.

It's important to note however that the first to file rule applies only to patent applications filed on or after March 16, 2013 and patents issued after that date. Therefore, courts must remain familiar with the old first to invent rule even after the new first to file rule takes effect.

IV. Changes to Section 102(b) Prior Art

The AIA also makes significant changes to what is considered prior art under Section 102(b) that will take effect on March 16, 2013. As discussed in Chapter 5.II.B.2, accused infringers may show that a patent is invalid for lack of novelty by pointing to prior art that anticipates the claimed invention.

The first change to Section 102(b) prior art has already been discussed: if an inventor discloses the invention and files for a patent within one year, the earlier disclosure is not considered prior art and the inventor may still be entitled to the patent. However, it remains to be seen exactly what the AIA means by "disclosure." It's possible that "disclosure" in the new Section 102(b) merely refers to the type of prior art discussed in Section 102(a). Under that reading, the inventor would qualify for the one-year grace period if he disclosed the invention "in a printed publication" or the invention was "in public use, on sale, or otherwise available to the public." However, other interpretations are possible, and it may be left either to PTO regulations or to the courts to determine exactly how much an inventor must disclose in order to gain the advantage of the one-year grace period.

The AIA also abolishes the distinction between public use or sale of an invention in the United States versus in other countries. Previously, only a public use or sale of the invention in the United States was considered prior art that could prevent an inventor from obtaining a patent (or invalidate a mistakenly issued patent). In a nod to our increasingly interconnected world, the AIA gets rid of this distinction. Prior public use or sale of the invention anywhere in the world is now considered prior art that can invalidate a patent.

The AIA's final change to prior art is the addition of the ambiguous words "otherwise available to the public" to the list of types of prior art. The AIA does not define this vague term, nor does it specifically direct the PTO to issue regulations on this phrase.

Therefore, it's likely that courts will define the term through patent disputes.

Although the Act leaves "otherwise available to the public" undefined, the phrase is similar to "known or used by others," a kind of prior art that the patent laws recognize until the new Section 102 takes effect on March 16, 2013. Decisions interpreting that phrase may provide a starting point for defining "otherwise available to the public." The Federal Circuit interpreted "known or used by others" to mean "knowledge or use which is accessible to the public."[1] The Federal Circuit clarified in 2004 that the "key inquiry is whether or not a reference has been made 'publicly accessible.'"[2] While these decisions certainly are not binding interpretations of the new "otherwise available to the public" category, these cases and their progeny may be a helpful starting point for courts as they interpret the AIA.

V. Changes to Defenses in Patent Litigation

The AIA makes three significant changes to defenses in patent litigation: it abolishes the "best mode" defense; it provides patent owners a method for curing inequitable conduct; and it expands the prior commercial use defense.

A. *Best Mode Defense is Abolished*

As discussed in Chapter 5.II.B.4, accused infringers often defend themselves by arguing that a patent is invalid for failure to disclose the "best mode" for carrying out the invention as required by 35 U.S.C. §112. Under the AIA, patent applicants still must disclose the best mode for carrying out the invention, but failure to do so is no longer a defense to infringement allegations. Thus, although patent examiners at the PTO still must concern themselves with the best mode issue, courts need no longer consider it. This provision took effect September 16, 2011, and it applies to all suits initiated on or after that date regardless of when the patent-in-suit issued.

---

[1] Carella v. Starlight Archery, 804 F.2d 135 (Fed. Cir. 1986).
[2] In re Klopfenstein, 380 F.3d 1345, 1348 (Fed. Cir. 2004).

B. *Inequitable Conduct and Supplemental Examination*

As mentioned in Part II.C of this chapter, the AIA creates a procedure under Section 257(a) called Supplemental Examination whereby a patentee may request the PTO to "consider, reconsider, or correct information believed to be relevant to the patent" after the patent has issued.

The primary impact of Supplemental Examination on district court actions is that it offers patentees a method of potentially curing some inequitable conduct. As discussed in Chapter 4.II.A, accused infringers may show that a patent is unenforceable if the original patent applicant failed to meet his duty of candor and good faith in pursuing the patent before the PTO. A patent applicant who obtains the patent through fraud has engaged in inequitable conduct, and a common form of inequitable conduct is intentionally withholding prior art references or other materials from the PTO's consideration.

Supplemental Examination gives patentees the opportunity to correct acts of inequitable conduct and in effect clean up their patents. Under the new Section 257(c)(2)(A), no materials that a patentee submits to the PTO for consideration under Supplemental Examination may later be used against the patentee as the basis for an inequitable conduct defense. This is true even if the patent applicant intentionally omitted the prior art reference in the original patent application.

There is however an exception to a patentee's ability to protect himself from charges of inequitable conduct if the patentee only learns about the prior art material from an accused infringer. Therefore, if an accused infringer pleads inequitable conduct "with particularity" in a pleading, the patentee may not then run to the PTO and submit material for Supplemental Examination in order to escape a claim of inequitable conduct. The only other minor exception is when the patentee learns about the material through a so-called Paragraph IV Hatch-Waxman letter, which relates to the FDA's procedure in approving generic drugs.

C. *The More Robust Prior Commercial Use Defense*

The AIA's third and final change to defenses in patent litigation is that it broadens the prior commercial use defense. Prior to the AIA, an accused infringer could defend based on his prior commercial use of a method disclosed in the patent-in-suit if he used such method at least one year prior to the filing date of the patent. However, this defense applied to method patents only. The AIA expands this defense to all patents issued on or after September 16, 2011. To succeed in the defense, the accused infringer must show that he "commercially used the subject matter in the United States, either in connection with an internal commercial use or an actual arm's length sale or other arm's length commercial transfer of a useful end result of such commercial use" at least one year prior to the patent's filing date (or the inventor's disclosure that triggers the one year–grace period, as discussed above).

VI. Miscellaneous Changes: Joinder and False Marking

There are two other changes that will affect patent litigation. First, the AIA prohibits plaintiffs from joining multiple defendants in a single action unless the plaintiff seeks joint and several liability or the claim arises out of the same "transaction, occurrence, or series of transactions or occurrences relating to the making, using, importing into the United States, offering for sale, or selling of the same accused product or process." The AIA does not prevent judges from officially relating cases or from coordinating similar cases for pretrial purposes. However, it appears that the AIA provides accused infringers the right to separate trials.

The AIA also eliminates the qui tam provision in false marking cases. Under the AIA, only the United States and a party who suffers actual "competitive injury" may bring false marking actions. And in private actions, the plaintiff is entitled only to compensatory damages. Many commentators have suggested that this will all but eliminate private false marking actions from the district courts.

VII. Chart Detailing the Effective Dates of Provisions in the Act

Various provisions in the AIA take effect on different dates and apply to different patents. The chart below details these effective dates for easy reference.

Post Grant Review	• September 16, 2012: for business method patents and patents involved in interference proceedings. • March 16, 2013: applicable to all patents.	See box to the left.
Inter Partes Review	September 16, 2012	Applicable to all patents after the nine-month window for Post Grant Review expires.
First to File Rule	March 16, 2013	Applies to all applications for patent on or after effective date.
Changes to §102 Prior Art	March 16, 2013	Applies to all patents issued or applied for on or after the effective date.
Best Mode Defense Abolished	September 16, 2011	Applies to all patents, regardless of when they were issued.
Inequitable Conduct—Curable Through Supplemental Examination	September 16, 2012	Applies to all patents, regardless of when they were issued.
Broader Prior Commercial Use Defense	September 16, 2011	Applies to patents issued on or after effective date.
Limitation on Joinder of Unrelated Defendants	September 16, 2011	Applies to all actions commenced on or after effective date.
Revision of False Marking Claims	September 16, 2011	Applies to all actions commenced on or after effective date.

3

The Complaint*

*Henry B. Gutman, Simpson Thacher & Bartlett LLP, New York, New York.
The author wishes to thank Michael Graif, Curtis, Mallet-Prevost, Colt & Mosle LLP, New York, New York, who prepared the original version of this chapter.

I. Pleading Infringement

A defendant may infringe directly or indirectly by inducing or contributing to the direct infringement of another person. As in other cases, well-pleaded patent complaints place the alleged infringer on notice as to the infringing acts and relief requested.[1]

The Federal Circuit has recently spoken on the impact of the heightened pleading requirements established by the Supreme Court in the *Twombly* and *Iqbal* cases upon the complaint in a patent infringement case. In *In re Bill of Lading Transmission*[2], the Federal Circuit resolved an issue that had divided the district courts, holding that for claims of *direct* patent infringement, simply conforming to the requirements of Form 18 of the Federal Rules of Civil Procedure was sufficient;[3] for claims of indirect infringement, however, the Federal Circuit held that the full-fledged *Iqbal* and *Twombly* plausibility analysis is required.[4] One commentator has suggested that in view of *In re Bill of Lading*, Form 18 should be eliminated.[5]

A. *Direct Infringement*

The Federal Circuit has held (pre-*Twombly*) that the following five elements are sufficient to state a claim of infringement: (1) ownership of the patent, (2) the infringer's name, (3) a citation to the infringed patent, (4) the infringing activity, and (5) citations to federal patent law.[6] This approach is consistent with the bare bones example of a patent complaint found in Form 18 of the Federal Rules of Civil Procedure. However, some post-*Twombly* district court decisions have required more. For example, in *Rovi*

---

[1] *See* Fed. R. Civ. P. 8.

[2] *In re Bill of Lading Transmission*, 681 F.3d 1323, 1335 (Fed. Cir. 2012).

[3] 681 F.3d at 1336.

[4] *Id.*

[5] Dennis Crouch, "Pleading Requirements for Direct Infringement; Inducing Infringement; and Contributory Infringement," *Patently-O*, http://www.patentlyo.com/patent/2012/06/pleading-requirements.html, (June 8, 2012) (last visited Sept. 28, 2012).

[6] Phonometrics, Inc. v. Hospitality Franchise Sys., Inc., 203 F.3d 790, 794 (Fed. Cir. 2000); Home & Nature, Inc. v. Sherman Specialty Co., 322 F. Supp. 2d 260, 265 (E.D.N.Y. 2004).

Corp. v. Hulu, LLC,[7] the court dismissed a complaint because it "fail[ed] to meet the standards required by the Supreme Court in the landmark cases of *Twombly* and *Iqbal.*"[8] As noted above, the Federal Circuit has now held in *In re Bill of Lading Transmission* that compliance with Form 18 is sufficient for direct infringement.[9]

B. Induced Infringement

Pursuant to 35 U.S.C. §271(b), "[w]hoever actively induces infringement of a patent shall be liable as an infringer." Active inducement requires a showing that a defendant intentionally encouraged patent infringement by another. The "alleged infringer must be shown... to have *knowingly* induced infringement," not merely knowingly induced the *acts* that constitute direct infringement.[10] Such intentional encouragement requires the defendant to have engaged in some affirmative act and not simply failed to take steps to prevent infringement.[11] In addition, a claim under Section 271(b) requires a showing that the activity induced by the defendant constitutes direct infringement.

Courts have taken different approaches toward allegations of induced infringement. Most have required that a claimant allege intent and direct infringement of the asserted patents. In some cases a claimant may allege intent by asserting that there was "specific intent and/or... the desire to actively induce infringement."[12] The Supreme Court's recent decision in *Global-Tech Appliances, Inc. v. SEB S.A.*,[13] should also be taken into consideration in evaluating the sufficiency of a complaint that alleges induced infringement. In *Global-Tech* the Court clarified that inducement cannot be sustained based on a "should have known," negligence type standard, but may be found where there is "willful blindness"—that is "(1) the defendant must subjectively believe that there is a

---

[7]No. 11-665, 2012 WL 261982, 2012 U.S. Dist LEXIS 10183 (D. Del. Jan. 27, 2012).

[8]681 F.3d at 1336.

[9]681 F.3d at 1336.

[10]DSU Med. Corp. v. JMS Co., 471 F.3d 1293, 1306 (Fed. Cir. 2006).

[11]Tegal Corp. v. Tokyo Electron Co., 248 F.3d 1376, 1378 (Fed. Cir. 2001).

[12]Takeda Chem. Indus., Ltd. v. Watson Pharm., Inc., 329 F. Supp. 2d 394, 401 (S.D.N.Y. 2004); *see also* Snap-on, Inc. v. Hunter Eng'g Co., 29 F. Supp. 2d 965, 970 (E.D. Wis. 1998) (finding the allegation that a defendant's conduct was "willful and deliberate" was sufficient to allege intent).

[13]131 S. Ct. 2060 (2011).

high probability that a fact exists and (2) the defendant must take deliberate actions to avoid learning of that fact."[14] As applied to inducement, actual knowledge of infringement is not required; a defendant may not escape inducement liability by deliberately avoiding actual knowledge that the acts it induces constitute patent infringement.[15] District courts synthesizing *Global-Tech* with *Iqbal* have found that "the question before the Court on [a] motion[] to dismiss is whether [the plaintiff] has plead sufficient facts . . . for the Court to *infer* that the defendant[] had knowledge of [the plaintiff's] patents and that their products infringed on those patents."[16]

With respect to the *Twombly* and *Iqbal* issue, the Federal Circuit has now held in *In re Bill of Lading Transmission*,[17] as noted above, that the heightened pleading standards established by the Supreme Court in those cases must be met for indirect infringement, including inducement.

C. Contributory Infringement

Pursuant to 35 U.S.C. §271(c), whoever sells a component of a patented machine for use in practicing a patented process that does not have a substantial noninfringing use shall be liable as a contributory infringer.

A plaintiff may allege generically that a defendant "infringed, induced and/or contributed to the infringement." Unlike induced infringement, however, contributory infringement does not require an allegation of intent. The statute requires only knowledge that an activity caused infringement.[18]

The language of Section 271(c) imposes liability for contributory infringement based on an offer to sell a component of a pat-

---

[14] *Global-Tech*, 131 S. Ct. at 2070.

[15] *See id.* at 2069–71.

[16] Trading Techs. Int'l, Inc. v. BCG Ptnrs., Inc., 2011 WL 3946581, *3, 2011 U.S. Dist. LEXIS 99415, *13–14 (N.D. Ill. Sept. 2, 2011) (emphasis in original).

[17] 681 F.3d at 1336.

[18] *See* Hewlett-Packard Co. v. Bausch & Lomb, Inc., 909 F.2d 1464 (Fed. Cir. 1990) ("proof of a defendant's *knowledge*, not *intent*, that his activity cause infringement was necessary to establish contributory infringement" (emphasis in original)).

ented invention even if an actual sale has not taken place.[19] In such cases it is sufficient for a claimant to plead that the defendant made an offer to sell to a third party who would have directly infringed had the sale taken place.

D. Infringement of Drug Patents

Subpart (1) of 35 U.S.C. §271(e) establishes a safe harbor for acts "solely for uses reasonably related to the development and submission of information under a Federal law which regulates the manufacture, use, or sale of drugs or veterinary biological products." This provision protects a company that is using a patented invention to generate data for an FDA filing, such as an Abbreviated New Drug Application (ANDA). It is, however, an act of infringement under subpart (2) to:

> Submit [either] an [ANDA or an application under §512 of the Federal Food, Drug, Cosmetic Act] if the purpose of such submission is to obtain approval under such Act to engage in the commercial manufacture, use, or sale of a drug or veterinary biologic product claimed in a patent or the use of which is claimed in a patent before the expiration of such patent.

Infringement under this section depends on whether the defendant "will likely market an infringing product" once the FDA approves the ANDA.[20] As such, allegations of infringement based on the filing of an ANDA require the plaintiff to assert that, if the application is approved, the accused infringer will infringe the asserted patent.

A complainant may also allege that the accused infringer's ANDA has induced a third party to directly infringe the asserted patent. In such cases, it must be found that the accused infringer knows or should know that its actions will induce infringement.[21] Courts have not ruled that such knowledge must be pled.

---

[19] *See* Finnsugar Bioproducts, Inc. v. Raytheon Engineers & Constructors, Inc., 1998 WL 703463 (N.D. Ill. 1998).

[20] Glaxo, Inc. v. Novopharm, Ltd., 110 F.3d 1562, 1568 (Fed. Cir. 1997).

[21] *See* Allergan, Inc. v. Alcon Labs., Inc., 324 F.3d 1322, 1332 (Fed. Cir. 2003) (citing Warner-Lambert v. Apotex, 316 F.3d 1348, 1354–55 (Fed. Cir. 2003)).

E. *Infringement for Supplying Components for Assembly into a Patented Product Outside of the United States*

Federal law also prohibits inducing or contributing to patent infringement outside the United States. It is an act of infringement under 35 U.S.C. §271(f) to:

> (1) [export] all or a substantial portion of the components of a patented invention ... in such manner as to actively induce the combination of such components outside of the [U.S.] in a manner that would infringe the patent if such combination occurred within the [U.S.]; or
>
> (2) [export] any component of a patented invention that is especially made or especially adapted for the use in the invention and not a staple article or commodity of commerce suitable for substantial noninfringing use, ... knowing that such component is so made or adapted and intending that such component will be combined outside of the [U.S.] in a manner that would infringe ... the patent if such combination occurred within the U.S.

Claimant may allege under subpart (1): (1) exportation of "all or a substantial portion" of the components of infringing product; and (2) intent to induce the combination of such components outside the United States in a manner that would infringe inside the United States.

Claimant may allege under subpart (2): (1) the exportation of a component that is especially adapted for an infringing use; (2) that the defendant knows that the component is so adapted; and (3) that the defendant intends that the component be combined abroad in a patented invention.[22]

F. *Infringement by a Product Made Outside the United States of a U.S. Patent Covering a Process*

According to 35 U.S.C. §271(g), it is considered an act of infringement to import into the United States or offer for sale, sell, or use within the United States a product made by a process patented in the United States. By the terms of the statute, a claimant alleging infringement under Section 271(g) should plead: (1) an act of importation into the United States, an offer to sell, sale, or

[22] *See* Microsoft v. AT&T, 127 S. Ct. 1746 (2007).

use of the product; and (2) that the accused act occurred during the term of the process patent.

G. *Willfulness*

Willful infringement is the "deliberate disregard" of another's patent rights.[23] A finding of willful infringement allows the court to multiply a patentee's damages up to threefold pursuant to 35 U.S.C. §284 and award attorneys' fees under 35 U.S.C. §285.[24] Because willfulness is not fraud, a plaintiff need not plead willful infringement with particularity.[25] Accordingly, willful infringement is usually pled by generally alleging that the infringement was and continues to be either "willful" or "willful and deliberate," together with a request for enhanced damages in the prayer for relief.[26]

II. Pleading Damages and Other Remedies

A plaintiff will typically request the following types of relief for patent infringement: (1) compensatory damages such as lost profits or reasonable royalty, (2) enhanced damages, (3) injunctive relief, and (4) attorneys' fees.[27]

---

[23] *See In re* Seagate Tech. LLC, 497 F.3d 1360, 1371 (Fed. Cir. 2007) (holding that "proof of willful infringement... requires at least a showing of objective recklessness." The court also held that in order to find objective recklessness "[(1)] a patentee must show by clear and convincing evidence that the infringer acted despite an objectively high likelihood that its actions constituted infringement... [and (2)] that this objectively-defined risk... was either known or so obvious that it should have been known to the accused infringer."); *see also* Vulcan Eng'g Co. v. FATA Aluminum, Inc., 278 F.3d 1366, 1378 (Fed. Cir. 2002).

[24] *See also* Read v. Portec, Inc., 970 F.2d 816, 826–31 (Fed. Cir. 1992).

[25] *See* Ferguson Beuregard/Logic Controls v. Mega Sys., LLC, 350 F.3d 1327, 1342–43 (Fed. Cir. 2003) ("the pleading requirement for willful infringement does not rise to the stringent standard required by Rule 9(b)").

[26] For information about separating willfulness issues from liability issues, see *infra* Chapter 11.II.B. For information about expert testimony on willfulness, see *infra* Chapter 11.IV.B.2.

[27] 35 U.S.C. §283 (injunctive relief), §284 (damages and enhanced damages) and §285 (attorneys' fees).

A. *Compensatory Damages*

Claimants may generically plead entitlement to all compensatory damages. For instance, "damages adequate to compensate," "damages according to proof," "general, special, actual and/or statutory damages," or "actual damages, including lost profits" are sufficient to preserve the plaintiff's right to all forms of compensatory damage.

B. *Enhanced Damages*

A claimant seeking enhanced damages for willful infringement must request that damages be enhanced, since such relief exceeds the compensatory relief to which a plaintiff is typically entitled. For instance, a claimant will often request that the "court award treble damages against defendant for its willful infringement.[28]

C. *Injunctions*

Federal law also allows courts to grant injunctions if necessary to prevent a violation of patent rights.[29] Claimants may request that a defendant be "preliminarily and permanently enjoined and restrained from making, importing, using, offering for sale, selling, or causing to be sold any product falling within, or designed to conduct a method falling within, the scope of any claim of the patents-in-suit, or otherwise infringing or contributing to or inducing infringement of any claim of the patents-in-suit." However, claimants also make general requests for an order "preliminarily and permanently enjoining [the defendant] from infringing the patents-in-suit."[30]

---

[28]See Rooklidge, Gooding, Johnson, Yen, *Compensatory Damages Issues in Patent Infringement Cases: A Pocket Guide for Federal District Judges*, (Federal Judicial Center 2011), *available at* http:www.fic.gov/public/pdf.nsf/lookup/damages patent.pdf/$file/damagespatent.pdf.

[29]35 U.S.C. §283 (2000); *see also* eBay, Inc. v. MercExchange LLC, 126 S. Ct. 1837 (2006).

[30]*See also infra* Chapter 13.VI.D.

D. Attorneys' Fees

Finally, most claimants request attorneys' fees pursuant to 35 U.S.C. §285, which allows for reasonable attorneys' fees to be awarded to the prevailing party "in exceptional cases." Attorneys' fees are awarded only in limited circumstances—they are an "exception to the American rule."[31] As such, a request for attorneys' fees under Section 285 must be pled before a successful party can be awarded such fees. Claimants may request, in accordance with the statute, that "the Court declare this to be an exceptional case and award claimant its attorneys' fees."[32]

---

[31]Forest Labs., Inc. v. Abbott Labs., 339 F.3d 1324, 1329 (Fed. Cir. 2003).
[32]*See also infra* Chapter 13.VI.D.

4

Motions to Dismiss, to Transfer, to Strike*

*Robert J. Gunther, Jr. and Nancy L. Schroeder, Wilmer Cutler Pickering Hale and Dorr, LLP New York, New York; and Daiske Yoshida, Latham & Watkins, LLP Tokyo, Japan.

I. Motion to Dismiss

A. *Lack of Subject-Matter Jurisdiction—Fed. R. Civ. P. 12(b)(1)*

A district court has subject-matter jurisdiction over a patent lawsuit under 28 U.S.C. §1338(a) only if the complaint establishes either that (1) the patent laws create the cause of action (e.g., a patent infringement claim, or a declaratory judgment action to declare a patent invalid or not infringed) or (2) the plaintiff's right to relief necessarily depends on the resolution of a substantial question of patent law. "[I]ssues of inventorship, infringement, validity and enforceability present sufficiently substantial questions of patent law to support jurisdiction under Section 1338(a)."[1] However, issues relating to ownership of patents do not.[2]

The mere presence of a claim that implicates patent issues does not necessarily create a cause of action arising under the patent laws.[3] If a claim is supported by alternative theories, there is no Section 1338(a) jurisdiction "unless patent law is essential to each of those theories." Thus, a district court has subject-matter jurisdiction over a patent lawsuit under 28 U.S.C. §1338(a) only if the complaint establishes either that: (1) the patent laws create the cause of action, or (2) the plaintiff's right to relief necessarily depends on the resolution of a substantial question of patent law.[4]

---

[1]Bd. of Regents v. Nippon Tel. & Tel. Corp., 414 F.3d 1358, 1363 (Fed. Cir. 2004); *see, e.g.*, U.S. Valves, Inc. v. Dray, 212 F.3d 1368, 1372 (Fed. Cir. 2000) (breach of contract claim in which it was necessary for plaintiff to show that its patents were infringed to prove the alleged breach raised substantial question of patent law); Univ. of Colo. Found. v. Am. Cyanamid Co., 196 F.3d 1366, 1372 (Fed. Cir. 1999) (plaintiff's claim of equitable title to a U.S. patent required determination of inventorship).

[2]Consolidated World Housewares, Inc. v. Finkle, 831 F.2d 261 (Fed. Cir. 1987).

[3]*Id.* at 265.

[4]Uroplasty, Inc. v. Advanced Uroscience, Inc., 239 F.3d 1277, 1280 (Fed. Cir. 2001) (claim that defendant improperly disclosed trade secret information in a patent application did not present a substantial question of patent law). Also, the presence of a patent law defense or counterclaim in answer to a complaint does not make the action arise under the patent laws for purposes of Section 1338(a). Christianson v. Colt Indus. Operating Corp., 486 U.S. 800, 809 (1988).

The Declaratory Judgment Act, 28 U.S.C. §2201, is regularly used in patent cases. For example, in the context of a patent license negotiation, the declaratory plaintiff often seeks a judgment declaring the patent-at-issue either invalid or not infringed by its current or planned activities. In a patent-based declaratory judgment action, the law of the Federal Circuit governs whether an actual controversy exists, and the inquiry is generally quite fact-intensive.[5] District courts must look at "all the circumstances."[6]

The Supreme Court, in *MedImmune, Inc. v. Genentech, Inc.*, clarified the meaning of "actual controversy" as used in the Declaratory Judgment Act.[7] *MedImmune* rejected the Federal Circuit's prior requirement that a patentee "create[] a reasonable apprehension" in the declaratory judgment plaintiff "that it will face an infringement suit."[8] Instead, the Court held that where the declaratory plaintiff is, in essence, forced to choose between a license on a patent it believes does not apply to its products or is invalid or unenforceable, and a potentially debilitating suit for patent infringement, and chooses the license "under protest," its claim for declaratory judgment is not extinguished.[9] In determining that a protesting licensee was not required to breach its license agreement before seeking declaratory relief, the Court considered "all the circumstances"[10] and drew from other legal contexts where a party seeking declaratory judgment was not required to expose itself to liability in the face of threatened action before challenging the basis for the threat.

In view of *MedImmune*, the Federal Circuit adjusted its declaratory judgment jurisprudence, most notably in *SanDisk Corp. v. STMicroelectronics, Inc.*[11] There, the Federal Circuit contrasted a situation in which a party merely becomes aware of the existence of another's patent, which would not give rise to declaratory jurisdic-

---

[5]MedImmune, Inc. v. Centocor, Inc., 409 F.3d 1376, 1378 (Fed. Cir. 2005).

[6]Teva Pharms. USA, Inc. v. Novartis Pharms. Corp., 482 F.3d 1330, 1339 (Fed. Cir. 2007) (quoting MedImmune, Inc. v. Genentech, Inc., 127 S. Ct. 764, 774 n.11 (2007)).

[7]MedImmune, Inc. v. Genentech, Inc., 549 U.S. 118 (2007), *rev'g* MedImmune, Inc. v. Centocor, Inc., 409 F.3d 1376, 1378 (Fed. Cir. 2005).

[8]*Id.* at 132 n.11.

[9]*Id.* at 136.

[10]*Id.* at 127 (quoting Md. Casualty Co. v. Pac. Coal & Oil Co., 312 U.S. 270, 273 (1941).

[11]SanDisk Corp. v. STMicroelectronics, Inc., 480 F.3d 1372, 1381 (Fed. Cir. 2007).

tion, with a situation where a party is faced with "some affirmative act by the patentee," which could give rise to jurisdiction, even if accompanied by a promise not to sue.[12] Thus, "where a patentee asserts rights under a patent based on certain identified ongoing or planned activity of another party, and where that party contends that it has the right to engage in the accused activity without license, an Article III case or controversy will arise and the party need not risk a suit for infringement by engaging in the identified activity before seeking a declaration of its legal rights."[13]

In *Cat Tech LLC v. TubeMaster, Inc.*, the Federal Circuit reaffirmed the second prong of its former reasonable apprehension test, requiring that the plaintiff also has made "meaningful preparation to conduct potentially infringing activity."[14] In *Cat Tech*, the Federal Circuit found that once a party's product design was "substantially fixed," indicating that the party did not "expect to make substantial modifications to its . . . designs once production beg[an]," the controversy became "real," and not hypothetical.[15]

---

[12] *Id.* (noting that "the outer boundaries of declaratory judgment jurisdiction . . . will depend on the application of the principles . . . to the facts and circumstances of each case"). In *SanDisk*, the court found that the district court erred in denying SanDisk's request for declaratory relief and vacated its judgment. The panel found that an Article III case or controversy arose because ST had asserted that it had a right to royalties from SanDisk "based on specific, identified activity," ST presented a detailed infringement analysis to SanDisk at a meeting; and because SanDisk disputed these assertions. *Id.* at 1382.

[13] *Id.* at 1381. Other Federal Circuit cases have further addressed this "affirmative act by the patentee" requirement. *See, e.g.*, Caraco Pharm. Labs., Ltd. v. Forest Labs., Inc., 527 F.3d 1278, 2008 WL 850330 (Fed. Cir. month day, 2008); Micron Tech., Inc. v. Mosaid Techs., Inc., 518 F.3d 897 (Fed. Cir. 2008); Adenta GmbH v. OrthoArm, Inc., 501 F.3d 1364 (Fed. Cir. 2007); Sony Elecs., Inc. v. Guardian Media Techs., Ltd., 497 F.3d 1271 (Fed. Cir. 2007); Teva Pharms. USA, Inc. v. Novartis Pharms. Corp., 482 F.3d 1330 (Fed. Cir. 2007) (jurisdiction conferred where "Novartis created a present and actual 'controversy' by choosing to sue under 35 U.S.C. §271(e)(2)(A) on Teva's single act of infringement, thereby placing into actual dispute the soundness of Teva's ANDA and Teva's ability to secure approval of the ANDA.").

[14] *Cat Tech LLC v. TubeMaster, Inc.*, 528 F.3d 871, 880 (Fed. Cir. 2008) ("[A]lthough *MedImmune* articulated a 'more lenient legal standard' for the availability of declaratory judgment relief in patent cases, . . . [i]f a declaratory judgment plaintiff has not taken significant, concrete steps to conduct infringing activity, the dispute is neither 'immediate' nor 'real' and the requirements for justiciability have not been met." (quoting Micron Tech., Inc. v. Mosaid Techs., Inc., 518 F.3d 897, 902–903 (Fed. Cir. 2008) and Lang v. Pac. Marine & Supply Co., 895 F.2d 761, 764 (Fed. Cir. 1990))).

[15] *Id.* at 882–83.

Because the Declaratory Judgment Act provides that a federal court "may" declare the rights of adverse parties, the authority to do so is discretionary. Thus, even when a case or controversy exists, a court has broad discretion to refuse to hear the suit in question.[16] The Federal Circuit applies an abuse-of-discretion standard to a trial court's refusal to hear a declaratory judgment case. An abuse of discretion "may occur if the trial court's decision was based upon an incorrect conclusion of law or clearly erroneous findings of fact, was devoid of any evidence in the record upon which the court rationally could have based its decision, or was clearly unreasonable or arbitrary."[17] In contrast, courts may not exercise discretion to hear a case when no ripe controversy yet exists and the appellate court reviews a denial of a motion to dismiss for lack of case or controversy without deference.[18]

Like other jurisdictional prerequisites, reasonable apprehension must exist at the time the suit is filed.[19] Though post-filing events "may not create jurisdiction where none existed at the time of filing... [t]he exercise of judicial power under Article III depends at all times on the existence of a case or controversy," and a district court may "properly consider[] post-filing events in its evaluation of continuing jurisdiction."[20] The declaratory plaintiff has the burden of establishing that jurisdiction existed at the time the complaint was filed and that the controversy has continued since.[21]

B. *Failure to Join a Necessary Party—Fed. R. Civ. P. 12(b)(7), 19*

A party may move to dismiss a claim for failure to join a necessary party under Rules 12(b)(7) and 19. Rule 19 requires a court to undertake a two-step analysis to determine whether a person in question should be joined.[22] First, the court must determine

---

[16]EMC Corp. v. Norand Corp., 89 F.3d 807, 814 (Fed. Cir. 1996).

[17]Genentech, Inc. v. Eli Lilly & Co., 998 F.2d 931, 936 (Fed. Cir. 1993).

[18]*See* Teva Pharms. USA, Inc. v. Pfizer, Inc., 395 F.3d 1324, 1332 (Fed. Cir. 2005); Gen-Probe, Inc. v. Vysis, Inc., 359 F.3d 1376, 1379 (Fed. Cir. 2004).

[19]Indium Corp. of Am. v. Semi-Alloys, Inc., 781 F.2d 879, 883 (Fed. Cir. 1985).

[20]Spectronics Corp. v. H.B. Fuller Co., 940 F.2d 631, 636 (Fed. Cir. 1991).

[21]*Id.* at 635.

[22]Vaupel Textilmaschinen KG v. Meccanica Euro Italia SPA, 944 F.2d 870, 876 (Fed. Cir. 1991).

whether a party is "necessary" under Rule 19(a); then, if the court determines that a party is necessary and cannot be joined, "the court shall determine whether in equity and good conscience the action should proceed among the parties before it, or should be dismissed" under the factors described in Rule 19(b).[23]

If a plaintiff has all substantial rights under the asserted patent, then the patentee is not a necessary party and need not be joined.[24] If a plaintiff, by contrast, does not have standing to sue under the patent, then it follows that the case should be dismissed for nonjoinder under Rule 19.[25]

C. Lack of Personal Jurisdiction—Fed. R. Civ. P. 12(b)(2)

1. Personal Jurisdiction Generally

A federal district court in a patent litigation also must have personal jurisdiction over the defendant as it would in any other type of matter.[26] A defendant's residence in the forum state is generally sufficient by itself to establish personal jurisdiction over that defendant.[27]

2. Standard for Personal Jurisdiction Under Federal Circuit Law

The Federal Circuit applies its own law, rather than that of the regional circuits, in determining whether personal jurisdiction exists over an out-of-state defendant in a patent suit.[28] If a suit involves both patent and nonpatent claims, Federal Circuit law also applies to personal jurisdiction for nonpatent claims if "the resolution of the patent infringement issue will be a significant factor" in determining liability under the nonpatent claims.[29] Federal Circuit law on personal jurisdiction focuses less on minimum

---

[23] *Id.* n.1; FED. R. CIV. P. 19.

[24] *Vaupel*, 944 F.2d at 876.

[25] Enzo APA & Son, Inc. v. Geapag A.G., 134 F.3d 1090, 1094 (Fed. Cir. 1998).

[26] VE Holding Corp. v. Johnson Gas Appliance Co., 917 F.2d 1574, 1583 n.20 (Fed. Cir. 1990).

[27] Milliken v. Meyer, 311 U.S. 457, 462–63 (1940).

[28] Beverly Hills Fan Co. v. Royal Sovereign Corp., 21 F.3d 1558, 1564 (Fed. Cir. 1994).

[29] 3D Sys., Inc. v. Aarotech Labs., Inc., 160 F.3d 1373, 1377 (Fed. Cir. 1998).

contacts than that of the forum state or the relevant circuit's interpretation of the forum state's law.

The district court must first examine whether the defendant has sufficient "minimum contacts" with the forum, such "that [it] should reasonably anticipate being haled into court there."[30] One basis for establishing purposeful minimum contacts is that the accused infringer placed a substantial amount of the infringing product into the "stream of commerce," conscious that such goods will be sold in the forum state.[31] This stream of commerce theory also applies where the defendant is the patentee.[32]

The court must next examine whether the claim "arises out of or relates to" the defendant's activities in the forum.[33] This analysis is largely fact-specific, and courts typically look to the quality of the activity in the forum and its relationship to the plaintiff's claim.[34] For example, in a declaratory judgment action, the patentee sending cease-and-desist letters to the forum is by itself insufficient to satisfy the jurisdictional requirement.[35] Such letters, however, may help establish jurisdiction in conjunction with other activities that provide additional contacts with the forum and relate to the underlying claim.[36]

Even if the first two prongs of the analysis are satisfied, a defendant may challenge jurisdiction if it can make "a compelling case that the presence of some other considerations would render jurisdiction unreasonable."[37] The factors that a court may consider in determining whether an exercise of jurisdiction would be unreasonable include: (1) the burden on the defendant; (2) the forum state's interest in adjudicating the dispute; (3) the plaintiff's interest in obtaining convenient and effective relief; (4) the

---

[30]Redwing Shoe Co. v. Hockerson-Halberstadt, Inc., 148 F.3d 1355, 1358 (Fed. Cir. 1998) (quoting World-Wide Volkswagen Corp. v. Woodson, 444 U.S. 286, 297 (1980)).

[31]*E.g.*, N. Am. Philips Corp. v. Am. Vending Sales, Inc., 35 F.3d 1576, 1580 (Fed. Cir. 1994); *Beverly Hills Fan*, 21 F.3d at 1566.

[32]*See* Viam Corp. v. Iowa Export-Import Trading Co., 84 F.3d 424, 428 (Fed. Cir. 1996).

[33]*See* Breckenridge Pharm., Inc. v. Metabolite Labs., Inc., 444 F.3d 1356, 1361 (Fed. Cir. 2006).

[34]*See* Akro Corp. v. Luker, 45 F.3d 1541, 1543 (Fed. Cir. 1995).

[35]*See Redwing Shoe*, 148 F.3d at 1360.

[36]*See, e.g.*, Genetic Implant Sys., Inc. v. Core-Vent Corp., 123 F.3d 1455, 1458 (Fed. Cir. 1997) (minimum contacts established where patentee engaged "in a program to develop a market" in the forum where accused infringer resided).

[37]*Akro*, 45 F.3d at 1549.

interstate judicial system's interest in obtaining the most efficient resolution of controversies; and (5) the "shared interest of the several States in furthering fundamental substantive social policies."[38] Here, the law is in flux with regard to this issue. The Federal Circuit has commented that, "[i]n general, these cases are limited to the rare situation in which the plaintiff's interest and the state's interest in adjudicating the dispute in the forum are so attenuated that they are clearly outweighed by the burden of subjecting the defendant to litigation within the forum."[39]

3. *Exercise of Jurisdiction Based on Extraterritorial Conduct*

The personal jurisdiction analysis set forth above may be used by a court to assert personal jurisdiction over a non-U.S. resident.[40] In addition, a party may be subject to jurisdiction in a U.S. court in certain instances in which the alleged infringing activities occurred outside of the United States.[41]

D. Improper Venue—Fed. R. Civ. P. 12(b)(3)

Venue in patent infringement cases is governed by 28 U.S.C. §1400(b), which provides that a patent infringement suit may be brought in any judicial district where: (1) "the defendant resides" or (2) "the defendant has committed acts of infringement and has a regular and established place of business."[42] Satisfying the venue requirement for patent cases is therefore much less rigorous than in other areas of the law, allowing substantial room for forum shopping. If the defendant is a corporation, it is deemed for purposes of venue to reside in any district where there would be personal jurisdiction over the corporation at the time the action is commenced.[43] If the defendant is an alien, it may be sued for infringement in any district, irrespective of Section 1400(b).[44]

---

[38] *Breckenridge*, 444 F.3d at 1367.

[39] *Beverly Hills Fan*, 21 F.3d at 1568.

[40] *See, e.g., id.* at 1567–68.

[41] *See* 35 U.S.C. §§271(h), (g) (2000).

[42] 28 U.S.C. §1400(b) (2000); VE Holding Corp. v. Johnson Gas Appliance Co., 917 F.2d 1574, 1577–78 (Fed. Cir. 1990).

[43] 28 U.S.C. §1391(c) (2000); *VE Holding*, 917 F.2d at 1578.

[44] 28 U.S.C. §1391(d) (2000); Brunette Mach. Works, Ltd. v. Kockum Indus., Inc., 406 U.S. 706, 706 (1972).

In declaratory judgment actions, the general venue provision, 28 U.S.C. §1391(b), applies rather than Section 1400(b).[45] Section 1400(b) also does not apply to a suit by a patent owner asserting rights under contract or tort law, for instance, even if the suit involves patent issues.[46]

If a court finds that venue is improper, it may in its discretion either dismiss the case or, "in the interest of justice," transfer the case to another district.[47] Because a dismissal for improper venue does not touch the merits and would be without prejudice,[48] a plaintiff may subsequently refile its lawsuit in any proper district provided the claim is not barred by any statute of limitations. Alternatively, in order to avoid "time-consuming and justice defeating technicalities," a court may transfer a case under Section 1406(a) (assuming the standards for transfer under that section are satisfied) regardless of whether it lacked personal jurisdiction over the defendants.[49] Recent Federal Circuit case law and the AIA make it more difficult to cherry pick venue.

E. Motion to Dismiss for Failure to State a Claim Upon Which Relief May Be Granted—Fed. R. Civ. P. 12(b)(6)

Under Rule 12(b)(6), a defendant may move to dismiss a claim for failure to state a claim upon which relief can be granted. Application of Rule 12(b)(6) in patent cases is a procedural question and is therefore governed by the law of the regional circuits.[50]

---

[45] *VE Holding*, 917 F.2d at 1583.

[46] Koratron Co. v. Deering Milliken, Inc., 418 F.2d 1314 (9th Cir. 1969), *cert. denied*, 398 U.S. 909 (1970).

[47] 28 U.S.C. §1406(a) (2000).

[48] *See In re* Cordis Corp., 769 F.2d 733, 737 (Fed. Cir. 1985).

[49] Goldlawr, Inc. v. Heiman, 369 U.S. 463, 466–67 (1962). Motions to transfer venue under 28 U.S.C. §1404(a) are addressed, *infra* III.

[50] Polymer Indus. Prods. Co. v. Bridgestone/Firestone, Inc., 347 F.3d 935, 937 (Fed. Cir. 2003).

II. Motion to Strike

A. *Inequitable Conduct*

1. Standard

Federal Rule of Civil Procedure 12(f) allows a court to strike from "any pleading any insufficient defense." Rule 9(b) requires that "in all averments of fraud or mistake, the circumstances constituting fraud or mistake shall be stated with particularity." Confirming the holdings of a majority of district courts,[51] the Federal Circuit held in *Exergen Corp. v. Walmart Stores, Inc.* that Rule 9(b)'s pleading particularity requirements apply to claims of inequitable conduct and fraud on the PTO and therefore require the specific allegations of the "who, what, when, where, and how of the material misrepresentation or omission committed before the PTO."[52] Furthermore, while knowledge and intent may usually be alleged generally, the party pleading inequitable conduct must "allege sufficient underlying facts from which a court may reasonably infer that a party acted with the requisite state of mind."[53]

Thus, in most district courts, Rule 12(f) in conjunction with Rule 9(b) allows either a party or the court upon its own initiative to strike an allegation of inequitable conduct if it is not pled with sufficient particularity.[54]

The Federal Circuit's 2011 en banc decision in *Therasense, Inc. v. Becton, Dickinson & Co.* further strengthened the requirements for proving inequitable conduct: "To prevail on a claim of inequitable conduct, the accused infringer must prove that the patentee acted with the *specific intent to deceive* the PTO. A finding that the misrepresentation or omission amounts to gross negligence or negligence under a 'should have known' standard does not satisfy this intent requirement. In a case involving nondisclosure of information, clear and convincing evidence must

---

[51] *See, e.g.*, Samsung Elec. Co. Ltd. v. Texas Instr., Inc., 39 USPQ2d 1673, 1675 (N.D. Tex. 1996); *but see* Quantum Corp. v. W. Digital Corp., 10 USPQ2d 1712, 1713 (N.D. Cal. 1988) (holding that allegations of inequitable conduct are not subject to Rule 9(b)).

[52] Exergen Corp. v. Walmart Stores, Inc., 575 F. 3d 1312, 1327 (Fed. Cir. 2009).

[53] *Id.* at 1327 & n.4.

[54] *See, e.g.*, Chiron v. Abbott Lab., 156 F.R.D. 219, 220–21 (N.D. Cal. 1994).

show that the applicant made a deliberate decision to withhold a known material reference."[55] Thus, parties may no longer plead gross negligence in place of specific intent. The court noted that the availability of the old, looser standard had resulted in a dramatic increase in the use of inequitable conduct defenses, often as litigation strategy to increase costs and thus settlement pressure,[56] or to create a cloud of impropriety over the patent and patentee.[57] Since *Therasense*, the Federal Circuit has continued to develop its new inequitable conduct jurisprudence.[58]

2. *Timing*

Under Rule 12(f), the motion to strike allegations of inequitable conduct for failure to plead with particularity must be made by a party within 20 days after service of the pleading. However, the court may bring the motion at any time on its own initiative.[59] Because many courts are loath to allow inequitable conduct claims to proceed in the absence of a good-faith basis for their assertion, courts often challenge the grounds for these claims at the first case-management conference.

---

[55]Therasense, Inc. v. Becton, Dickinson & Co., 649 F.3d 1276, 1290 (Fed. Cir. 2011) (internal quotation marks and citations omitted).

[56]For example, the Eastern District of Virginia recently granted a patentee attorneys' fees under 35 U.S.C. §285, in relation to the defendant's continued pursuance of an inequitable conduct defense after the *Therasense* decision issued, given that in light of the new standard, the defendant's claim was "objectively baseless" with "utterly no evidence as to either" materiality or intent. *See* Pfizer, Inc. v. Teva Pharma. USA, Inc., No. 2:10cv128, 2011 WL 4943984, at *4 (E.D. Va. Oct. 17, 2011).

[57]*Therasense*, 649 F.3d at 1288.

[58]*See, e.g.*, Powell v. Home Depot U.S.A., Inc., 663 F.3d 1221 (Fed. Cir. 2011) (affirming finding of no inequitable conduct based on but-for materiality standard); Cordis Corp. v. Boston Sci. Corp., 658 F.3d 1347 (Fed. Cir. 2011) (affirming district court's rejection of the defense after remand for consideration of materiality and intent); Delano Farms Co. v. Cal. Table Grape Comm'n, 655 F.3d 1337 (Fed. Cir. 2011) (reversing and remanding holding that declaratory judgment plaintiff had sufficiently pled inequitable conduct); Am. Calcar, Inc. v. Am. Honda Motor Co., 651 F.3d 1318 (Fed. Cir. 2011) (vacating district court's finding of inequitable conduct where district court applied wrong standard and provided insufficient findings). For information on bifurcation of inequitable conduct from the case in chief, see *infra* Chapter 11.II.A.

[59]Fed. R. Civ. P. 12(b).

III. Motion to Transfer

In a series of mandamus decisions, the Federal Circuit has ordered transfer in a number of cases, requiring that more weight be given to the public and private interest factors set forth in the language of Section 1404. In the first such decision, *In re TS Tech USA Corp.*, the Federal Circuit granted the defendant's mandamus petition and required a district court in the Eastern District of Texas to transfer the patent case to the Southern District of Ohio.[60] The court accepted the defendant's argument that transfer was proper because its key witnesses and evidence were located within that district; furthermore, the case had no connection with the venue because neither of the parties were incorporated in Texas nor had offices in the District.[61]

The Federal Circuit reviewed the district court's decision under a "clear abuse of discretion,"[62] and applied Fifth Circuit law regarding transfer, which required transfer when the "transferee venue is 'clearly more convenient' than the venue chosen by the plaintiff."[63] The Federal Circuit found that the district court had: (1) given too much weight to plaintiff's choice of venue; (2) failed to follow the Fifth Circuit's "100-mile rule," which provided that the inconvenience factor increased proportionately to the distance a witness had to travel to testify; (3) failed to consider the relative ease of access to sources of proof, as required under §1404(a); and (4) failed to appropriately consider the weight of public interests where the only contact with the forum was that "several of the vehicles were sold in that venue."[64]

Subsequent to its decision in *TS Tech*, the Federal Circuit has granted several similar mandamus petitions, each directing the transfer of a patent action to a more convenient venue. Recurring facts supporting transfer include that one or more of the parties had headquarters in the transferee venue; cost and convenience for attendance of witnesses; availability of compulsory process in

---

[60] *In re* TS Tech. USA Corp., 551 F.3d 1315, 1323 (Fed. Cir. 2008).
[61] *Id.* at 1318.
[62] *Id.*
[63] *Id.* at 1319.
[64] *Id.* at 1320–21.

transferee venue; and lack of contacts with the plaintiff's chosen venue.[64a]

In requiring transfer, the Federal Circuit rejected a district court's assertion that it was the most "centrally located" venue with respect to the parties and/or witnesses.[65] In addition, "negligible judicial efficiencies" should not counterbalance other factors strongly favoring transfer.[66] On the other hand, the district court's substantial experience with the patent at issue in another pending case may weigh in favor of retaining jurisdiction and denying transfer.[67]

Section 299 of The America Invents Act, passed in the fall of 2011[68], makes joinder of multiple defendants in a single patent infringement case more difficult by narrowing the grounds for joinder currently allowed under Federal Rule of Civil Procedure 20(a).[69] Section 299 makes it more difficult for patentees to try a single case against multiple alleged infringers. It will also likely make it more difficult for patentees to sue multiple defendants in a single venue, given the likelihood that the defendants will be

---

[64a] *See, e.g., In re Link_A_Media Devices Corp.*, 662 F.3d 1221 (Fed. Cir. 2011); *In re Verizon Bus. Network Servs.*, 635 F.3d 559 (Fed. Cir. 2011); *In re Microsoft Corp.*, 630 F.3d 1361 (Fed. Cir. 2011); *In re Acer America Corp.*, 626 F.3d 1252 (Fed. Cir. 2010); *In re Zimmer Holdings, Inc.*, 609 F.3d 1378 (Fed. Cir. 2010); *In re Nintendo Co., Ltd.*, 589 F.3d 1194 (Fed. Cir. 2009); *In re Hoffmann-La Roche Inc.*, 587 F.3d 1333 (Fed. Cir. 2009); *In re Genentech, Inc.*, 566 F.3d 1338 (Fed. Cir. 2009).

[65] *See, e.g., In re Genentech*, 566 F.3d at 1344–45.

[66] *See In re Zimmer*, 609 F.3d at 1382.

[67] *See., e.g. In re* Vistaprint Ltd., 628 F.3d 1342 (Fed. Cir. 2010). Where, however, a district court denied transfer because of its supposed experience with the case, settled over 5 years earlier but regarding the patent at issue in the pending case, the Federal Circuit found clear error in light of convenience factors strongly favoring transfer. *See In re Verizon*, 635 F.3d at 562.

[68] See Chapter 2, *supra.*

[69] The Leahy-Smith America Invents Act of 2011, §299, 125 Stat. 284-341 (2011): Multiple "accused infringers may be joined in one action as defendants or counter claim defendants, or have their actions consolidated for trial, or counterclaim defendants only if: (1) any right to relief is asserted against the parties jointly, severally, or in the alternative with respect to or arising out of the same transaction, occurrence or series of transactions or occurrences relating to the making, using, importing into the United States, offering for sale, or selling of the same accused product or process; and (2) questions of fact common to all defendants or counterclaim defendants will arise in the action. (b) ALLEGATIONS INSUFFICIENT FOR JOINDER.—For purposes of this subsection, accused infringers may not be joined in one action as defendants or counterclaim defendants, or have their actions consolidated for trial, based solely on allegations that they each have infringed the patent or patents in suit."

geographically dispersed, shifting more of the burden of costly and time-consuming multi-defendant infringement cases to the patentee.[70]

[70] *See* Rodney R. Sweetland, III & Jeffrey Frey, Avoiding America Invents Act Section 299 Via ITC, http://www.law360.com/articles/277161.

5

Answer and Counterclaims*

*Lawrence B. Goodwin, Kasowitz Benson Torres & Friedman LLP, New York, New York.

I. Introduction

In a patent case, after the usual denial of most of the allegations in the complaint, the defendant will assert defenses. Section 282 of the patent statute identifies several defenses, including noninfringement, invalidity, and unenforceability. Other defenses, such as laches, estoppel, and misuse, are based on common law. Because many of these defenses are asserted as a matter of course in all patent cases (as if by script), many district courts inquire at the case-management conference to determine which are really at issue. The defenses in patent cases themselves require substantial discovery and motion practice, so it is just as important to narrow the defenses early in the case as it is to rein in the claims asserted by the plaintiff.

The defendant may also assert counterclaims for declaratory judgment that mirror defenses and independent claims.

II. Affirmative Defenses

A. *Noninfringement*

Section 282 specifically lists noninfringement as an affirmative defense. The party asserting a noninfringement defense simply asserts that the patent claims, as properly construed as a matter of law by the court, do not cover the things alleged to infringe. The party asserting infringement has the burden to prove infringement by a preponderance of the evidence.

Under Section 271 of the patent statute, infringement can be direct infringement (Section 271(a)), induced infringement (Section 271(b)) or contributory infringement (Section 271(c)). Direct infringement under Section 271(a) can be innocent—even if the infringer does not know about the patent he can be liable for infringement. On the other hand, those accused of indirect infringement—i.e., induced or contributory infringement, can assert a defense that they did not have knowledge of the allegedly infringed patent, and therefore cannot be liable for induced or contributory infringement.[1]

In the America Invents Act,[2] (the AIA), an amendment[3] to Section 273 provides a noninfringement defense if the accused infringer can prove, by clear and convincing evidence, that he commercially used the claimed invention internally within his company, within the United States, at least one year before the earlier of (i) the filing date of the patent or (ii) the inventor's disclosure of the invention.

B. *Invalidity of the Patent*

Patents are presumed valid under 35 U.S.C. §282, and the party asserting invalidity has the burden of proof by clear and convincing evidence. Some bases to assert invalidity are detailed in the subsections below.

1. *Section 101*

One defense, based on 35 U.S.C. §101, alleges that the claimed invention is not within the statutory classes of subject matter (e.g., a process or machine) but instead is directed to a pure idea or mental process, or is inoperable. Although Section 101 historically has not often been asserted, a defense under this section has become much more prevalent as a result of *Bilski v. Kappos*,[4] which held that a patent on a method of hedging financial losses in the energy industry was not patentable subject matter. The Supreme Court's more recent decision in *Prometheus Laboratories, Inc. v. Mayo Collaborative Services*,[5] holding that a method for optimizing the administration of a drug for gastrointestinal disorders was

---

[1]Global-Tech Appliances, Inc. v. SEB S. A., 131 S. Ct. 2060 (2011). Note that this defense will not be available to an indirect infringer who does not have actual knowledge of the infringement because of "willful blindness."

[2]Public Law 112–29, 125 Stat. 284 (2011), to be codified as 35 U.S.C. §299.

[3]This amendment applies to any patent issued on or after September 16, 2011.

[4]130 S. Ct. 3218, 561 US 130, 177 L. Ed. 2d 792 (2010).

[5]No. 10-1150 (Mar. 20, 2012).

an attempt to claim a law of nature and therefore unpatentable under 35 USC §101 will certainly increase the assertion of this defense.

Another Section 101-based (but little-used) defense is double patenting, which may be asserted when two patents issue for the same or similar inventions. The doctrine seeks to prevent the unjustified extension of patent exclusivity beyond the term of a patent.

2. *Section 102*

A patented invention must be new. If any one of the conditions set forth in Section 102 is not met, an invention is not new, and thus a patent on that invention would be invalid. If the "prior art" "anticipates" the claimed invention, the anticipated claims are invalid. Anticipation is a fact issue and must be proved by clear and convincing evidence.

The AIA will substantially change the way in which Section 102 is applied—but only for patents that have an effective filing date[6] on or after March 16, 2013. Accordingly, this discussion is in two parts: first, for those patents having a filing date prior to March 16, 2013; and second, for those patents filed thereafter.

a. *For Those Patents Having an Effective Filing Date Prior to March 16, 2013:*

Under Section 102(a), if the claimed invention was known or used in the United States, or patented or described in a publication anywhere in the world, before the patentee's *date of invention*, the claim lacks novelty and is invalid. Similarly, under Section 102(e), if the claimed invention was described in a U.S. patent application filed in the United States before the plaintiff patentee's *date of invention*, the claim lacks novelty and is invalid. In many cases, if defenses are raised under either Section 102(a) or (e), the patentee will assert that the invention date predates the defendant's alleged prior art, and thus the patent is not invalid.

Section 102(b) defines prior art as disclosures of the invention in patents or publications anywhere in the world, or public use or sale of the invention in the United States, more than one year before the U.S. filing date of the application for the plaintiff's patent. Thus, unlike Section 102(a) and (e), prior art under Section 102(b) will invalidate the

---

[6]The "effective filing date" is either the actual filing date or the filing date of the earliest application to which the patent claims priority.

patent regardless of the date of the patentee's invention so long as the prior art predates the patent's filing date by more than one year.

Although less commonly asserted, a defendant may raise bases of invalidity under Section 102(c) (abandonment), Section 102(d) (foreign patent application filed more than one year before the date of the patentee's U.S. filing), or Section 102(f) (the inventor did not himself invent the claimed subject matter).

Section 102(g) is the so-called "interference" statute that allows a defendant to prove that someone invented the claimed subject matter in the United States before the patentee's invention. Section 102(g) is sometimes invoked by the defendant in response to the plaintiff patentee's assertion that his or her invention date was prior to the filing date of a prior patent that otherwise would have been prior art under Section 102(e).

b. For Those Patents Having an Effective Filing Date on or After March 16, 2013:

New Section 102 from the AIA does away with Sections (a)-(g) from the current law and implements what is commonly referred to as a "first-to-file" system. Under the new Section 102, the *date of the invention* is irrelevant for purposes of novelty—the only date that matters is the filing date. Thus, under Section 102(a)(1), if the claimed invention was patented, described in a printed publication, or in public use, on sale, or otherwise available to the public anywhere in the world before the effective filing date of the claimed invention, the claim lacks novelty and is invalid. Similarly, under Section 102(a)(2), if the claimed invention was described in another person's earlier-filed patent, the claim lacks novelty and is invalid.

New Section 102(b) includes an important exception to the rules stated in the new Section 102(a): The publication or other disclosure of the inventor's own work will not invalidate the claimed invention as long as the inventor files the patent application within one year of the disclosure.

3. Section 103

Section 103 requires the patented subject matter to be "nonobvious."[7] Thus, even if no single prior art reference anticipates the claimed invention, Section 103 can operate as a defense if the defendant can show, by clear and convincing evidence, that a person of ordinary skill in the art would have found the claimed

[7] *See* KSR Int'l Co. v. Teleflex, Inc., 127 S. Ct. 1727 (2007).

invention obvious in view of prior art defined in Section 102(a), (b), (e), or (g) (or Section 102(a) of the AIA).

The only difference between the current Section 103 and the new Section 103 under the AIA relates to timing: under the current law, obviousness is to be judged at the time of the invention; under the new law, obviousness is to be judged at the time of filing of the application.

4. *Section 112*

Invalidity may also be based on noncompliance with Section 112. Paragraph 1 of Section 112 contains the enablement and written-description requirements of patentability. To meet the enablement requirement, a patent's specification must enable those skilled in the relevant art to make and use the invention without undue experimentation. To comply with the written-description requirement, a patent's specification must contain information sufficient "to show that the inventor possessed the claimed invention at the time of the original disclosure." Paragraph 1 of Section 112 also requires that the patent set forth the best mode contemplated by the inventor for carrying out his invention (the so-called "best-mode" requirement).

The AIA does not substantively change the existing Section 112. Note, however, that Section 282 of the AIA states that "the failure to disclose the best mode shall not be a basis on which any claim of a patent may be canceled or held invalid or otherwise unenforceable."[8]

Paragraph 2 of Section 112 can also serve as a defense if the claims are indefinite, i.e., they do not clearly point out and distinctly claim the inventive subject matter. If a person skilled in the relevant art would not be able to discern the meaning of the claims, the claims violate paragraph 2 of Section 112.

5. *Other Matters Relating to an Invalidity Defense*

Validity is analyzed on a claim-by-claim basis. Each claim of a patent must be separately assessed for validity. For example, an independent claim might be invalid under Section 102 because of an on-sale bar (i.e., the product embodying the defined inven-

---

[8]This provision applies to proceedings commenced on or after September 16, 2011.

tion was on sale more than one year before the patent application was filed), but a dependent claim, or another independent claim, might not be invalid because it contains limitations that were not in the product on sale. In some cases, there are so many asserted patent claims that analysis becomes unwieldy. If the parties stipulate that a certain claim is representative of a group of claims, then the validity resolution of the representative claim applies to all the other claims in the group.

A finding of noninfringement does not render a counterclaim for invalidity moot. A party seeking declaratory judgment of invalidity presents a claim independent of the patentee's charge of infringement. Moreover, the determination of validity has greater public importance than infringement.

C. *Inequitable Conduct in Obtaining the Patent*

People involved in the prosecution of a patent application have a duty of candor and good faith in dealing with the Patent and Trademark Office. The intentional failure to meet the duty of candor and good faith constitutes inequitable conduct. The duty is breached by a misrepresentation of a material fact or failure to disclose material information. Inequitable conduct related to any of the claims in the patent bars enforcement of the entire patent by the patent holder.

To establish that a patent is unenforceable, the defendant must show by clear and convincing evidence that: (1) the information withheld or misrepresented was material to the patentability of the invention; and (2) the duty of candor was breached with intent to deceive or mislead the Patent and Trademark Office. Once the challenger has shown the requisite levels of materiality and intent, then the district court must weigh the equities to determine whether the applicant's conduct before the patent office warrants rendering the entire patent unenforceable.

The Federal Circuit, in *Therasense, Inc. v. Becton, Dickinson and Co.*,[9] held that for the court to find the withheld information or misrepresentation to be "material," the party asserting the defense has the burden to prove, that but for the deception, the patent office would not have allowed the patent claim to issue.

[9] 649 F.3d 1276 (Fed. Cir. 2011) (*en banc*).

The Federal Circuit has also held, in *Exergen Corp. v. Wal-Mart Stores, Inc.*,[9a] that a party pleading the defense of inequitable conduct must do so with specificity, meeting the standards established by Rule 9(b), Fed.R.Civ.P., for fraud claims.

D. License or Implied License

Infringement is the unauthorized use of the patented product or process. Thus, a showing by the defendant that the use was authorized will defeat the claim of infringement. The term "use" in this context refers generally to the accused infringing activity. One way to establish that the use was noninfringing is based on a license or implied license. When the patentee and accused infringer are parties to an express license agreement, the dispute may be over whether the products are covered by the license.

The implied license defense is often based on the first-sale or exhaustion doctrine. Once the patentee already receives due compensation for the sale of a product, the patentee is not entitled to double or repeated compensation for subsequent sales or uses of that product. For example, resale of a product that was purchased from an authorized seller cannot constitute infringement. "To invoke the protection of the first sale doctrine, the authorized first sale must have occurred under the United States Patent."[10]

Another common circumstance giving rise to an implied license is when the patentee sells equipment for making its patented invention. In the absence of circumstances tending to show the contrary, if the plaintiff sells a product or equipment that has no noninfringing uses, that sale includes an implied license to practice the invention. This principle was applied to a case where the patentee sold two components separately but the patent covered only the combination of the two parts. The court found that the customers who purchased one of the components from the patentee had an implied license to practice the invention, which was a defense against contributory infringement by an unauthorized seller of the second component.

The existence of an implied license is a question of law, based on underlying facts that the defendant must prove by a preponderance of the evidence.

[9a] 575 F.3d 1312 (Fed. Cir. 2009).

[10] Jazz Photo Corp. v. United States ITC, 264 F.3d 1094 (Fed. Cir. 2001).

E. Limitations on Damages

Under 35 U.S.C. §286, the period for damages is limited to six years before filing the complaint or the counterclaim for infringement. The infringement suit may be filed after the patent expires, provided the damages are limited to the period starting not more than six years before filing the lawsuit and ending no later than the patent expiration.

Section 287 is the "marking and notice" statute. It provides a limitation on damages that occur prior to actual notice of infringement, under certain circumstances. If the patent owner, or someone with his or her authority (a licensee), makes, sells, or offers to sell in the United States a product covered by the patent, damages are only available after the patent owner notifies the alleged infringer of its infringement. The actual notice requirement is satisfied when the recipient is informed of the identity of the patent and the activity that is believed to be an infringement, accompanied by a proposal to abate the infringement, whether by license or otherwise. If actual notice of infringement is required, it must be given even if the accused infringer is independently aware of the patent. Notice may also be satisfied by marking the patentee or licensee's products with the patent number. Section 287 does not apply if the patent owner, or anyone with his or her authority, does not make, sell, or offer to sell any products under the patent in the United States. Also, this limitation typically does not apply to patents containing exclusively method claims; however, if a patent contains both method and apparatus claims, or if the method covers uses of a patented apparatus, marking may be required.[11]

F. Equitable Defenses: Laches and Estoppel

The premise underlying the equitable defenses of laches and estoppel is that the patentee's delay or misleading conduct tips the scales of justice in favor of the defendant. By engaging in improper conduct, the patentee forfeits what would otherwise be rightful compensation for the defendant's infringement.

---

[11] *See* Devices for Medicine, Inc. v. Boehl, 822 F.2d 1062 (Fed. Circ. 1987).

1. *Laches*

"Two elements underlie the defense of laches: (a) the patentee's delay in bringing the suit was unreasonable and inexcusable, and (b) the alleged infringer suffered material prejudice attributable to the delay."[12]

The patentee may negate the laches defense by establishing an excuse or justification for the delay. Excuses that may be offered in some instances include negotiations with the accused infringer, poverty or illness under limited circumstances, wartime conditions, and dispute over patent ownership and extent of infringement. Another excuse is when the patentee is involved in other litigation, and generally (though not a rigid rule) the defendant is aware of the other pending litigation. Sometimes the inequity of the patentee's conduct is negated by evidence of egregious conduct on the part of the defendant. For example, when the patentee can demonstrate that the defendant deliberately copied or otherwise knowingly infringed the patent, this evidence may temper the evidence of patentee's laches.

When the delay is more than six years from the time that the patentee has knowledge of the infringement, there is a rebuttable presumption of laches. The defendant at all times bears the burden of persuasion to establish the laches defense. Upon proof that the delay exceeded six years, by reason of the presumption, absent other equitable considerations, the defendant makes a prima facie defense of laches. If the patentee presents sufficient evidence that, if believed, would preclude a finding in favor of the infringer, then the presumption evaporates and the infringer is left to its proof. The courts may have chosen the six-year limit because it is the statutory limitation on damages; however, these two six-year periods are in theory completely unrelated.

Where the defense of laches is established, the court may bar the patentee from recovering damages that accrued before the lawsuit.

2. *Equitable Estoppel*

Equitable estoppel completely bars a patentee's claim. There are three elements for establishing equitable estoppel: "(a) The

---

[12]A.C. Aukerman Co. v. R.L. Chaides Constr. Co., 960 F.2d 1020 (Fed. Cir. 1992) (*en banc*).

patentee, through misleading conduct, leads the alleged infringer to reasonably infer that the patentee does not intend to enforce its patent against the alleged infringer. 'Conduct' may include specific statements, action, inaction, or silence where there was an obligation to speak. (b) The alleged infringer relies on that conduct. (c) Due to its reliance, the alleged infringer will be materially prejudiced if the patentee is allowed to proceed with his claim."[13]

Equitable estoppel does not require the passage of an unreasonable period of time before filing the suit. To contrast the two defenses: Laches focuses on the reasonableness of the plaintiff's delay; equitable estoppel focuses on what the defendant is lead to believe from the plaintiff's conduct.

The defense of equitable estoppel requires some sort of communication between the parties. The patentee must have communicated something to the infringer in a misleading way. To contrast the two defenses: Laches may be established with or without communication between the parties before the lawsuit; equitable estoppel will only be established with evidence of communication from or conduct by the patentee before the lawsuit.

The infringer must show that the patentee's communication or conduct supports an inference that the patentee did not intend to press an infringement claim against the infringer. Again, to contrast the two defenses: Laches may be established even though the infringer did not know of the patentee or the patent before the lawsuit; for equitable estoppel, the infringer must have known of the patentee and the patent, and the patentee must have had knowledge of the infringer's activities.

Where an alleged infringer establishes the defense of equitable estoppel, the patentee's claim for damages, as well as injunctive relief, may be entirely barred.

G. *Patent Misuse*

The defense of patent misuse "relates generally to the use of patent rights to obtain or to coerce an unfair commercial advantage [so to] extend the economic effect beyond the scope of the patent grant."[14] "The concept of patent misuse arose to restrain

---

[13]*Id.* at 1028.

[14]C.R. Bard, Inc. v. M3 Sys., Inc., 157 F.3d 1340, 1372 (Fed. Cir. 1998).

practices that did not in themselves violate any law, but that draw anticompetitive strength from the patent right, and thus were deemed to be contrary to public policy."[15]

Patent misuse is viewed as a broader wrong than an antitrust violation because of the economic power that may be derived from a patentee's right to exclude. Thus, misuse may arise even when there are no violations of antitrust law. The key inquiry in patent misuse is determining whether, by imposing conditions that derive their force from the patent, the patentee has impermissibly broadened the scope of the patent grant with anticompetitive effect. "In cases where the patentee imposes restrictions on the use of its invention, if the restriction is reasonably within the patent grant, the patent misuse defense can never succeed. In cases in which a condition controlling the use of a patented invention extends beyond the patentee's statutory right to exclude, however, either a per se rule of patent misuse or a rule of reason analysis must be applied."[16] Patent misuse arises in equity, and a holding of misuse renders the patent unenforceable until the misuse is purged; misuse does not, of itself, invalidate the patent.

Congress, however, has expressly defined certain practices as not constituting patent misuse. Below is the excluded conduct set forth in the patent statute:

1. deriving revenue from acts that would otherwise constitute contributory infringement of the patent;
2. licensing or authorizing another to perform acts that would otherwise constitute contributory infringement of the patent;
3. seeking to enforce patent rights against infringement or contributory infringement, such as bringing a lawsuit;
4. refusing to license or use any rights to the patent; or
5. in the absence of the relevant market power, using a tying arrangement, i.e., conditioning a patent license or the sale of the patented product on the license of another patent or purchase of a separate product.[17]

[15] *Id.* (quoting Mallinckrodt, Inc. v. Medipart, Inc., 976 F.2d 700, 703–04 (Fed. Cir. 1992)).

[16] Monsanto Co. v. Homan McFarling, 363 F.3d 1336, 1341 (Fed. Cir. 2004) (internal citations omitted).

[17] 35 U.S.C. §271(d) (2000).

III. COUNTERCLAIMS

A. *Antitrust Counterclaims*

Patentees have a statutory right to bring a civil suit in federal court against infringers. However, some conduct may incur antitrust liability, including: (1) the enforcement of a patent known to be obtained by fraud; (2) bringing a sham litigation; (3) tying the license of a patent to the purchase of unpatented goods; or (4) creating an overall scheme to use the patent to violate the antitrust laws.

The two most common antitrust counterclaims involve allegations that the patentee has violated the antitrust laws by enforcing a patent knowingly obtained by fraud or by bringing a sham litigation. These counterclaims are referred to as *Walker Process*[18] and *PRE*[19] claims, respectively. To prove a *Walker Process* claim, a defendant must demonstrate that the patentee: (1) obtained the patent by knowingly and willfully misrepresenting facts to the Patent Office, and (2) was aware of the fraud at the time the suit was brought. If these elements are met, a patentee may be stripped of its exemption from the antitrust laws, and antitrust liability exists if the defendant can establish the necessary additional elements of a violation of the antitrust laws. A defendant asserting an antitrust counterclaim based on a *PRE* sham-litigation theory must demonstrate that: (1) the lawsuit is objectively baseless, and (2) the baseless lawsuit "conceals an attempt to interfere directly with the business relationships of a competitor" through the litigation process—as opposed to the plaintiff seeking to protect its rights through litigation. Evidence of anticompetitive intent or purpose alone cannot transform otherwise legitimate activity into a sham.

B. *Unfair Competition Claims*

The defendant may also assert a counterclaim for unfair competition under the Lanham Act or state law. Such claims typically center around statements made by the patentee to the defendant's

---

[18] *See* Walker Process Equip., Inc. v. Food Mach. & Chem. Corp., 382 U.S. 172 (1965).

[19] *See* Prof'l Real Estate Investors, Inc. v. Columbia Pictures Indus., Inc., 508 U.S. 49, 58–60 (1993).

customers claiming that customers and/or the defendant infringe. While a patentee has the right to publicize its patent rights and to make allegations of infringement, such claims cannot be made in bad faith. For example, if a patentee knows that its patent is invalid or not infringed, yet represents to the marketplace that a competitor is infringing, such conduct would constitute bad faith and support a claim of unfair competition.

C. *Tortious Interference Claims*

A defendant may also assert counterclaims based on state-law tort causes of action, such as tortious interference with contracts, prospective contracts, and business relations. As with unfair-competition claims, such claims are often founded on the patentee's improper behavior in the marketplace, e.g., by making baseless claims regarding infringement to a defendant's customers.

D. *Declaratory Judgment of Noninfringement, Invalidity, or Unenforceability*

In addition to pleading noninfringement, invalidity, and/or unenforceability as affirmative defenses, a defendant will usually assert a counterclaim for a declaratory judgment on these grounds as well. This allows the defendant to seek affirmative relief on these grounds even when a patentee dismisses its claims against the defendant or when the court enters judgment against a patentee at any stage of the proceedings. Thus, for example, under Federal Rule of Civil Procedure 58, an order of final judgment may not be entered following summary judgment of noninfringement on all of plaintiff's claims where counterclaims of invalidity have been asserted. Instead, the court must proceed to adjudicate those claims, even if it finds it unnecessary to do so to resolve the infringement claims that prompted the litigation in the first instance.

6

Preliminary Injunction Motions*

I. Introduction

Although 35 U.S.C. §283 specifically provides that preliminary injunctions may be issued in patent cases, they remain an extraordinary remedy "not to be routinely granted."[1] Courts have discretion as to whether or not to grant a preliminary injunction, based on the four traditional equitable factors for such an injunction:

- the likelihood of success on the merits of the underlying litigation;

---

*George F. Pappas, Covington & Burling LLP, Washington, D.C. The author wishes to thank Ranganath Sudarshan for his assistance in preparing this chapter revision and Joseph A. Calvaruso, Orrick, Herrington & Sutcliffe, New York, New York, who prepared the original version of this chapter.

[1]High Tech Med. Instrumentation, Inc. v. New Image Indus., Inc., 49 F.3d 1551, 1554 (Fed. Cir. 1995).

- whether immediate irreparable harm will result if the relief is not granted;
- whether the balance of hardships to the parties weighs in the movant's favor; and
- whether the public interest is best served by granting the injunctive relief.

II. Likelihood of Success on the Merits

To establish a likelihood of success on the merits, a patentee must show that it will likely prove infringement, and that it will likely withstand challenges, if any, to the validity of the patent.[2] These determinations follow the same substantive law used to determine these issues at trial, but with some adjustment to the relative burdens of going forward with evidence and persuasion. For example, while the patentee must demonstrate a likelihood of success in light of the presumptions and burdens that will inhere at trial, an accused infringer need only raise a "substantial question" concerning validity, enforceability, or infringement.[3]

A. *Infringement*

A showing of infringement at the preliminary injunction stage follows the same two-step process used to determine infringement at trial: construing the claims of the patent-in-suit and comparing them to the accused device. Thus, the Federal Circuit has directed district courts to begin any preliminary injunction analysis with construction of those claims upon which the request for preliminary relief is premised. However, claim construction conducted at the preliminary injunction stage need not be considered final for the rest of the case, because it is usually based on an incomplete record and an accelerated process. The court may therefore alter or expand on its claim construction to the extent appropriate at later stages of the litigation.[4]

---

[2]Titan Tire Corp. v. Case New Holland, Inc., 566 F.3d 1372, 1376 (Fed. Cir. 2009).

[3]*See, e.g.*, Abbott Labs. v. Andrx Pharms., Inc., 452 F.3d 1331 (Fed. Cir. 2006).

[4]For more on infringement, see *supra* Chapter 3.

B. Invalidity

Unlike at trial, where the accused infringer must prove invalidity by clear and convincing evidence, a preliminary injunction should be denied if the accused infringer asserts an invalidity defense that raises a "substantial question" regarding validity. "The fact that, at trial on the merits, the proof of invalidity will require clear and convincing evidence is a consideration for the judge to take into account in assessing the challenger's case at the preliminary injunction stage; it is not an evidentiary burden to be met preliminarily by the challenger."[5] In turn, the conclusion as to whether a "substantial question" has been raised by the defendant is reached after considering the evidence on both sides of the validity issue.[6] After considering both the patentee's and the defendants' validity arguments, if the alleged infringer has presented an invalidity defense that the patentee has not shown lacks "substantial merit," the trial court should conclude that the patentee has not succeeded in showing likelihood of success on the merits.[7]

III. Irreparable Harm

The patentee must also demonstrate that it will suffer irreparable harm in order to receive a preliminary injunction. There is no presumption of irreparable harm upon a showing of likelihood of success.[8]

The patentee may demonstrate irreparable harm by showing potential lost sales, loss of market share and goodwill, or the accused infringer's inability to satisfy a judgment for damages. Nevertheless, a showing of potential lost sales is insufficient to demonstrate irreparable harm if other factors weigh against irreparable harm. Moreover, simply showing that an accused infringer has sufficient funds to fully compensate the patentee with monetary damages is insufficient to negate irreparable harm because it ignores the accused infringer's effect on the patentee's right to market exclusivity.

---

[5] *Titan Tire*, 566 F.3d at 1380.

[6] *Id.* at 1379.

[7] *Id.*; New England Braiding Co. v. A.W. Chesterton Co., 970 F.2d 878, 883 (Fed. Cir. 1992).

[8] Robert Bosch LLC v. Pylon Mfg. Corp., 659 F.3d 1142, 1149 (Fed. Cir. 2011).

The defendant may attempt to negate a finding of irreparable harm by showing, e.g., that: (1) the accused infringer has ceased or will soon cease the allegedly infringing activities, thus making an injunction unnecessary; (2) the patentee has engaged in a pattern of granting licenses under the patent, such that it may be reasonable to expect that invasion of the patent right can be recompensed with a royalty rather than with an injunction; or (3) the patentee unduly delayed in bringing suit. The patentee may rebut a claim that it unduly delayed suit by showing that the delay was caused by settlement negotiations, pursuing suits against other infringers, or other defenses to a claim of laches.[9] As a general matter, evidence of irreparable harm cannot be rebutted by a showing that the patentee's business is being harmed by other infringers, market conditions, or poor business decisions made by the patentee, rather than the accused infringer's conduct. However, evidence of other infringers may support a finding of unreasonable delay in bringing suit, willingness to accept royalties in lieu of market exclusivity, or indifference in enforcing one's patent.

IV. Balance of Hardships

To obtain a preliminary injunction, the patentee need not prove that the balance of hardships weighs in its favor, but it will typically make the same arguments it used to demonstrate irreparable harm. The court may also consider the relative sizes of the parties, whether the patentee had an exclusive position in the market, the relative effect on the business of the parties, or the relative timing of the parties' entry into the market. The mere fact that an accused infringer might be put out of business by the injunction does not insulate it when the other preliminary injunction factors tip the balance in favor of the patentee.

V. Public Interest

In most cases, the public interest in enforcing valid patents outweighs the lower prices afforded by competition, resulting in

---

[9] *See supra* Chapter 5.II.F.1.

this factor favoring the patentee. Nevertheless, the public interest may favor the accused infringer when enjoining the accused product would otherwise affect public health or safety. Moreover, district courts may decline to enter a permanent injunction where the patentee has no plans to market a useful product and the injunction would deprive the public of such a product.

7

The Case-Management Conference*

I. Introduction

Successfully handling a patent case begins with the case-management conference. Patent cases typically involve complex technologies, challenging legal questions, and unique discovery issues not found in other civil litigation. It thus behooves the court and the parties to appreciate early the unique aspects of a patent case.

---

*George F. Pappas, Covington & Burling LLP, Washington, D.C. The assistance of Kevin B. Collins, Scott C. Weidenfeller, and Ranganath Sudarshan in preparing this material is greatly appreciated.

II Conference Checklist

Below is a checklist of issues for the case-management conference that courts can consider discussing with the parties:

Ask for an informal description of the technology

Require a brief statement/summary of claims and defenses by each party

- Is the alleged infringement:
  - Literal
  - Indirect: inducement or contributory
- Does the doctrine of equivalents apply?
- Special issues relating to willfulness:
  - Timing of the assertion of the claim
  - Timing of the reliance on any opinion of counsel
  - Possibility of bifurcation
  - Possibility of disqualification of counsel
- Is alleged invalidity based on:
  - Anticipation
  - Obviousness
  - On-sale bar
  - Prior public use
  - Lack of written description
  - Lack of enablement
  - Failure to disclose best mode
- If inequitable conduct is pleaded, the parties should:
  - Identify material misrepresentations or omissions
  - Identify evidence of intent to mislead
  - Address possible disqualification of counsel who obtained the patent
- Antitrust claims/unfair competition claims:
  - Should they be severed?
- Relief sought:
  - Permanent injunction
  - Damages:
    - Reasonable royalty
    - Lost profits
    - Price erosion
    - Convoyed sales

- Limitations on damages:
  - Laches
  - Estoppel
  - Notice and marking
- Discussion of alternative dispute resolution (ADR):
  - Usefulness
  - Timing
  - Mediation or arbitration

Determine whether a protective order will be needed

- Seek agreement of the parties
- Access to confidential information often limited based on:
  - Sensitivity of information and whether disclosure could cause substantial harm to opposing party's competitive position
  - Whether individual is engaged in "competitive decision making," e.g., patent strategy, licensing negotiations, sales and marketing, and research and development in relevant product market
- Have a form protective order if no agreement within specified period

Consider an order on electronic discovery issues

- Rule 16 provides that court may provide for disclosure and discovery of electronically stored information or include agreements reached by parties
- Encourage agreements as to scope of search, including search terms, custodians and witnesses to respond, relevant time period
- Need to require preservation of electronically stored information
- Consider default standard absent agreement between the parties
- Consider adopting Model Order on electronic discovery in patent cases[1]

In determining the length of time needed for fact discovery:

- Consider bifurcating discovery:
  - Claim construction/infringement issues

---

[1]The Model Order is available at http://www.cafc.uscourts.gov/images/stories/thecourt/Ediscovery_Model_Order.pdf.

  - Infringement/validity/inequitable conduct issues
  - Infringement/willful infringement issues
  - Liability/damages issues
- Ask if foreign discovery will be necessary:
  - Depositions of foreign nationals in their respective countries (Hague Convention or by agreement)
  - Depositions of foreign nationals in United States (with translators)
  - Document production in foreign countries
  - Volume of documents requiring translations

Determine length of time needed for expert discovery

- Usually three rounds—party with burden of proof or burden of production goes first:
  - First round—plaintiff on infringement, defendant on invalidity and inequitable conduct
  - Second round—each party files responsive reports and plaintiff produces opinions on objective factors on nonobviousness
  - Third round—defendant responds only to opinions on objective factors of nonobviousness

Consider limitations on discovery

- Number of total hours for fact witnesses or number of depositions; should you vary from federal or local rules?
- Location of depositions
- Discoverability of invention disclosures, opinions of counsel, and patents closely related to those at issue in the case

Determine need for tutorials

- How do you want to learn about the technology in the case?
  - Tutorial by counsel in court
  - Tutorial by experts in court
  - DVDs from each side for use by court at any time
  - Court-appointed expert

Set timing and procedures for *Markman* process

- Prior to construing claims, require a joint statement identifying what claims are in dispute, the parties' respective interpretations, and all evidentiary support for their proposed construction
- Decide when to construe claims
  - Close of fact discovery
  - Close of expert discovery
  - Other appropriate time

- Limit the disputed claim terms to those that are essential to resolving the case
- Require simultaneous opening legal briefs and responsive briefs
- Decide whether to hold a hearing
- If a hearing is held:
  - Prior to or at the hearing, expect a "walk through" of the patent identifying each of its parts, the file history, and any other proceedings before the PTO, such as an interference or reexamination, that bear on the claims to be construed
  - Consider whether to allow parties to call witnesses, e.g., the inventor or experts on the technology at issue and state of the art at the time of the invention
  - Encourage parties' use of graphics, animations and other visual displays to aid in understanding the technology and disputed claim terms

Determine timing of dispositive motions

- For threshold dispositive issues, motions prior to any claim construction
- Conduct a separate *Markman* hearing, followed by dispositive motions
- Combined *Markman* and summary judgment hearing

III. Local Rules

Overall, the court and the parties may wish to use all or a portion of local rules that have been adopted by various district courts across the country.[2] Alternatively, the court may wish to create a scheduling order tailored to the unique aspects of an individual case.

---

[2]At present, at least sixteen federal district courts have enacted local patent rules. These include: the Northern District of California, Southern District of California, Northern District of Georgia, Northern District of Illinois, Southern District of Indiana, District of Massachusetts, District of Minnesota, Eastern District of Missouri, District of New Jersey, Eastern District of North Carolina, Southern District of Ohio, Western District of Pennsylvania, Eastern District of Texas, Northern District of Texas, Southern District of Texas, Western District of Washington.

Any patent case is almost certain to proceed more efficiently if the issues identified in the checklist above are considered.

Most local patent rules impose deadlines for a plaintiff to serve infringement contentions, for a defendant to serve invalidity contentions, and for the parties to exchange proposed claim constructions. Most local patent rules also contain provisions addressing the production of opinions of counsel by a party wishing to rely on such opinions as a defense to an allegation of willful infringement.

Below are some issues that are addressed by certain local patent rules, but not all:

- Proceedings under 21 U.S.C. §355 ("Hatch-Waxman Act") (e.g., D. N.J., N.D. Ohio)
- Settlement and Alternative Dispute Resolution (e.g., S.D. Cal., D. Minn., S.D. Ohio, W.D. Pa.)
- Litigation stays pending completion of reexamination at the U.S. Patent & Trademark Office (e.g., N.D. Ill.)

The full text of local patent rules may be found at the following links:

N.D. Cal.	http://www.cand.uscourts.gov/filelibrary/177/LocalRules-Patent-12-2009.pdf
S.D. Cal.	http://www.casd.uscourts.gov/uploads/Rules/Local%20Rules/LocalRules.pdf
N.D. Ga.	http://www.gand.uscourts.gov/pdf/NDGARulesPatent.pdf
N.D. Ill.	http://www.ilnd.uscourts.gov/home/LocalRules.aspx?rtab=patentrules
S.D. Ind.	http://www.insd.uscourts.gov/Forms/Patent%20CMP%20-%20Track%203.pdf
D. Mass.	http://www.mad.uscourts.gov/general/pdf/LC/LOCALRULEScombined.pdf (Rule 16.6)
D. Minn.	http://www.mnd.uscourts.gov/local_rules/forms/FORM-4.doc
E.D. Mo.	http://www.moed.uscourts.gov/sites/default/files/LocalPatentRules.pdf
D. N.J.	http://www.njd.uscourts.gov/rules/completeRulesOctober2011.pdf (Section 9.3)

E.D.N.C	http://www.nced.uscourts.gov/localRules/LocalRules.htm (Rules 301-305)
S.D. Ohio	http://www.ohsd.uscourts.gov/localrules/ohsdpatentrules.pdf
W.D. Pa.	http://www.pawd.uscourts.gov/Documents/Forms/LocalPatentRules.pdf
E.D. Tex.	http://www.txed.uscourts.gov/cgi-bin/view_document.cgi?document=1179&download=true
N.D. Tex.	http://www.txnd.uscourts.gov/pdf/misc_orders/misc62_11-17-09.pdf
S.D. Tex.	http://www.txs.uscourts.gov/district/rulesproc/patent/schedulingorder.pdf
W.D. Wash.	http://www.wawd.uscourts.gov/documents/HomePageAnnouncements/2009%20Local%20Rules/Patent%20Rules%20-%20final.pdf

8

Discovery Issues Unique to Patent Cases*

*George E. Bowles, FACTL, and Roy W. Hardin, Locke Lord LLP, Dallas, Texas.

I. Introduction

As noted in Chapter 7, several districts have adopted local patent rules, most of which are versions of the rules in the Northern District of California; these rules govern discovery in a patent case. Even in districts that have not adopted such rules, many courts have adopted scheduling orders unique to patent cases, or the parties can agree to a case-management plan that mimics a designated set of local patent rules or a modified version of them. A number of district courts have enacted these local rules or scheduling orders pursuant to the Patent Pilot Program that went into effect in 2011.[1] In addition, the Federal Circuit Advisory Council recently adopted a Model Order designed to streamline e-discovery in patent cases and provides for cost shifting under certain circumstances where the burdens fall disproportionately on one party.[2]

II. Scheduling Considerations

Key scheduling considerations that the Federal Rule of Civil Procedure 26(f) conference can be used to resolve include the timing and presentation of claim construction (*Markman*) issues (see Chapter 9), limits on fact and expert discovery, and the possibility of using phased discovery for claim construction and other issues.

---

[1]Those pilot districts are as follows: Eastern District of New York, Southern District of New York, Western District of Pennsylvania, District of New Jersey, District of Maryland, Northern District of Illinois, Southern District of Florida, District of Nevada, Eastern District of Texas, Northern District of Texas, Western District of Tennessee, Central District of California, Northern District of California, and Southern District of California.

[2]The Model Order is available at http://www.cafc.uscourts.gov/images/stories/the-court/Ediscovery_Model_Order.pdf.

III. Disclosure of Infringement and Invalidity Contentions and Claim Construction Issues

Many patent rules provide for an orderly process of disclosure of the parties' contentions regarding the three main issues of every patent case: infringement, invalidity, and claim construction. To encourage full disclosure, the patent rules limit the parties' ability to amend their contentions.

A. Patentee's Infringement Contentions

The patent rules require that the patentee disclose its infringement contentions first, identifying each product or process it alleges infringes. The patentee uses a "claim chart" setting forth the limitations of each asserted claim and pointing out completely and specifically how the accused products/processes satisfy each limitation, either literally or under the doctrine of equivalents.

The patent rules also require the patentee to disclose documents or other information in its possession that could be used to challenge the validity of the patent. Such information includes the patentee's sales or offers to sell products or processes covered by the patents-in-suit, which may not otherwise be available to the accused infringer.

B. Accused Infringer's Invalidity Contentions

The patent rules give the accused infringer some time to complete its searches for prior art after the accused infringer receives the patentee's specific infringement allegations and invalidity information, at which time it must present, again in claim chart form, its invalidity contentions. The patentee's contentions often indicate how the patentee construes its own claims, and the accused infringer may respond accordingly.

The accused infringer must set forth in detail which prior-art publication or practice allegedly satisfies each limitation of the asserted patent claims. If a combination of references is required to satisfy all limitations of a claim, the accused infringer must disclose the evidence on which it relies to combine the references in that manner.

The patent rules also require the accused infringer to produce documents or other information in its possession that show how the allegedly infringing products are constructed and operate, such as instructions, drawings, or source code. This information is necessary for the patentee to make out its infringement case.

C. Parties' Contentions Regarding Contested Claim Interpretation Issues

If the court decides that a separate *Markman* hearing procedure is warranted, it has become common practice to ask the parties to identify claim terms in issue by way of a claim chart identifying each such term, listing each party's proposed constructions of those terms, and setting forth the evidentiary support for each party's proposed constructions. This process narrows the issues and focuses the court on only the claim terms in dispute.

Because the parties' proposed claim constructions often reveal their theories in the case, the patent rules set forth a three-stage process for preparing the claim chart to ensure neither party is placed at a disadvantage:

- First, the parties confer and agree on the terms in dispute. This exercise forces the parties to tell each other where the issues of the case lie.
- Second, the parties simultaneously exchange proposed definitions, so neither party can adjust its position in light of the definitions proposed by the other.
- Third, the parties again confer to determine if they can agree to the construction of additional terms and then construct the claim chart that they submit to the court.

The patent rules also require complete disclosure of documents and witness statements to be used in the claim construction process and require that deposition and other discovery be completed within a short time after the final claim chart is prepared.

IV. Relevance and Limits of Discovery

Federal Circuit law controls whether particular written or other materials are discoverable in a patent case, because a determination of relevance implicates the substantive law of patent validity and infringement.[3] However, regional circuit law governs purely procedural discovery issues, such as discovery under the provisions of Rule 56(f).[4]

V. Attorney-Client Privilege and Waiver Issues

Questions of privilege and waiver arise frequently in patent litigation, most often in two areas. First, in applying for a patent, inventors and their counsel have a duty of candor and good faith before the Patent and Trademark Office. Failure to comply constitutes inequitable conduct that renders a patent unenforceable. Facts that counsel learn through communications with the inventors can end up being at the center of an inequitable conduct defense.

Second, to defend against an allegation of willful infringement or enhanced damages for an exceptional case, the accused infringer may argue that it exercised due care upon learning of the patent at issue.[5] A well-reasoned opinion from patent counsel can be a basis for a defense against such charges, but the accused infringer must produce the opinion, waiving the attorney-client privilege, to benefit from it.

A. *Questions of What Qualifies as Privileged*

The application of attorney–client privilege principles to communications between inventors and patent attorneys is an issue of substantive patent law to which Federal Circuit law, not regional circuit law, applies.[6] However, regional circuit law governs

---

[3]Truswal Sys. Corp. v. Hydro-Air Eng'g, Inc., 813 F.2d 1207, 1212 (Fed. Cir. 1987); *see also* Commissariat A L'Energie Atomique v. Chi Mei Optoelectronics Corp., 395 F.3d 1315, 1323 (Fed. Cir. 2005) (request for jurisdictional discovery analyzed under Federal Circuit law).

[4]Vivid Techs., Inc. v. Am. Sci. & Eng'g, Inc., 200 F.3d 795, 807 (Fed. Cir. 1999).

[5]*See In re* Seagate Tech. LLC, 497 F.3d 1360 (Fed. Cir. 2007), *cert. denied*, 552 U.S. 1230 (2008); *see also* Leahy-Smith America Invents Act, Pub. L. No. 112-29, §17 (codified at 35 U.S.C. §298).

[6]*In re* Spalding, 203 F.3d 800 (Fed. Cir. 2000) (applying Seventh Circuit law to hold community-of-interest existed between patentee and exclusive licensee].

whether the privilege applies to communications with two different clients under the community-of-interest doctrine.[7]

B. Waiver—Its Scope and Effect

Federal Circuit law applies to the issue of the extent to which a party waives its attorney-client privilege and work-product immunity when it asserts the advice-of-counsel defense in response to a charge of willful infringement. The assertion of such a defense waives the privilege in communications delivered to the client regarding infringement or validity, but the attorney work-product doctrine protects documents on those same issues if the documents have not been communicated to the client.[8]

C. The Timing Issue

Because an assertion of the advice-of-counsel defense acts as a waiver of privilege, the accused infringer ordinarily seeks to postpone disclosing any opinion of counsel as long as possible. As a result, discovery disputes can occur over when the accused infringer must elect to assert the advice-of-counsel defense and permit related discovery by the patentee. The patent rules handle this issue by providing for a specific date by which the accused infringer must produce relevant documents and a privilege log, or waive its right to rely on the defense.

VI. Summary of the Discovery Order and Timing Suggested by Patent Rules

Start: Case-management conference

10 days: Disclosure of asserted claims and preliminary infringement contentions:
- Infringement claim chart

---

[7] *In re* Regents of the Univ. of Cal., 101 F.3d 1386, 1390 n.2 (Fed. Cir. 1997), *cert. denied*, 520 U.S. 1193 (2007).

[8] *In re* EchoStar Communications Corp., 448 F.3d 1294 (Fed. Cir. 2006), *cert. denied*, 549 U.S. 1096 (2006).

	• Production of information related to prior sales, conception, reduction to practice, design and development, and the prosecution history of the patent
55 days:	Disclosure of preliminary invalidity contentions: • Invalidity claim chart • Production of specifications, source code, schematics, formulas, and flow charts sufficient to show operation of each accused instrumentality • Production of copies of the cited prior art
65 days:	Exchange of proposed terms and claim elements for construction
85 days:	Simultaneous exchange of preliminary claim constructions
115 days:	Joint claim construction and prehearing statement
145 days:	Completion of claim construction discovery
160 days:	Opening claim construction briefs Responsive briefs 14 days later Reply by party asserting infringement seven days after responsive briefs

9

Claim Construction—The *Markman* Hearing*

---

*John L. Cooper, FACTL, Farella Braun + Martel LLP, San Francisco, California.

I. General Principles

The patent claims define the metes and bounds of the patentee's right to exclude others from practicing its invention. Because claim construction is necessary for both the infringement and invalidity analyses in patent infringement actions, it is a key task.

The court must construe the claims,[1] but it has substantial discretion in the process it undertakes to construe the claim terms at issue, including:

- when during the course of the lawsuit to construe the claim terms at issue;
- whether and how to conduct a tutorial on the underlying technology or to rely on expert testimony prior to construing the claims;
- whether to have a formal evidentiary hearing, often called a "Markman hearing" after the seminal Supreme Court case,"[2] involving testimony from witnesses, and how much time to devote to each party at such a hearing; and
- the order in which it may consider evidence relevant to the construction of any particular claim.

II. Key Elements in Claim Construction

A. *Claims*

Claims are typically written in a form that has three sections: the "preamble," the "transition," and the "body."

The preamble sets out the type of invention being claimed, such as "A pharmaceutical product." The preamble may shed light on the meaning of claim terms. However, the preamble limits the claim only in the rare instances when it recites "essential structure

[1]Markman v. Westview Instruments, Inc., 517 U.S. 370 (1996).
[2]*Id.*

or steps, or if it is 'necessary to give life, meaning, and vitality' to the claim."[3]

The transition is a phrase that links the preamble to the body, such as "comprising," "consisting of," or "consisting essentially of." These terms have special meaning in patent law. "Comprising" is open-ended, meaning that the invention can include additional elements, so long as it includes all of the elements listed in the claim. In contrast, "consisting of" is closed, prohibiting any elements other than those claimed. "Consisting essentially" of is a variant of the closed form, permitting only unclaimed elements "that do not materially affect the basic and novel properties of the invention."[4]

The body of the claim sets forth a series of phrases delineating the structural limitations, elements, or steps in the invention. Thus, the claim construction typically focuses on the limitations in the body of the claim.

1. *Independent v. Dependent Claims*

Independent claims stand alone, while dependent claims expressly refer to an earlier claim, such as "The method of claim 1, further comprising. . . ." A dependent claim incorporates all of the limitations of the claim from which it depends and adds further limitations specific to the dependent claim. Thus, it is necessarily narrower than the claim from which it depends. Independent claims are typically the most important because they have the broadest coverage.

2. *Means-Plus-Function or Step-Plus-Function Claims*

A patentee may use a shorthand technique to draft a claim limitation by invoking the written description of the patent, pursuant to 35 U.S.C. §112, ¶ 6, which provides:

> An element in a claim for a combination may be expressed as a means or step for performing a specified function without the recital of structure, material, or acts in support thereof, and such

---

[3]Am. Med. Sys., Inc. v. Biolitec, Inc., 618 F.3d 1354, 1358 (Fed. Cir. 2010) (citing Catalina Mktg. Int'l, Inc. v. Coolsavings.com, Inc., 289 F.3d 801, 808 (Fed. Cir. 2002)).

[4]PPG Indus. v. Guardian Indus. Corp., 156 F.3d 1351, 1354 (Fed. Cir. 1998).

> claim shall be construed to cover the corresponding structure, material, or acts described in the specification and equivalents thereof.[5]

Known as "means-plus-function," "step-plus-function," or "112/6" claim limitations, these limitations frequently use the language "means for [performing a function]" or "step for [performing a function]," and Section 112, paragraph 6 presumptively applies when these phrases are used.

Use of this technique limits the claim term to the specific structure disclosed in the written description and to equivalents of that structure. For example, a claim reciting "a fastener" may encompass nails, screws, clips, buttons, buckles, glue, Velcro, and other fasteners, while a claim reciting "a means for fastening" may be limited to nails and the equivalents of nails if the written description of the patent describes only nails.

B. Intrinsic Evidence

Patents must include a "specification," which is the written body of the patent, other than the claims.

The "prosecution history" of a patent, which is also called the "file history" or "file wrapper," is the complete record of the examination proceedings before the Patent and Trademark Office, including the prior art cited during the examination. The prosecution history provides evidence of the Patent and Trademark Office's and the inventor's understanding of the patent, and it can be used to define or narrow the claimed invention.

III. Timing of Claim Construction

The timing of claim construction may significantly affect the course of patent litigation. An early claim construction may focus discovery, streamline the issues to be tried, and enhance settlement prospects, but construing the claims before discovery has been completed may result in constructions based on an incomplete record, or even construction of claim terms that have no bearing on the ultimate infringement issues to be resolved. Thus, many local patent rules set claim construction several months

---

[5] 35 U.S.C. §112, ¶¶1-6 (2000).

after the initial case-management conference.[6] Nonetheless, the particular facts and technology involved in a particular case may affect the timing of claim construction.

IV. Issues to Consider During a Claim Construction Hearing

The parties usually bear the responsibility of isolating terms and phrases for the court to construe, but certain courts limit the number of claim terms that they will construe during a claim construction hearing because patent cases typically turn on the construction of only a few key terms or phrases. Indeed, courts have noted that patent infringement cases usually "resolve by motion or settlement" soon after these terms or phrases are construed. Additional terms can be construed at the summary judgment or trial phases of the action, or a party may request leave to designate additional terms and demonstrate good cause for doing so.

V. Evidence to Consider When Construing Patent Claim Terms

The Federal Circuit laid out the basic principles of claim construction in *Phillips v. AWH Corp.*[7] The words of a claim are generally given their ordinary and customary meaning as understood by a person of ordinary skill in the field of the invention, called a "person of ordinary skill in the art," at the time of the invention. The evidence used to determine the ordinary and customary meaning is divided into "intrinsic evidence," which is the claims themselves, the specification, and the prosecution history; and "extrinsic evidence," which includes a range of different sources, such as expert testimony, dictionaries, and technical treatises. "The sequence of steps used by the judge in consulting various sources is not important; what matters is for the court to attach the appropriate weight to be assigned to those sources in light of the statutes and policies that inform patent law."[8]

---

[6]See *supra* Chapter 7.

[7]415 F.3d 1303 (Fed. Cir. 2005) (en banc).

[8]*Id.* at 1324.

A. *Use of Intrinsic Evidence in Construing Claim Terms*

The most important evidence to consider in interpreting patent claims is the language of the patent claims at issue. The usage of the claim term in the context of both the claim under construction and other claims in the patent can prove highly informative. For example, *Phillips* noted that the use of the term "steel baffles" implied that the term "baffles" was not limited to steel objects. Moreover, claim terms are generally used consistently and have the same meaning throughout the patent. Finally, differences between the claims, both asserted and unasserted, can help determine the meaning of a claim term.

The patent is treated as a fully integrated written instrument, which includes the specification and concludes with claims, and the specification "is always highly relevant to the claim construction analysis."[9] The specification may indicate how the patentee views the scope of the invention, although the court must remain wary not to import limitations from the specification into the claims. The specification must also be reviewed to determine whether the patentee acted as his or her own lexicographer, using a special definition for a term that may differ from the term's ordinary and customary meaning. The specification may also provide a clear disclaimer, or disavowal, of claim scope by the inventor, which is dispositive.

The claim construction should also consider the prosecution history of the patent, although the use of the prosecution history in claim construction may in some cases be secondary to the specification. The written dialogue between the Patent and Trademark Office and the patent applicant may include statements with which the applicant was attempting to explain the invention and the claim terms and to distinguish the invention and the claim terms from the prior art to obtain the patent. The prosecution history may therefore include helpful, if not controlling, statements.

There is some dispute at the Federal Circuit over whether courts should interpret claims in light of what was "actually invented," or whether claims should be construed entirely in the abstract. Although *Phillips* does not support construing claims in relation to the invention, Judges Moore and Rader have written that there is "a clear intra-circuit split on the claim construction

---

[9] *Id.* at 1315.

process" on this point.[10] Until this issue is settled, the better practice is not to allow the invention to interfere with the claim construction process.

B. Use of Extrinsic Evidence in Construing Claim Terms

While the Federal Circuit has placed significant emphasis on the use of intrinsic evidence in construing patent claims, it has held that courts may also consider extrinsic evidence in construing claim terms. Extrinsic evidence is less significant than intrinsic evidence, though.

Technical dictionaries and treatises are a potentially helpful form of extrinsic evidence that can help the court understand the underlying technology and the way in which a person of ordinary skill in the art might use the claim terms. In addition, expert testimony can be used: (1) to provide background on the technology at issue; (2) to explain how an invention works; (3) to help ensure that the court's understanding of the technology in the patent comports with that of a person of ordinary skill in the art (including testimony that will ground the court's analysis in the science as it was understood when the patent was filed); and (4) to help establish that a particular term in the patent or the prior art had a particular meaning in the pertinent field during the relevant time frame. However, conclusory, unsupported assertions by experts regarding the definition of a claim term, and assertions that are at odds with the claim construction based on the intrinsic record, should be rejected. Thus, courts regularly reject testimony from "patent experts" whose sole or primary function is to opine about how claims should be construed. Many courts view such testimony as an intrusion on the court's function.

The Federal Circuit has noted several reasons that extrinsic evidence may be less reliable than intrinsic evidence. For example, extrinsic evidence was not created for the purpose of explaining the patent or the meanings of terms in the patent. Extrinsic publications may not be written by or for those skilled in the art, so they may not reflect the meaning of a term to such a person.

---

[10]Retractable Techs., Inc. v. Becton, Dickinson & Co., 659 F.3d 1369, 1372–3 (Fed. Cir. 2011) (Moore, J. and Rader, J., dissenting) (arguing that the court in its panel opinion had impermissibly "chang(ed) the plain meaning of a claim term to tailor its scope to what the panel believed was the 'actual invention'").

Moreover, expert reports and testimony may suffer from litigation bias. Finally, the universe of extrinsic evidence is very large, and each party will choose the most favorable extrinsic evidence to support its arguments. Accordingly, extrinsic evidence must always be considered in the context of the intrinsic record, which carries more weight in claim construction.

VI. Appeal of a Claim Construction Ruling

The Federal Circuit reviews claim construction rulings without deference on appeal. Nevertheless, the Federal Circuit has generally been unwilling to hear interlocutory appeals of claim construction issues.

10

Summary Judgment Motions*

*Kenneth S. Weitzman, Weitzman Law Offices LLC, Roseland, New Jersey.

I. Applying the Summary Judgment Standard to Burdens of Proof in Patent Litigation

Summary judgment is as appropriate in a patent case as it is in any other case.[1] Before discussing the specific burdens of proof in patent litigation, however, it is important to differentiate between a movant seeking summary judgment who does not ultimately bear the burden of proof at trial and one who does. "When the moving party does not have the burden of proof on the issue that is the subject of the summary judgment motion ... the movant nonetheless bears the initial burden of coming forward with sufficient evidence to demonstrate that there is no material issue of fact that would preclude summary judgment, and that it is entitled to judgment as a matter of law."[2] The moving party may meet its initial burden by either providing evidence that negates an essential element of the opposing party's case or by showing that there is no material issue of fact and that the nonmoving party will be unable to prove an essential element of its case.[3] Once the movant satisfies its initial burden, then the burden of coming forward shifts to the party opposing the motion.[4] "The opposing party does not, at this stage, have the burden of establishing that it is entitled to judgment in its favor; it need only show either that the movant did not establish that it is entitled to judgment on undisputed facts or on the opposer's version of the facts, or that there are material issues of fact which require resolution at trial."[5]

In contrast, "where the moving party has the burden of proof on a claim or defense raised in a summary judgment motion, it must show that the undisputed facts establish every element of

---

[1]Desper Prods., Inc. v. QSound Labs, Inc., 157 F.3d 1325, 1332 (Fed. Cir. 1998) (quoting C.R. Bard, Inc. v. Advanced Cardiovascular, Inc., 911 F.2d 670, 672 (Fed. Cir 1990)); *see also* Avia Group Int'l, Inc. v. L.A. Gear Cal., Inc., 853 F.2d 1557, 1561 (Fed. Cir. 1988), *abrogated on other grounds by* Egyptian Goddess, Inc. v. Swisa, Inc., 543 F.3d 665 (Fed. Cir. 2008); Spectra Corp. v. Lutz, 839 F.2d 1579, 1581 n.6 (Fed. Cir. 1988). Summary judgment may be particularly appropriate in patent cases where the only real dispute between the parties is that of claim construction—which is a question of law for the court to decide.

[2]Vivid Techs., Inc. v. Am. Science & Eng'g, Inc., 200 F.3d 795, 806 (Fed. Cir. 1999).

[3]*Id.* at 807.

[4]*Id.* at 806.

[5]*Id.* at 806–07.

the claim or defense."[6] In other words, even in the absence of an adequate response by the nonmovant, a moving party who bears the ultimate burden of proof on the issue raised in the summary judgment motion must demonstrate that it is entitled to judgment as a matter of law.[7]

A. *Summary Judgment of Infringement/Noninfringement*

Summary judgment on the issue of infringement or noninfringement is available in patent litigation.[8]

A claim for patent infringement must be proven by a preponderance of the evidence.[9] Patent infringement is a two-step inquiry. First, the court must construe the asserted patent claim(s) as a matter of law.[10] Second, the fact finder—here, the court for purposes of summary judgment—must determine whether the accused product, composition, system, or process contains each limitation of the properly construed claims, either literally or under

---

[6]Meyers v. Brooks Shoe, Inc., 912 F.2d 1459, 1461 (Fed. Cir. 1990), *overruled on other grounds,* A.C. Aukerman Co. v. R.L. Chaides Constr. Co., 960 F.2d 1020 (Fed. Cir. 1992); *see also* Meyers v. Asics Corp., 974 F.2d 1304, 1307 (Fed. Cir. 1992).

[7]*See* Saab Cars USA, Inc. v. United States, 434 F.3d 1359, 1368 (Fed. Cir. 2006) (citation omitted).

[8]*See, e.g.*, Flex-Rest, LLC v. Steelcase, Inc., 455 F.3d 1351 (Fed. Cir. 2006); Semitool, Inc. v. Dynamic Micro Sys. Semiconductor Equip. GmbH, 444 F.3d 1337, 1447 (Fed. Cir. 2006); Schoenhaus v. Genesco, Inc., 440 F.3d 1354, 1359–60 (Fed. Cir. 2006); Lawman Armor Corp. v. Winner Int'l, LLC, 437 F.3d 1383, 1384 (Fed. Cir. 2006), *abrogated on other grounds by* Egyptian Goddess, Inc. v. Swisa, Inc., 543 F.3d 665 (Fed. Cir. 2008); MicroStrategy, Inc. v. Business Objects, S.A., 429 F.3d 1344, 1353 (Fed. Cir. 2005); Invitrogen Corp. v. Clontech Labs., Inc., 429 F.3d 1052, 1081 (Fed. Cir. 2005); Nystrom v. TREX Co., 424 F.3d 1136, 1138 (Fed. Cir. 2005); Biagro W. Sales, Inc. v. Grow More, Inc., 423 F.3d 1296, 1304–07 (Fed. Cir. 2005); Network Commerce, Inc. v. Microsoft Corp., 422 F.3d 1353, 1364 (Fed. Cir. 2005); Tap Pharm. Prods., Inc. v. Owl Pharms., LLC, 419 F.3d 1346, 1348–49 (Fed. Cir. 2005); Terlep v. Brinkmann Corp., 418 F.3d 1379, 1380 (Fed. Cir. 2005); Pause Tech., LLC v. TiVo, Inc., 419 F.3d 1326, 1336 (Fed. Cir. 2005); CollegeNet, Inc. v. ApplyYourself, Inc., 418 F.3d 1225, 1236 (Fed. Cir. 2005); Lisle Corp. v. A.J. Mfg. Co., 398 F.3d 1306, 1317 (Fed. Cir. 2005); Frank's Casing Crew & Rental Tools, Inc. v. Weatherford Int'l, Inc., 389 F.3d 1370, 1379–80 (Fed. Cir. 2004). *See also supra* Chapter 2.A.

[9]Advanced Cardiovascular Sys., Inc. v. SciMed Life Sys., Inc., 261 F.3d 1329, 1336 (Fed. Cir. 2001).

[10]Markman v. Westview Instruments, Inc., 517 U.S. 370, 372–74 (1996); Cybor Corp. v. FAS Techs., Inc., 138 F.3d 1448, 1454 (Fed. Cir. 1998) (en banc).

the doctrine of equivalents. The first step is a question of law; the second step is a question of fact.[11]

Summary judgment is particularly appropriate in patent cases where the only real dispute between the parties concerns the proper meaning of the patent claims.[12]

Because claim construction is a question of law for the court to decide, disputes over the proper meaning of claim terms do not alone raise genuine issues of material fact sufficient to preclude the grant of summary judgment.[13] For this reason, some judges combine summary judgment and *Markman* hearings.

"Summary judgment on the issue of infringement (or non-infringement) is proper when no reasonable jury could find that every limitation recited in a properly construed claim either is or

---

[11] *Markman,* 517 U.S. at 372–74; Ferguson Beauregard v. Mega Sys., Inc., 350 F.3d 1327, 1338 (Fed. Cir. 2003).

[12] *See* Voice Techs. Group, Inc. v. VMC Sys., Inc., 164 F.3d 605, 612 (Fed. Cir. 1999) ("Upon construction of the claims, summary judgment may follow when it is shown that the infringement issue can be reasonably decided only in favor of the movant, when all reasonable factual inferences are drawn in favor of the non-movant"); Vivid Techs., Inc. v. Am. Science & Eng'g, Inc., 200 F.3d 795, 806 (Fed. Cir. 1999).

[13] *See* Laitram Corp. v. Morehouse Indus., Inc., 143 F.3d 1456, 1461 (Fed. Cir. 1998) ("Because the parties did not dispute the structure of the accused devices . . . once the issue of claim construction is settled, [the] summary judgment motion for noninfringement did not implicate any issues of fact"); General Mills, Inc. v. Hunt-Wesson, Inc., 103 F.3d 978, 983 (Fed. Cir. 1997); Athletic Alternatives, Inc. v. Prince Mfg., Inc., 73 F.3d 1573, 1578 (Fed. Cir. 1996) ("Where, as here, the parties do not dispute any relevant facts regarding the accused product but disagree over which of two possible meanings of Claim 1 is the proper one, the question of literal infringement collapses to one of claim construction and is thus amenable to summary judgment."); Southwall Techs., Inc. v. Cardinal IG Co., 54 F.3d 1570, 1578 (Fed. Cir. 1995) ("disagreement over the meaning of a term within a claim does not necessarily create a genuine issue of material fact"); Transmatic, Inc. v. Gulton Indus., Inc., 53 F.3d 1270, 1278 (Fed. Cir. 1995) ("The structure of the accused device was undisputed; the parties' disagreement over the meaning of the claim did not preclude a grant of summary judgment."); Intellicall, Inc. v. Phonometrics, Inc., 952 F.2d 1384, 1387 (Fed. Cir. 1992); Tilotson, Ltd. v. Walbro Corp., 831 F.2d 1033, 1037 (Fed. Cir. 1987) ("Claim scope or construction is a question of law and the existence of a dispute as to that legal issue does not preclude summary judgment"); Howes v. Medical Components, Inc., 814 F.2d 638, 643 (Fed. Cir. 1987) ("Claim construction is a question of law and the mere existence of a dispute as to that legal issue does not preclude summary judgment.").

is not found in the accused device either literally or under the doctrine of equivalents."[14]

To be entitled to summary judgment of noninfringement, the moving party must demonstrate that the facts and inferences, when viewed in the light most favorable to the nonmoving party, would not persuade a reasonable jury to return a verdict in favor of the nonmoving party—the patent owner.[15]

B. Summary Judgment of Validity/Invalidity

It is common for a defendant in a patent litigation to move for summary judgment that one or more claims of the asserted patent(s) are invalid. Similarly, although less common, a patentee may move for summary judgment that its patent claims are not invalid.[16]

---

[14]PC Connector Solutions LLC v. SmartDisk Corp., 406 F.3d 1359, 1364 (Fed. Cir. 2005) (citing Bai v. L & L Wings, Inc., 160 F.3d 1350, 1353–54 (Fed. Cir. 1998)); *see also* Chimie v. PPG Indus., Inc., 402 F.3d 1371, 1376 (Fed. Cir. 2005); Frank's Casing Crew & Rental Tools, Inc. v. Weatherford Int'l, Inc., 389 F.3d 1370, 1376 (Fed. Cir. 2004) (citing Gart v. Logitech, Inc., 254 F.3d 1334, 1339 (Fed. Cir. 2001)). In other words, "[s]ummary judgment is appropriate when it is apparent that only one conclusion as to infringement could be reached by a reasonable jury." TechSearch, LLC v. Intel Corp., 286 F.3d 1360, 1369 (Fed. Cir. 2002) (citing ATD Corp. v. Lydall, Inc., 159 F.3d 534, 540 (Fed. Cir. 1998)).

[15]Bus. Objects, S.A. v. Microstrategy, Inc., 393 F.3d 1366, 1371–72 (Fed. Cir. 2005) (citing Anderson v. Liberty Lobby, Inc., 477 U.S. 242, 255 (1986)).

[16]*See, e.g.*, IPXL Holdings, LLC v. Amazon.com, Inc., 430 F.3d 1377, 1378 (Fed. Cir. 2005) (affirming grant of summary judgment of invalidity); Sentry Protection Prods., Inc. v. Eagle Mfg. Co., 400 F.3d 910, 911 (Fed. Cir. 2005) (same); University of Rochester v. G.D. Searle & Co., 358 F.3d 916, 917 (Fed. Cir. 2004) (same); Minton v. Nat'l Ass'n of Sec. Dealers, Inc., 336 F.3d 1373, 1381 (Fed. Cir. 2003) (same); New Railhead Mfg., LLC v. Vermeer Mfg. Co., 298 F.3d 1290, 1297 (Fed. Cir. 2002) (same); Teleflex, Inc. v. Ficosa N. Am. Corp., 299 F.3d 1313, 1329–30 (Fed. Cir. 2002) (affirming grant of partial summary judgment of no invalidity); Apotex USA, Inc. v. Merck & Co., 254 F.3d 1031, 1033 (Fed. Cir. 2001) (affirming grant of summary judgment of invalidity); Shockley v. Arcan, Inc., 248 F.3d 1349, 1353 (Fed. Cir. 2001) (affirming grant of summary judgment of no invalidity); Nat'l Presto Indus., Inc. v. West Bend Co., 76 F.3d 1185, 1189 (Fed. Cir. 1996) (same).

Because a patent is presumed valid pursuant to 35 U.S.C. §282, the party seeking to invalidate a patent claim has the burden to do so by clear and convincing evidence.[17]

Thus, in the context of summary judgment, a moving party seeking to invalidate a patent bears the burden of proof and "must submit such clear and convincing evidence of invalidity so that no reasonable jury could find otherwise."[18] In contrast, if the patentee moves for summary judgment that its patent claims are not invalid, the movant—who does not bear the burden of proof at trial—must show that the non-moving party "failed to produce clear and convincing evidence on an essential element of a defense upon which a reasonable jury could invalidate the patent."[19]

Since a court considering summary judgment must view the evidence through the prism of the evidentiary burden the parties would have faced at trial,[20] it is important to recognize that the issue of invalidity may be a question of fact (such as in the case of anticipation, lack of written description, or best-mode violation), a question of law based on underlying facts (such as in the case of obviousness, inventorship, derivation, or lack of enablement), or a pure question of law (such as in the case of indefiniteness).

As with infringement, the first step in any invalidity analysis is determining the proper meaning of the relevant claim terms in dispute.[21] Because claim construction is a question of law, disputes with respect to the proper meaning of claim terms do not

---

[17]Invitrogen Corp. v. Biocrest Mfg., L.P., 424 F.3d 1374, 1378 (Fed. Cir. 2005); Norian Corp. v. Stryker Corp., 363 F.3d 1321, 1326 (Fed. Cir. 2004); Group One, Ltd. v. Hallmark Cards, Inc., 254 F.3d 1041, 1045–46 (Fed. Cir. 2001); Connell v. Sears Roebuck & Co., 722 F.2d 1542, 1549 (Fed. Cir. 1983). This standard of proof applies equally in the summary judgment context. *Nat'l Presto,* 76 F.3d at 1189.

[18]Eli Lilly & Co. v. Barr Labs., Inc., 251 F.3d 955, 962 (Fed. Cir. 2001).

[19]*Id.*

[20]Apple Computer, Inc. v. Articulate Sys., Inc., 234 F.3d 14, 20 (Fed. Cir. 2000).

[21]*See* Akamai Techs., Inc. v. Cable & Wireless Internet Servs., Inc., 344 F.3d 1186, 1195 n.4 (Fed. Cir. 2003); Omega Eng'g, Inc. v. Raytek Corp., 334 F.3d 1314, 1335 (Fed Cir. 2003); SIBIA Neurosciences, Inc. v. Cadus Pharm. Corp., 225 F.3d 1349, 1355 (Fed. Cir. 2000) ("[t]he first step in any invalidity analysis is claim construction").

alone raise genuine issues of material fact sufficient to preclude the grant of summary judgment.[22]

Like claim construction, some invalidity defenses are questions of law that are amenable to summary judgment. For instance, because the determination of whether a claim is indefinite and thus invalid under 35 U.S.C. §112, ¶ 2, is a question of law,[23] summary judgment of invalidity for indefiniteness is appropriate where one or more patent claims are "not amenable to construction" or "insolubly ambiguous."[24] Summary judgment of invalidity for indefiniteness is not appropriate, however, where the "meaning of the claim is discernible, even though the task may be formidable and the conclusion may be one over which reasonable persons will disagree."[25]

Other invalidity defenses are questions of law based on underlying factual issues. For example, while the ultimate determination of invalidity based on obviousness under 35 U.S.C. §103 is a legal issue for the court, it is based on subsidiary factual issues, such as the scope and content of the prior art, differences between the prior art and the claim(s) being challenged, the level of ordinary skill in the art, and so-called "secondary considerations" of nonobviousness.[26] Where the underlying factual issues are not in dispute, summary judgment may be appropriate even if the ultimate legal conclusion of obviousness is disputed.[27]

However, a patentee cannot defeat summary judgment of obviousness simply by pointing to disputes on these underlying

---

[22] *See* Southwall Techs., Inc. v. Cardinal IG Co., 54 F.3d 1570, 1578 (Fed. Cir. 1995) ("disagreement over the meaning of a term within a claim does not necessarily create a genuine issue of material fact"); Tillotson, Ltd. v. Walbro Corp., 831 F.2d 1033, 1037 (Fed. Cir. 1987) ("Claim scope or construction is a question of law and the existence of a dispute as to that legal issue does not preclude summary judgment"); Howes v. Med. Components, Inc., 814 F.2d 638, 643 (Fed. Cir. 1987) ("Claim construction is a question of law and the mere existence of a dispute as to that legal issue does not preclude summary judgment").

[23] Cross Med. Prods., Inc. v. Medtronic Sofamor Danek, Inc., 424 F.3d 1293, 1303 (Fed. Cir. 2005).

[24] Datamize, LLC v. Plumtree Software, Inc., 417 F.3d 1342, 1347 (Fed. Cir. 2005).

[25] Bancorp Servs., LLC v. Hartford Life Ins. Co., 359 F.3d 1367, 1371 (Fed. Cir. 2004); *see also* Xerox Corp. v. 3Com Corp., 458 F.3d 1310 (Fed. Cir. 2006).

[26] *See* Graham v. John Deere Co., 383 U.S. 1, 17–18 (1966); Group One Ltd. v. Hallmark Cards, Inc., 407 F.3d 1297, 1303 (Fed. Cir. 2005).

[27] Newell Cos. v. Kenney Mfg. Co., 864 F.2d 757, 763 (Fed. Cir. 1988).

factual inquiries.[28] In such circumstances, the court must weigh "'the materiality of the dispute, i.e., whether resolution of the dispute one way or the other makes a difference to the final determination of obviousness.'"[29] So long as the court views all the factual disputes in the light most favorable to the nonmoving party, the court can grant summary judgment of invalidity based on obviousness if it finds that resolution of those factual disputes does not affect the outcome.[30] If, however, the ultimate determination of obviousness depends on resolution of those factual disputes, then summary judgment is not appropriate.

Like obviousness, the issue of invalidity from lack of enablement under 35 U.S.C. §112, ¶ 1, is a question of law based on underlying factual issues.[31] In this context, "[w]hether undue experimentation is needed is not a single, simple factual determination, but rather is a conclusion reached by weighing many factual considerations," such as: "(1) the quantity of experimentation necessary, (2) the amount of direction or guidance presented, (3) the presence or absence of working examples, (4) the nature of the invention, (5) the state of the prior art, (6) the relative skill of those in the art, (7) the predictability or unpredictability of the art, and (8) the breadth of the claims."[32] If there are no genuine issues of material fact, then the court may grant summary judgment on the enablement issue.[33] However, if the ultimate determination of invalidity depends on resolution of these factual disputes, then summary judgment is not appropriate.

Likewise, invalidity because of improper inventorship or derivation under 35 U.S.C. §102(f) is a question of law based

---

[28] *See* Chore-Time Equip., Inc. v. Cumberland Corp., 713 F.2d 774, 778 (Fed. Cir. 1983) ("The mere incantation of the fact findings listed in *Graham* cannot establish the impropriety of issuing a summary judgment when there is no material issue of fact requiring a trial to resolve, and the facts of record require a holding of patent invalidity.").

[29] Rockwell Int'l Corp. v. United States, 147 F.3d 1358, 1362 (Fed. Cir. 1998) (quoting Monarch Knitting Mach. Corp. v. Sulzer Morat GmbH, 139 F.3d 877, 881 (Fed. Cir. 1998)).

[30] *See* Union Carbide Corp. v. Am. Can Co., 724 F.2d 1567, 1571 (Fed. Cir. 1984).

[31] *See* Liquid Dynamics Corp. v. Vaughan Co., 449 F.3d 1209, 1224 (Fed. Cir. 2006).

[32] *In re* Wands, 858 F.2d 731, 737 (Fed. Cir. 1988).

[33] *See* Nat'l Recovery Techs., Inc. v. Magnetic Separation Sys., Inc., 166 F.3d 1190, 1194 (Fed. Cir. 1999).

on underlying factual issues.[34] If there are no genuine issues of material fact, then the court may grant summary judgment on this issue. If, however, the ultimate determination of invalidity depends on resolution of factual disputes, then summary judgment is not appropriate.

Other invalidity defenses raised in patent litigation are questions of fact. For instance, anticipation based on the prior art under 35 U.S.C. §102 is a question of fact.[35] Nevertheless, "[a]lthough anticipation is a question of fact, it still may be decided on summary judgment if the record reveals no genuine dispute of material fact."[36] "Summary judgment is proper if no reasonable jury could find that the patent is not anticipated."[37]

Like anticipation, invalidity for lack of written description under 35 U.S.C. §112, ¶ 1, is a question of fact, judged from the perspective of one of ordinary skill in the art as of the relevant filing date.[38] Where a patentee moves for summary judgment that its patent claims are not invalid for failure to satisfy the written description requirement, the nonmoving party—who bears the burden of proof on the invalidity issue—must come forward with evidence raising at least a genuine issue of fact regarding whether the patents failed the written description requirement.[39]

Similarly, invalidity for failure to comply with the best-mode requirement under 35 U.S.C. §112, ¶ 1, is a question of fact that involves a two-pronged inquiry.[40] The first prong is subjective, focusing on the inventor's state of mind at the time of filing the patent application, and asks whether the inventor considered a particular mode of practicing the invention to be superior to all

---

[34]Checkpoint Sys., Inc. v. All-Tag Sec. S.A., 412 F.3d 1331, 1338 (Fed. Cir. 2005) (citing Bd. of Educ. v. Am. Bioscience, 333 F.3d 1330, 1337 (Fed. Cir. 2003)).

[35]IPXL Holdings, LLC v. Amazon.com, Inc., 430 F.3d 1377, 1380 (Fed. Cir. 2005).

[36]Telemac Cellular Corp. v. Topp Telecom, Inc., 247 F.3d 1316, 1327 (Fed. Cir. 2001) (citing Gen. Elec. Co. v. Nintendo Co., 179 F.3d 1350, 1353 (Fed. Cir. 1999)).

[37]*Telemac*, 247 F.3d at 1327.

[38]*See* Vas-Cath, Inc. v. Mahurkar, 935 F.2d 1555, 1563–64 (Fed. Cir. 1991).

[39]*See* Invitrogen Corp. v. Clontech Labs., Inc., 429 F.3d 1052, 1072–73 (Fed. Cir. 2005) (citing Novartis Corp. v. Ben Venue Labs., Inc., 271 F.3d 1043, 1046 (Fed. Cir. 2001)).

[40]N. Telecom Ltd. v. Samsung Elecs. Co., 215 F.3d 1281, 1286 (Fed. Cir. 2000).

other modes at the time of filing.[41] The second prong is objective and asks whether the inventor adequately disclosed the mode he or she considered to be superior.[42] If there are no genuine issues of material fact, then the court may grant summary judgment on the issue of failure to satisfy the best-mode requirement. On the other hand, if the ultimate determination of invalidity depends on resolution of factual disputes, then summary judgment on the best-mode issue is not appropriate.

C. Summary Judgment of Unenforceability

Although less common than summary judgment of invalidity or non-infringement, courts have granted summary judgment that a patent is unenforceable because of inequitable conduct committed during the prosecution of the patent application(s) leading to the patent-in-suit.[43]

The Federal Circuit has "'urge[d] caution' in making an inequitable conduct determination at the summary judgment stage."[44] This is particularly so because the existence of the requisite intent to deceive the U.S. Patent and Trademark Office (PTO) is an inherently factual issue and "cannot be inferred solely from the fact that information was not disclosed; there must be a factual basis for a finding of deceptive intent.'"[45] However, courts regularly grant summary judgment where no evidence of intent to mislead is shown and it is inappropriate to infer such intent.

A patent may be rendered unenforceable because of inequitable conduct if a patent applicant, with intent to mislead or deceive the examiner in the PTO, fails to disclose material information or submits materially false information to the PTO dur-

---

[41] *Id.*

[42] *See* Amgen, Inc. v. Chugai Pharm. Co., 927 F.2d 1200, 1212 (Fed. Cir. 1991).

[43] *See* Digital Control, Inc. v. Charles Mach. Works, 437 F.3d 1309, 1313 (Fed. Cir. 2006) ("Determining at summary judgment that a patent is unenforceable for inequitable conduct is permissible, but uncommon."); Ferring B.V. v. Barr Labs., Inc., 437 F.3d 1181, 1186–87 (Fed. Cir. 2006).

[44] M. Eagles Tool Warehouse, Inc. v. Fisher Tooling Co., 439 F.3d 1335, 1340 (Fed. Cir. 2006) (quoting Paragon Podiatry Lab., Inc. v. KLM Labs., Inc., 984 F.2d 1182, 1190 (Fed. Cir. 1993)).

[45] *M. Eagles*, 439 F.3d at 1340 (quoting Hebert v. Lisle Corp., 99 F.3d 1109, 1116 (Fed. Cir. 1996)).

ing prosecution of the patent application.[46] The party asserting inequitable conduct must prove a threshold level of materiality and intent by clear and convincing evidence.[47] The court must then determine whether the patent applicant's conduct amounts to inequitable conduct by weighing the evidence of intent to deceive "independent[ly] of its analysis of materiality."[48] The Federal Circuit has emphasized that "[i]ntent and materiality are separate requirements" and that "a district court may not infer intent solely from materiality."[49]

This recent restatement of the inequitable conduct test in *Therasense* rejected a previous understanding of the test that allowed courts to weigh materiality and intent to deceive in light of each other.[50] Under *Therasense*, proof "that the applicant knew of a reference, should have known of its materiality, and decided not to submit it to the PTO does not prove specific intent to deceive."[51]

Summary judgment on inequitable conduct is only appropriate if "the facts of materiality or intent are not reasonably disputed."[52] Otherwise, "the issue is not amenable to summary disposition."[53] A genuine issue of material fact is not raised by the submission of "merely conclusory statements or completely insupportable, specious, or conflicting explanations or excuses."[54] Thus, the Federal Circuit has affirmed grants of summary judgment on inequitable conduct where, for example, "the affidavits submitted to explain the representations made to the PTO were 'bare declaration[s] of lack of intent to mislead' and the explanations provided in the affidavits were either 'nonresponsive' or lacked evidentiary support."[55]

---

[46]Norian Corp. v. Stryker Corp., 363 F.3d 1321, 1330–31 (Fed. Cir. 2004).

[47]Molins PLC v. Textron, Inc., 48 F.3d 1172, 1178 (Fed. Cir. 1995).

[48]Therasense, Inc. v. Becton, Dickinson & Co., 649 F.3d 1276, 1290 (Fed. Cir. 2011).

[49]*Id.*

[50]*See* Am. Hoist & Derrick Co. v. Sowa & Sons, Inc., 725 F.2d 1350, 1363 (Fed. Cir. 1984), *overruled by Therasense.*

[51]*Therasense,* 649 F.2d at 1290.

[52]*Baker Oil,* 828 F.2d at 1566 (citing KangaROOS U.S.A., Inc. v. Caldor, Inc., 778 F.2d 1571, 1577 (Fed. Cir. 1985)); *see also Ferring,* 437 F.3d at 1199.

[53]*Id.*

[54]Monsanto Co. v. Homan McFarling, 363 F.3d 1336, 1340 (Fed. Cir. 2004) (quoting *Paragon,* 984 F.2d at 1191–92).

[55]*Id.* (quoting *Paragon,* 984 F.2d at 1191–92). As the Federal Circuit noted in *Ferring*:

II. Timing of Summary Judgment Motions

The court has wide discretion in determining when summary judgment motions should be heard.[56] Assuming that the summary judgment motion raises issues relating to the interpretation of the asserted patent claims, the court has the discretion to: (1) construe the relevant disputed claim terms at the time of summary judgment without conducting a separate *Markman* hearing; (2) schedule a *Markman* hearing prior to hearing the summary judgment motion; or (3) combine the summary judgment hearing with a *Markman* hearing. Some commentators have encouraged courts to consider a "dual track" approach to summary judgment, arguing that some summary judgment motions are best decided prior to or in conjunction with a limited claim construction hearing.[57] Considerations related to these procedures are discussed below.

A. *Where Not All Claims Have Been Construed*

It is proper for a court to hear a summary judgment motion prior to construing all of the disputed claim terms. There is no requirement that the court conduct a Markman hearing and construe claims prior to hearing summary judgment motions.

The court has discretion to construe claims, if needed, in the context of a summary judgment motion.[58] The court need only

---

> [W]e have recognized, in cases such as Paragon, that summary judgment is appropriate on the issue of intent if there has been a failure to supply highly material information and if the summary judgment record establishes that (1) the applicant knew of the information; (2) the applicant knew or should have known of the materiality of the information; and (3) the applicant has not provided a credible explanation for the withholding.

Ferring, 437 F.3d at 1191 (citations omitted).

[56] *See* CytoLogix Corp. v. Ventana Med. Sys., Inc., 424 F.3d 1168, 1172 (Fed. Cir. 2005) ("the district court has considerable latitude in determining when to resolve issues of claim construction"); Lab. Corp. of Am. Holdings v. Chiron Corp., 384 F.3d 1326, 1333 (Fed. Cir. 2004) ("District courts are granted broad latitude in managing the cases before them."); Nutrinova Nutrition Specialties & Food Ingredients GmbH v. Int'l Trade Comm'n, 224 F.3d 1356, 1360 (Fed. Cir. 2000).

[57] *See* Peter S. Menell et al., *Patent Claim Construction: A Modern Synthesis and Structured Framework*, 25 Berk. Tech. L.J. 711, 806–13 (2010).

[58] *See* Markman v. Westview Instruments, Inc., 52 F.3d 967, 981 (Fed. Cir. 1995) (en banc), *aff'd*, 517 U.S. 370 (1996).

construe the disputed claim language "to the extent necessary to resolve the controversy."[59] Some purely legal questions that do not turn on complicated factual determinations may be especially appropriate for disposition through this type of early summary judgment.[60]

B. *After All Claims Have Been Construed Through a Formal* Markman *Hearing*

The court has wide discretion in determining whether to and when to hold a *Markman* hearing. In exercising this discretion, the court may defer summary judgment motions until after the court has construed the disputed terms in the patent claims.[61] Indeed,

---

[59]Vivid Techs., Inc. v. Am. Science & Eng'g, Inc., 200 F.3d 795, 803 (Fed. Cir. 1999); *see also* Ballard Med. Prods. v. Allegiance Healthcare Corp., 268 F.3d 1352, 1358 (Fed. Cir. 2001) ("If the district court considers one issue to be dispositive, the court may cut to the heart of the matter and need not exhaustively discuss all other issues presented by the parties."); Biovail Corp. Int'l v. Andrx Pharms., Inc., 239 F.3d 1297, 1301 (Fed. Cir. 2001) (finding it unnecessary to construe claim term that was not relevant to outcome of the case). *In re* Gabapentin Patent Litig., 395 F. Supp. 2d 153, 158 n.3 (D.N.J. 2005) (deciding summary judgment motion without *Markman* hearing); Aspex Eyewear, Inc. v. E'lite Optik, Inc., No. 3:98-CV-2996D, 2001 WL 204775, at *2 (N.D. Tex. Feb. 27, 2001) ("In cases such as this one, where the technology is accessible to the court and the claims are relatively straightforward, a *Markman* hearing is unnecessary.").

[60]*See* Menell et al, *supra* note 177, at 811–13 (suggesting that lack of patentable subject matter under Section 101, enablement motions under Section 112, and even some obviousness motions may be appropriate for early summary judgment treatment).

[61]*See* Genzyme Corp. v. Transkaryotic Therapies, Inc., 346 F.3d 1094, 1096–97 (Fed. Cir. 2003) (summary judgment affirmed where motions were filed after *Markman* hearing); *In re* Cruciferous Sprout Litig., 301 F.3d 1343, 1346 (Fed. Cir. 2002) (affirming summary judgment granted after *Markman* hearing); Wolf Designs, Inc. v. DHR & Co., 231 F.R.D. 430, 440 (N.D. Ga. 2005) ("Typically, in a case involving a utility patent, claim construction would occur before summary judgment motions were filed."); Digi Int'l Inc. v. Lantronix, Inc., 2005 WL 1397010, at *3 (D. Minn. June 13, 2005); McNulty v. Taser Int'l, 217 F. Supp. 2d 1058 (C.D. Cal. 2002) (summary judgment granted after *Markman* hearing), *aff'd*, 106 Fed. App'x 15 (Fed. Cir. 2004); Control Res., Inc. v. Delta Elecs., Inc., 133 F. Supp. 2d 121, 126 (D. Mass. 2001) ("[A]s is the practice of this Court, a *Markman* hearing was conducted prior to and entirely independently of the summary judgment hearing.").

at least one district court has expressed the view that summary judgment briefing should follow the *Markman* hearing.[62]

C. *Combining* Markman *and Summary Judgment*

If a summary judgment motion raises issues relating to the interpretation of the asserted patent claims, the court has discretion to combine the summary judgment motion with a *Markman* hearing.[63] Conducting a *Markman* hearing in connection with summary judgment motions has the advantage of placing the dispute in proper context and can limit the number of disputed claim terms that the court must resolve in order to decide summary judgment. Some courts have found this combined summary judgment and limited claim construction procedure especially useful to decide the issue of non-infringement when the court can dispose of the case by construing a very small number of claims.[64] If the dispute

---

[62]Magarl, LLC v. Crane Co., No. IP 02-0478-C-T/L, 1:03-CV-01255-JDT-TW, 2004 WL 2750252, at *15 (S.D. Ind. Sept. 29, 2004).

[63]*See* V-Formation, Inc. v. Benetton Group SpA, 401 F.3d 1307, 1310 (Fed. Cir. 2005) (affirming grant of summary judgment where district court heard summary judgment argument at same time as *Markman* hearing); Holmes Group, Inc. v. RPS Prods., Inc., 424 F. Supp. 2d 271, 282 (D. Mass. 2006) ("it is appropriate to address claim [] construction in the context of a motion for summary judgment"); Old Town Canoe Co. v. Glenwa, Inc., 229 F. Supp. 2d 1151, 1155 (D. Or. 2002) ("A summary judgment motion may create the appropriate setting in which to conduct a *Markman* hearing."), *aff'd in part and vacated on other grounds*, 55 Fed. App'x 918 (Fed. Cir. 2003); *Amgen*, 126 F. Supp. at 78 n.4 (timing of *Markman* hearing was "optimal" because "[a] motion for summary judgment is, of course, an excellent vehicle to frame the essential questions of patent claim construction"); Biogen v. Berlex Labs., Inc., 113 F. Supp. 2d 77, 81 (D. Mass. 2000) ("the court held a '*Markman* hearing,' for the purpose of deciding how to construe the relevant claims, in connection with the hearings on the motions for summary judgment"), *aff'd in part*, 318 F.3d 1132 (Fed. Cir. 2003); Ahlstrom Mach., Inc. v. Clement, 13 F. Supp. 2d 45, 46 (D.D.C. 1998) (holding oral argument on summary judgment and *Markman* hearing together), *aff'd*, 217 F.3d 860 (Fed. Cir. 1999) (table); MediaCom Corp. v. Rates Tech., Inc., 4 F. Supp. 2d 17, 22 & n.2 (D. Mass. 1998) ("[s]ince *Markman*, claim construction has most frequently been handled in conjunction with a hearing on a motion for summary judgment"; "the Rule 56 summary judgment motion is a perfectly appropriate vehicle in which to conduct a *Markman* hearing").

[64]*See* Schoenhaus v. Genesco, Inc., 440 F.3d 1354, 1356 (Fed. Cir. 2006) (affirming a "carefully crafted summary judgment opinion" that "construed two limitations of claim 1 of the patent" instead of a full claim construction order); *see also* Planet Bingo v. Gametech Int'l, 472 F.3d 1338, 1340 (Fed. Cir. 2006) (affirm-

is clearly limited to a small number of claims, an early summary judgment hearing combined with limited claim construction can save both the court and the parties time and resources.

III. Evidence to Support or Oppose Summary Judgment

A. *Expert Evidence Supporting Summary Judgment*

"Where the nonmoving party will bear the burden of proof at trial on a dispositive issue, a summary judgment motion may properly be made in reliance solely on the pleadings, depositions, answers to interrogatories, and admissions on file."[65] Thus, for example, in the context of summary judgment of noninfringement, the Federal Circuit has held "that nothing more is required than the filing of a summary judgment motion stating that the patentee had no evidence of infringement and pointing to the specific ways in which accused systems did not meet the claim limitations."[66]

Most often, however, moving parties support motions for summary judgment by submitting affidavits from fact and expert witnesses. Expert evidence, however, is not always necessary to support summary judgment motions in patent cases where the technology is "'easily understandable without the need for expert explanatory testimony.'"[67]

Expert testimony may be important in patent cases involving complex technology. Under Federal Rule of Civil Procedure 56(e), such supporting affidavits must be made on personal knowledge, show that the affiant is competent to testify, and set forth facts that

---

ing early summary judgment when construction of a single claim disposed of entire suit).

[65]Celotex Corp. v. Catrett, 477 U.S. 317, 324 (1986).

[66]Exigent Tech., Inc. v. Atrana Solutions, Inc., 442 F.3d 1301, 1308 (Fed. Cir. 2006).

[67]Centricut, LLC v. Esab Group, Inc., 390 F.3d 1361, 1369 (Fed. Cir. 2004), *cert. denied*, 126 S. Ct. 337, 163 L. Ed. 2d 49 (2005) (quoting Union Carbide Corp. v. Am. Can Co., 724 F.2d 1567, 1573 (Fed. Cir. 1984)); *see also* Prima Tekil, LLC v. Polypap, S.A.R.L., 412 F.3d 1284, 1290 n.7 (Fed. Cir. 2005) ("Expert testimony was not required; the technology being easily understood without expert testimony."); Iron Grip Barbell Co. v. USA Sports, Inc., 392 F.3d 1317, 1323 n.3 (Fed. Cir. 2004).

would be admissible at trial. General and conclusory opinions of experts will not be sufficient to support summary judgment.[68]

B. Expert Evidence Opposing Summary Judgment

It is common for the nonmovant to oppose summary judgment based on an affidavit of its retained expert.[69] Under Rule 56(e), and like supporting affidavits, any such opposing affidavits must be made on personal knowledge, show that the affiant is competent to testify, and set forth facts that would be admissible at trial.

It is not always necessary for the nonmovant to oppose the motion with affidavits or other evidence. "[A] non-movant need not always provide affidavits or other evidence to defeat a summary judgment motion. If, for example, the movant bears the burden of proof and its motion fails to satisfy that burden, the non-movant is 'not required to come forward' with opposing evidence."[70]

Conclusory statements of counsel or of a witness on the ultimate issue do not raise a genuine issue of material fact.[71] "It is well settled that an expert's unsupported conclusion on the ultimate issue of infringement is insufficient to raise a genuine issue of material fact, and that a party may not avoid that rule simply by

---

[68] *See* Koito Mfg. Co. v. Turn-Key-Tech, LLC, 381 F.3d 1142, 1152 & n.4 (Fed. Cir. 2004) (expert's failure to provide explanatory testimony linking prior art to the asserted claims insufficient to find claims invalid over prior art); Phillips Petroleum Co. v. Huntsman Polymers Corp., 157 F.3d 866, 876 (Fed. Cir. 1998) (conclusory expert declarations devoid of facts upon which the conclusions were reached fail to raise a genuine issue of material fact that would preclude summary judgment).

[69] *See* Schwing GmbH v. Putzmeister Aktiengesellschaft, 305 F.3d 1318, 1326 (Fed. Cir. 2002) (acknowledging that expert declarations are often offered to avoid summary judgment).

[70] Saab Cars USA, Inc. v. United States, 434 F.3d 1359, 1368 (Fed. Cir. 2006) (citing Adickes v. S.H. Kress & Co., 398 U.S. 144, 160 (1970)); *see also Exigent Tech.*, 442 F.3d at 1307–08. "If the motion is brought by a party with the ultimate burden of proof, the movant must still satisfy its burden by showing that it is entitled to judgment as a matter of law even in the absence of an adequate response by the nonmovant'", *Saab*, 434 F.3d at 1368 (citing 11 James Wm. Moore et al., Moore's Federal Practice ¶ 56.13[1] (3d ed. 2005)).

[71] *See Schwing*, 305 F.3d at 1326 ("[expert's] conclusory statement is insufficient to raise a genuine evidentiary dispute for trial"); Biotec Biologische Naturverpackungen GmbH & Co. KG v. Biocorp, Inc., 249 F.3d 1341, 1353 (Fed. Cir. 2001); Applied Cos. v. United States, 144 F.3d 1470, 1475 (Fed. Cir. 1998).

framing the expert's conclusion as an assertion that a particular critical claim limitation is found in the accused device."[72] "The party opposing the [summary judgment] motion must point to an evidentiary conflict created on the record at least by a counter statement of a fact or facts set forth in detail in an affidavit by a knowledgeable affiant. Mere denials or conclusory statements are insufficient."[73]

"It is not the trial judge's burden to search through lengthy technologic documents for possible evidence. The public interest in invalidating invalid patents does not override the well established procedure requiring the nonmovant to come forward with evidence sufficient to negate the movant's position."[74] Although expert testimony is not always required to prove infringement when the technology is complex, a patentee will be unable to satisfy its burden of proof if it fails to present expert testimony in response to that offered by an accused infringer to negate infringement.[75]

IV. Appealability of Partial Summary Judgment

Orders granting summary judgment disposing of the entire case generally can be appealed as a final judgment. Orders granting partial summary judgment are not final judgments.[76]

If a party wishes to immediately appeal an order granting partial summary judgment, it must ordinarily obtain certification from the district court under Rule 54(b).[77] If an order granting partial summary judgment is appealed prior to obtaining Rule

[72]Dynacore Holdings Corp. v. U.S. Philips Corp., 363 F.3d 1263, 1277–78 (Fed. Cir. 2004) (citing Arthur A. Collins, Inc. v. N. Telecom Ltd., 216 F.3d 1042, 1046 (Fed. Cir. 2000); Zelinski v. Brunswick Corp., 185 F.3d 1311, 1317 (Fed. Cir. 1999); *Phillips Petroleum*, 157 F.3d at 876)).

[73]Barmag Barmer Maschinenfabrik AG v. Murata Machinery, Ltd., 731 F.2d 831, 836 (Fed. Cir. 1984).

[74]*Biotec Biologische*, 249 F.3d at 1353.

[75]Centricut, LLC v. Esab Group, Inc., 390 F.3d 1361, 1370 (Fed. Cir. 2004).

[76]CAE Screenplates Inc. v. Heinrich Fiedler GmbH & Co., 224 F.3d 1308, 1314 (Fed. Cir. 2000) ("An order granting partial summary judgment is not a final appealable order because ... it does not dispose of all claims raised."); Syntex Pharms. Int'l, Ltd. v. K-Line Pharms., Ltd., 905 F.2d 1525, 1526 (Fed. Cir. 1990).

[77]*CAE Screenplates*, 224 F.3d at 1313.

54(b) certification, the notice of appeal will ripen upon the entry of a proper Rule 54(b) certification.[78] Once there is a final judgment disposing of all claims in the case, an order granting partial summary judgment is considered to "merge" with the final judgment and becomes ripe for appeal.[79]

---

[78] State Contracting & Eng'g Corp. v. Florida, 258 F.3d 1329, 1335 (Fed. Cir. 2001).

[79] *See* Invitrogen Corp. v. Clontech Labs., Inc., 429 F.3d 1052, 1069 (Fed. Cir. 2005) (citing Hendler v. United States, 952 F.2d 1364, 1368 (Fed. Cir. 1991)); Fifth Third Bank of W. Ohio v. United States, 402 F.3d 1221, 1236 (Fed. Cir. 2005); Glaros v. H.H. Robertson Co., 797 F.2d 1564, 1573 (Fed. Cir. 1986) (stating that grant of partial summary judgment "from which no immediate appeal lies" is "merged" into the final judgment and reviewable on appeal from that judgment).

11

Pretrial Issues and Motions In Limine*

*Morgan Chu, Christine W.S. Byrd & Alexander C.D. Giza, Irell & Manella LLP, Los Angeles, California.

I. Introduction

Patent litigation raises unique pretrial issues regarding bifurcation (or other separation of issues for trial), time for trial, and motions in limine.

II. Separation of Issues for Trial

Patent trials are sometimes bifurcated (or trifurcated) among several different issues. For example, the issue of inequitable conduct is often bifurcated from the jury trial for a separate bench trial.[1] Courts have allowed other divisions of issues in appropriate situations.

Under Federal Rule of Civil Procedure 42(b), the court has discretion to order a separate trial of any claim or issue, or of any number of claims or issues, always preserving inviolate the right of trial by jury under the Seventh Amendment or pursuant to a statute. Considerations include convenience, avoiding prejudice, expedition, and economy.[2] Specific factors considered vary by the jurisdiction, but commonly considered factors include: (1) whether the issues are to be tried before a jury or to the court; (2) whether the issues have common questions of law or fact; (3) whether settlement of the claims or judicial economy would be facilitated; (4) whether prejudice would be avoided; (5) whether the pos-

---

[1] *See, e.g.*, Micro Motion, Inc. v. Kane Steel Co., 894 F.2d 1318, 1320 (Fed. Cir. 1990) (noting that district court trifurcated case: inequitable conduct (tried to the court), infringement, and damages).

[2] Fed. R. Civ. P. 42(b).

ture of discovery on the issues favors a single trial or bifurcation; (6) whether a single trial of all issues would create the potential for jury bias or confusion; and (7) whether the documentary and testimonial evidence on the issues overlap.[3]

A. *Inequitable Conduct From Case in Chief*

The Federal Circuit has specifically approved of bifurcating the issue of inequitable conduct from the remainder of a patent case and trying the inequitable conduct issue to the court without a jury.[4] In resolving the issue of the right to a jury trial,[5] the court concluded: "Thus the *conduct-of-the-applicant-in-the-PTO* issue raised in the nonjury trial and the separated infringement/validity issues are distinct and without commonality either as claims or in relation to the underlying fact issues."[6] Of course, the court has discretion to allow bifurcation, and the analysis could be more complicated if other Rule 42(b) factors are involved, e.g., if there are antitrust issues (*Handgards, Walker Process*) with common questions of fact for the jury.

Having a separate bench trial on inequitable conduct also extends, when otherwise appropriate, to bifurcation of other issues reserved for the court, e.g., laches, equitable estoppel, and unclean hands. Nevertheless, courts may, and often do, choose to use advisory juries for issues otherwise left to the courts.

---

[3] *See, e.g.*, Morris v. Northrop Grumman Corp., 37 F. Supp. 2d 556, 580 (E.D.N.Y. 1999); THK Am., Inc. v. NSK Co., 151 F.R.D. 625, 632 (N.D. Ill. 1993); Reading Indus. v. Kennecott Copper Corp., 61 F.R.D. 662, 664 (S.D.N.Y. 1974).

[4] Agfa Corp. v. Creo Prods. Inc., 451 F.3d 1366, 1371–75 (Fed. Cir. 2006); Gardco Mfg., Inc. v. Herst Lighting Co., 820 F.2d 1209, 1212–13 (Fed. Cir. 1987).

[5] *See, e.g.*, Beacon Theatres, Inc. v. Westover, 359 U.S. 500, 503–04 (1959).

[6] *Gardco*, 820 F.2d at 1213 (emphasis in original).

B. Willfulness From Liability

Courts have sometimes bifurcated the issue of willfulness from the issue of infringement.[7] Willful infringement is a question of fact[8] appropriate for decision by a jury.[9] This type of bifurcation separates the trial into two stages—first infringement, then willfulness—and the two stages are tried before the same jury, before two different juries, or to the court.

In the past, the main factor in favor of bifurcation of willfulness was prejudice to the accused infringer based on the *Quantum* dilemma—the problem of choosing between relying on advice of counsel as a willfulness defense and maintaining attorney-client privilege to prevent disclosure of materials on infringement that are potentially prejudicial.[10] The Federal Circuit has "suggested the advisability of separate trials in appropriate cases."[11]

In some cases, courts have found "no significant overlap between issues of liability for patent infringement and willfulness," and, having already decided to bifurcate damages into a second stage of trial, also include willfulness in the second stage.[12]

---

[7] *See, e.g.*, Kimberly A. Moore, *Empirical Statistics on Willful Patent Infringement*, 14 Fed. Cir. B.J. 227, 235 (2004) (reporting that from 1999–2000 willfulness was bifurcated in 34.5 percent of the cases that went to trial).

[8] *See, e.g.*, Golden Blount, Inc. v. Robert H. Peterson Co., 438 F.3d 1354, 1367 (Fed. Cir. 2006).

[9] Christopher B. Seaman, *Willful Patent Infringement and Enhanced Damages After* In re Seagate: *An Empirical Study*, 97 Iowa Law Rev. 417, 436 n.132 (2012).

[10] Quantum Corp. v. Tandon Corp., 940 F.2d 642, 643–44 (Fed. Cir. 1991).

[11] *Id.* at 644. *See also, e.g.*, Johns Hopkins Univ. v. Cellpro, 160 F.R.D. 30, 37 (D. Del. 1995) (discussing motion to bifurcate discovery and trial on damages and willfulness, ultimately denying motion but granting leave to renew at pretrial conference); Neorx Corp. v. Immunomedics, Inc., 28 USPQ2d 1395, 1396–97 & n.4 (D.N.J. 1993) (vacating magistrate court's denial of bifurcation and remanding for in camera review of privileged materials and consideration of other factors). This may change in light of *Knorr-Bremse*, where the Federal Circuit held that "an adverse inference that a legal opinion was or would have been unfavorable shall not be drawn from invocation of the attorney–client and/or work product privileges or from failure to consult with counsel." Knorr-Bremse Systeme fuer Nutzfahrzeuge GmbH v. Dana Corp., 383 F.3d 1337, 1347 (Fed. Cir. 2004) (en banc). Moreover, *In re Seagate Tech. LLC*, No. Misc. 830, 2007 WL 2358677 (Fed. Cir. Aug. 20, 2007), may have reduced the need to obtain and rely on opinions of counsel.

[12] Novopharm Ltd. v. Torpharm, Inc., 181 F.R.D. 308, 312 (E.D.N.C. 1998); Princeton Biochemicals, Inc. v. Beckman Instruments, Inc., 180 F.R.D. 254, 260 (D.N.J. 1997).

C. Liability From Damages

Bifurcation of liability issues from damages issues might be appropriate in some patent cases.[13] "Patent cases are often uniquely amenable to bifurcation because of the complex nature of the damages determination and the extensive discovery that is often necessary to prove the nature and extent of those damages."[14] "A preliminary finding on the question of liability may well make unnecessary the damages inquiry, and thus result in substantial saving of time of the Court and counsel and reduction of expense to the parties."[15] "Moreover, separate trial of the issue of liability may present counsel the opportunity to obtain final settlement of that issue on appeal without having reached the often time-consuming and difficult damages question."[16]

D. Infringement From Invalidity

Less frequently, courts bifurcate infringement issues from invalidity issues.[17]

---

[13]*E.g.*, WMS Gaming, Inc. v. Int'l Game Tech., 184 F.3d 1339, 1345 (Fed. Cir. 1999); Central Soya Co. v. Geo. A. Hormel & Co., 723 F.2d 1573, 1575 (Fed. Cir. 1983); Princeton Biochemicals, Inc. v. Beckman Instruments, Inc., 180 F.R.D. 254, 259 (D.N.J. 1997); Amgen, Inc. v. Chugai Pharm. Co., 13 USPQ2d 1737, 1741 (D. Mass. 1989); Am. Standard, Inc. v. Pfizer, Inc., 722 F. Supp. 86, 90 (D. Del. 1989); E.I. duPont de Nemours & Co. v. Phillips Petroleum Co., 656 F. Supp. 1343, 1346 (D. Del. 1987).

[14]*Novopharm Ltd.*, 181 F.R.D. at 310; *accord* Eaton Corp. v. Auburn Gear Inc., 8 USPQ2d 1373, 1375 (N.D. Ind. 1988).

[15]Swofford v. B & W, Inc., 34 F.R.D. 15, 20 (S.D. Tex. 1963). *See also* MOORE, *supra* note 7, at 235 (reporting that the fact finder found no liability in 42.8 percent of cases that were tried from 1983–2000).

[16]*Swofford*, 34 F.R.D. at 20.

[17]*See* Inland Steel Co. v. LTV Steel Co., 364 F.3d 1318, 1319 (Fed. Cir. 2004) (noting that district court trifurcated into infringement, invalidity, and damages trials); Tec Air, Inc. v. Denso Mfg. Mich., Inc., 192 F.3d 1353, 1357 (Fed. Cir. 1999) (same); Allen Organ Co. v. Kimball Int'l, Inc., 839 F.2d 1556, 1558 (Fed. Cir. 1988) (noting parties' agreement to bifurcate infringement issue from validity and enforceability issues); Stambler v. RSA Security, Inc., 123 Fed. App'x 982, 986 (Fed. Cir. 2005) (unpublished) (finding no abuse of discretion in district court decision to bifurcate invalidity and infringement issues).

E. Antitrust From Patent Issues

Courts may also bifurcate patent issues from antitrust issues.[18] A court noted what it described as the "now-standard practice of separating for trial patent issues and those raised in an antitrust counterclaim."[19] "[T]he major consideration is directed toward the choice most likely to result in a just final disposition of the litigation."[20] A recurring concern is the complexity of patent issues and antitrust issues:

> Patent validity and infringement claims and antitrust actions both involve large and complex bodies of laws. Antitrust actions frequently require protracted trials. The burden placed on a trier of fact, be it judge or jury, in a case involving patent validity, patent infringement, patent misuse, unfair competition, antitrust violations, and an unlawful interference with contractual relationships, is at best a heavy one to bear.[21]

While many courts indicate a strong preference for bifurcating patent and antitrust issues, such separation is still discretionary.

---

[18] *E.g.*, Purdue Pharma L.P. v. Endo Pharms., Inc., 438 F.3d 1123, 1128 (Fed. Cir. 2006) (noting that the trial court bifurcated patent issues from antitrust and unfair trade claims); Arthrocare Corp. v. Smith & Nephew, Inc., 406 F.3d 1365, 1367 (Fed. Cir. 2005) (noting that the trial court bifurcated patent issues of infringement, invalidity, and inequitable conduct in first phase from damages, willfulness, and the antitrust counterclaim in second phase); Medtronic, Inc. v. Daig Corp., 789 F.2d 903, 904 (Fed. Cir. 1986) (noting that the trial court trifurcated case with the issues of patent validity and infringement to be tried first, the issues of damages relating to patent infringement to be tried second, and the issues of liability and damages relating to the antitrust and unfair competition claims to be tried last); Ashland Oil, Inc. v. Delta Oil Prods. Corp., 806 F.2d 1031, 1032 (Fed. Cir. 1986); Technicon Instruments Corp. v. Alpkem Corp., 866 F.2d 417, 418 (Fed. Cir. 1989).

[19] *In re* Innotron Diagnostics, 800 F.2d 1077, 1084 (Fed. Cir. 1986). *See also* Henan Oil Tools, Inc. v. Eng'g Enters., Inc., 262 F. Supp. 629, 631 (S.D. Tex. 1966) ("It is common for courts to sever antitrust issues from patent validity and infringement issues."); Brandt, Inc. v. Crane, 97 F.R.D. 707, 708 (N.D. Ill. 1983) ("As a general rule, separate trials of patent and antitrust claims further the interests of convenience, expediency and economy."); Alarm Device Mfg. Co. v. Alarm Prods. Int'l, Inc., 60 F.R.D. 199, 202 (E.D.N.Y. 1973) ("More often than not, separate trials of patent validity–infringement claims and misuse–antitrust claims have been found to be salutary.").

[20] *In re* Innotron Diagnostics, 800 F.2d 1077, 1084 (Fed. Cir. 1986).

[21] *Henan Oil Tools*, 262 F. Supp. at 631. *See also* Dentsply Int'l, Inc. v. New Tech. Co., Civ. A. No. 96-272 MMS, 1996 WL 756766, at *4–5 (D. Del. Dec. 19, 1996) (stating that avoiding jury confusion and expediting trial "[are] the primary end[s] to which any order of separate trials under Rule 42(b) [are] directed").

"[I]n any patent infringement suit in which antitrust is the basis of defense, or counterclaims, the court, pursuant to Rule 42(b) of the Federal Rules of Civil Procedure, should order separate trials of the antitrust and patent issues.... Several members disagree with this recommendation. They feel that judicial discretion, not restricted by a presumption in favor of separate trials, suffices to meet the problem."[22]

III. Time Limits at Trial

The court's inherent power to control cases includes the discretionary power to set time limits for a trial.[23] The time required for a patent trial can depend on many factors, including the complexity of the technology, the number of patents in suit, the number of asserted claims, the number of parties, and the number of different accused products. For example, the District of Delaware and the Eastern District of Texas currently schedule two weeks for a patent trial. Courts sometimes provide a time limit in hours for each party's entire presentation of evidence. Courts may also allow a separate amount of time for each of the following: jury voir dire, opening statements, interim summations, and closing arguments.

IV. Motions In Limine

Patent cases raise many issues for motions in limine that are unique to patent litigation. Recurring issues include: (1) limitations concerning inventor testimony, (2) expert testimony, (3) comparison of the accused products to embodiments of the patent, (4) commercial success of the patented invention, (5) a

---

[22] *Alarm Device Mfg.*, 60 F.R.D. at 202 (quoting *Report of the Attorney General's National Committee to Study the Antitrust Laws* 249 (1955)). *See also, e.g.*, Genentech, Inc. v. Wellcome Found. Ltd., 14 USPQ2d 1363, 1373 (D. Del. 1990) (denying bifurcation in part because "both the validity of the patents and the defense of fraudulent and inequitable conduct will require exploration of much of the same evidence that will be presented on Defendants' antitrust claim").

[23] *See, e.g.*, Duquesne Light Co. v. Westinghouse Elec. Corp., 66 F.3d 604, 609 (3d Cir. 1995); Monotype Corp. PLC v. Int'l Typeface Corp., 43 F.3d 443, 450 (9th Cir. 1994); Johnson v. Ashby, 808 F.2d 676, 678 (8th Cir. 1987).

finding of validity of the same patent in other litigation, (6) reference to reissue or reexamination proceedings, (7) use of the word "monopoly," (8) evidence of foreign patents and proceedings, and (9) evidence relating to equitable issues tried separately before the court.

A. Inventor Testimony

Courts may grant motions in limine to limit inventor testimony on the patent-in-suit depending on the subject of the proposed testimony. For example, inventor testimony "may not be used to vary, contradict, expand, or limit the claim language from how it is defined, even by implication, in the specification or file history."[24] Also, an inventor may not have "particularized knowledge and experience in the structure and workings of [an] accused device."[25]

On the other hand, inventors can explain the invention consistent with the specification and claims:

> An inventor is a competent witness to explain the invention and what was intended to be conveyed by the specification and covered by the claims. The testimony of the inventor may also provide background information, including explanation of the problems that existed at the time the invention was made and the inventor's solution to these problems.[26]

In addition, inventors may generally testify about enablement, conception, and reduction to practice.[27]

B. **Daubert** *and Expert Testimony*

Federal Rule of Evidence 702 allows testimony by experts if, among other requirements, it will "assist the trier of fact to under-

---

[24]Bell Atl. Network Servs., Inc. v. Covad Communications Group, Inc., 262 F.3d 1258, 1269 (Fed. Cir. 2001) (citing Vitronics Corp. v. Conceptronic, Inc., 90 F.3d 1576, 1584–85 (Fed. Cir. 1996)).

[25]Air Turbine Tech., Inc. v. Atlas Copco AB, 410 F.3d 701, 714 (Fed. Cir. 2005); Cordis Corp. v. Boston Scientific Corp., No. Civ. 03-027 SLR, 2006 WL 1305227, at *14 (D. Del. May 11, 2006).

[26]Voice Techs. Group v. VMC Sys., Inc., 164 F.3d 605, 615 (Fed. Cir. 1999).

[27]*See, e.g.*, MEMC Elec. Materials, Inc. v. Mitsubishi Materials Silicon Corp., No. C 01-4925 SBA, 2006 WL 463525, at *11 (N.D. Cal. Feb. 24, 2006).

stand the evidence or to determine a fact in issue."[28] The rule also specifies the necessary qualifications of an expert and the appropriate basis for the expert's opinion. Under Rule 702, an expert qualified "by knowledge, skill, experience, training, or education" may provide opinion testimony "if (1) the testimony is based upon sufficient facts or data, (2) the testimony is the product of reliable principles and methods, and (3) the witness has applied the principles and methods reliably to the facts of the case." While the general principles of Rule 702 apply equally to both patent and nonpatent cases, patent cases have some different and special limitations, including limitations on expert testimony relating to inadequate, untimely, or lack of disclosure; limitations on expert testimony on willfulness; and limitations on expert testimony regarding Patent Office procedures.

1. *Limitations Relating to Inadequate, Untimely, or Lack of Disclosure*

According to the Federal Rules of Civil Procedure, expert testimony must be appropriately disclosed and supplemented, or it may be precluded from trial.[29] In patent cases, statutes and special Patent Rules add disclosure requirements for infringement contentions, invalidity contentions, and notice of prior art pursuant to 35 U.S.C. §282. Inadequate, untimely, or lack of disclosure can appropriately lead to preclusion.[30]

2. *Limitations on Expert Testimony on Willfullness*

Accused infringers often move under Federal Rules of Evidence 702 and 403 to preclude testimony by experts on the issue of whether infringement was willful. Courts may allow expert

---

[28]Daubert v. Merrell Dow Pharms., Inc., 509 U.S. 579, 590 (1993).

[29]Fed. R. Civ. P. 26(a)(2), 26(e)(1) & 37(c)(1).

[30]*See, e.g.*, TiVo v. EchoStar Communications Corp., No. 2:04-cv-1-DF, at 5 (E.D. Tex. Jan. 26, 2006) (precluding EchoStar's experts from referring to reverse doctrine of equivalents because of failure to appropriately disclose opinions); Immersion Corp. v. Sony Computer Entm't Am., Inc., No. C 02-0710 CW, at 3 (N.D. Cal. July 6, 2004) (precluding Sony from relying on any prior art not disclosed in its final invalidity contentions).

testimony on willfulness.[31] Some courts specifically preclude expert testimony on the law of willfulness, but otherwise allow expert testimony.[32]

3. Limitations on Expert Testimony Regarding PTO Procedures

While some courts allow expert testimony on PTO procedures, courts may also preclude expert testimony that indicates that PTO procedures are shoddy.[33] Courts view such testimony as an improper "attempt to undermine the presumption of validity under 35 U.S.C. §282 by inviting the jury to speculate about possible defects, errors, or omissions in the application process that led to the issuance of the patent-in-suit."[34]

---

[31]*In re* Hayes Microcomputer Prods., Inc. Patent Litig., 982 F.2d 1527, 1543 (Fed. Cir. 1992) (affirming decision allowing expert witness to testify in order to impeach defendant's defense that "a reasonable basis [existed] for believing in good faith that the [patent–in–suit] was invalid").

[32]*E.g.*, Clintec Nutrition Co. v. Baxa Corp., No. 94 C 7050, 1998 WL 560284, at *9 (N.D. Ill. Aug. 26, 1998) (precluding expert testimony on the law regarding willfulness); Oxford Gene Tech., Ltd. v. Mergen Ltd., 345 F. Supp. 2d 431, 443 (D. Del. 2004) ("[The plaintiff's patent law expert] will not, however, be permitted to testify as to the legal standard for willfulness. Nor will she be permitted to testify as to whether [the defendant's] behavior met the standard of reasonableness, . . . or regarding [the defendant's] intent, motive, or state of mind, or evidence by which such state of mind may be inferred."). *But cf.* Pioneer Hi-Bred Int'l, Inc. v. Ottawa Plant Food, Inc., 219 F.R.D. 135, 142–43 (N.D. Iowa 2003) ("[T]he testimony of [the patent expert] regarding the sufficiency of the evidence of willful infringement is nevertheless inadmissible. This is so, because willful infringement is not an issue on which the court finds that expert testimony will assist the trier of fact to understand the evidence or determine the issue. *See* FED. R. EVID. 702 (prerequisites to admission of expert testimony). Rather, 'willful infringement' is a matter for jury determination, in light of facts well within their understanding and appropriate instructions from the court.").

[33]*See, e.g.*, Applied Materials, Inc. v. Advanced Semiconductors Materials Am., Inc., No. C 92-20643 RMW, 1995 WL 261407, at *3 (N.D. Cal. Apr. 25, 1995) (excluding expert testimony concerning overwork at the PTO and other matters insinuating that the PTO does not do its job properly as "irrelevant speculation"); Bausch & Lomb, Inc. v. Alcon Labs., Inc., 79 F. Supp. 2d 252, 255–56 (W.D.N.Y. 2000) (ruling inadmissible testimony on "the problems Examiners encounter with the completeness or 'file integrity' of the 'shoes' maintained at the PTO," "the difficulties Examiners face in discovering and obtaining prior art references other than patents," and "the time constraints under which Examiners in the PTO must operate"; "generalized testimony about 'problems' in the PTO is not admissible").

[34]*Bausch & Lomb*, 79 F. Supp. 2d at 255. *See also, e.g.*, W. Elec. Co. v. Piezo Tech., Inc., 860 F.2d 428, 433 (Fed. Cir. 1988) ("It is no more appropriate to

Some judges like to show the jury the Federal Judicial Center's videotape on the Patent Office and its procedures, especially early in the case, to educate the jury on patents in general and to help them understand the appropriate context.[35]

C. Comparison of Accused Product With Embodiments of Patent

Under some circumstances, courts have granted motions to preclude evidence of the patentee's embodiment of the invention. Comparing the accused products to the patentee's embodiment of the invention is contrary to longstanding principles of patent law. "Specifications teach. Claims claim.... Infringement, literal or by equivalence, is determined by comparing an accused product not with a preferred embodiment described in the specification, or with a commercialized embodiment of the patentee, but with the properly and previously construed claims in suit."[36]

D. Commercial Success of the Patented Invention

Evidence related to the patentee's invention can be relevant to secondary considerations of nonobviousness and, in particular,

---

question a patent examiner's technical expertise than it is to question the quality of a judge's law school education or judicial experience."); Neutrino Dev. Corp. v. Sonosite, Inc., 410 F. Supp. 2d 529, 544 (S.D. Tex. 2006) ("The Court finds that, to the extent that [the expert's] testimony simply addresses the potential pressures and potential for error at the PTO, such testimony is inadmissible. Such general testimony tends to undermine the presumption of validity.") (citation omitted).

[35] *See, e.g.*, Minebea Co. v. Papst, No. Civ.A. 97-0590(PLF), 2005 WL 1459704, at *7 (D.D.C. June 21, 2005) (stating "that the jury will be shown a videotape prepared by the Federal Judicial Center on the practices and procedures of the USPTO immediately after the Court's preliminary instructions"); *see also* An *Introduction to the Patent System* (Federal Judicial Center 2002).

[36] SRI Int'l v. Matsushita Elec. Corp. of Am., 775 F.2d 1107, 1121 & n.14 (Fed. Cir. 1985) (en banc); *accord* Phillips v. AWH Corp., 415 F.3d 1303, 1323 (Fed. Cir. 2005) (en banc) ("[A]lthough the specification often describes very specific embodiments of the invention, we have repeatedly warned against confining the claims to those embodiments."); Laitram Corp. v. Cambridge Wire Cloth Co., 863 F.2d 855, 865 (Fed. Cir. 1988) ("References to a preferred embodiment, such as those often present in a specification, are not claim limitations.").

commercial success.[37] The Federal Circuit noted that "evidence rising out of the so-called 'secondary considerations' must always when present be considered en route to a determination of obviousness."[38] As a limit on evidence of commercial success, "[a] nexus is required between the merits of the claimed invention and the evidence offered."[39] This is to ensure that evidence of commercial success is attributable to the inventions of the claims at issue, "rather than to extraneous factors such as advertising and marketing or to the features" outside the claims.[40]

E. Finding of Validity of Same Patent in Other Litigation

The effect of a first litigation regarding the validity of a patent may be the subject of a motion in limine in a second litigation. Generally, a prior judgment of no invalidity does not preclude a different accused infringer from arguing that the same patent is invalid in the second litigation.[41]

In a second litigation between the same parties regarding the same patent, the first settlement or judgment "would operate to bar a challenge to the validity of the patent claims at issue in the first suit only if the accused device was 'essentially the same' as the previous device admitted to infringe, or that any changes were merely 'colorable' or 'unrelated to the limitations in the claims of the patent.'"[42] "[I]f the devices were not essentially the same, in which case the suit was based on a different claim—i.e., a cause of action for infringement different from the cause of action in the

---

[37] *See* Graham v. John Deere Co., 383 U.S. 1, 17 (1966).

[38] Stratoflex, Inc. v. Aeroquip Corp., 713 F.2d 1530, 1538 (Fed. Cir. 1983).

[39] *Id.* at 1539; *In re* GPAC Inc., 57 F.3d 1573, 1580 (Fed. Cir. 1995) ("Because GPAC has not met its burden . . . to demonstrate that the commercial success of [the] invention resulted directly from the subject matter claimed in the [patent–in–suit], we conclude that the nexus requirement of *Stratoflex* is not satisfied."); *In re* Paulsen, 30 F.3d 1475, 1482 (Fed. Cir. 1994) ("When a patentee offers objective evidence of nonobviousness, there must be a sufficient relationship between that evidence and the patented invention.").

[40] *Paulsen*, 30 F.3d at 1482.

[41] Grayson v. McGowan, 543 F.2d 79, 81 (9th Cir. 1976) (citing Blonder-Tongue Labs., Inc. v. Univ. of Ill. Found., 402 U.S. 313, 329 (1971)).

[42] Hallco Mfg. Co. v. Foster, 256 F.3d 1290, 1295 (Fed. Cir. 2001) (citing Foster v. Hallco Mfg., 947 F.2d 469, 479–80 (Fed. Cir. 1991)).

earlier litigation—...there would be no claim preclusion to bar the attack on validity."[43]

F. Reference to Reissue or Reexamination Proceedings

A court may preclude evidence of a reissue or reexamination proceeding in the PTO on a motion in limine pursuant to Federal Rule of Evidence 403.[44]

Considering grants of requests for reexaminations, for example, courts have recognized that "the Patent Office's decision to grant reexamination casts the validity of the patent into some doubt, but only to a small degree."[45] On the other hand, the potential prejudice when calling into doubt the presumption of validity is significant.[46] Whether documents in a reexamination other than the PTO's initial grant of reexamination should be precluded is a closer question.[47]

G. Use of the Word "Monopoly"

A court may preclude an accused infringer from using the term "monopoly" in reference to the patent-in-suit as being

---

[43] *Hallco,* 256 F.3d at 1295.

[44] *See, e.g.,* Amphenol T&M Antennas Inc. v. Centurion Int'l Inc., 69 USPQ2d 1798, 1800 (N.D. Ill. 2002); Lemelson v. Gen. Mills, Inc., No. 77 C 4558, 1987 WL 16226, at *1 (N.D. Ill. Aug. 24, 1987) (denying reconsideration of order granting motion in limine to exclude evidence of reissue proceeding because "the probative value of testimony concerning the reissue proceedings is substantially outweighed by the danger of unfair prejudice, confusion of the issues and misleading the jury").

[45] *Amphenol,* 69 USPQ2d at 1800. *See also* Hoechst Celanese Corp. v. BP Chems. Ltd., 78 F.3d 1575, 1584 (Fed. Cir. 1996) ("[T]he grant by the examiner of a request for reexamination is not probative of unpatentability."); Soverain Software LLC v. Amazon.com, Inc., 356 F. Supp. 2d 660, 662 (E.D. Tex. 2005) (observing that "over 90% of all reexamination requests are granted"); IMAX Corp. v. In-Three, Inc., 385 F. Supp. 2d 1030, 1033 n.1 (C.D. Cal. 2005) ("Only 12% of requests for reexamination from third parties result in claims being eliminated.").

[46] *Amphenol,* 69 USPQ2d at 1800.

[47] Price v. Code-Alarm, Inc., No. 91 C 699, 1992 WL 390895, at *4 (N.D. Ill. Dec. 16, 1992) (deferring decision until trial).

prejudicial.[48] Other case-specific circumstances may change the balancing under Rule 403.[49]

H. Evidence of Foreign Patents and Proceedings

Courts have considered whether to preclude evidence of foreign patents and proceedings under Federal Rule of Evidence 403.[50] A court could conclude in a particular case that foreign patents and proceedings would cause jury confusion, prejudice, and waste of time and thus preclude the foreign patent materials.

I. Evidence Related to Decisions for the Court

A court may limit or preclude evidence if the jury may be improperly affected by evidence it hears relating to issues it does not decide. In patent cases, these issues include inequitable conduct, injunction, and treble damages.[51] For example, regarding the issue of injunctive relief, the court in *THK America, Inc. v. NSK, Ltd.*[52] recognized that an accused infringer may try "to exploit the notion of injunctive relief in a way designed to elicit sympathy to [it] for the effects of the injunctive relief upon its work force or

---

[48] *See, e.g.,* Jamesbury Corp. v. Litton Indus. Prods., Inc., 756 F.2d 1556, 1559 (Fed. Cir. 1985); Panduit Corp. v. Stahlin Bros. Fibre Works, Inc., 575 F.2d 1152, 1160 n.8 (6th Cir. 1978) (noting "monopoly" is a "pejorative term").

[49] *See* THK Am., Inc. v. NSK, Ltd., 917 F. Supp. 563, 571 (N.D. Ill. 1996) (denying motion to preclude use of term "monopoly" before the jury because the term existed in other documentary evidence and could not be excised from the documents without destroying the context).

[50] *E.g.,* Max Daetwyler Corp. v. Input Graphics, Inc., 583 F. Supp. 446, 457 (E.D. Pa. 1984) (denying motion and stating that any prejudice can be addressed by allowing additional evidence or a curative or limiting instruction). Courts recognize that foreign patent law and procedures are different and have no affect on validity or infringement of claims in U.S. patents. *E.g.,* Application of Dulberg, 472 F.2d 1394, 1398 (C.C.P.A. 1973) ("We need not even consider the actions taken in foreign countries with regard to the patentability of this application under our law. The granting of a patent on an 'invention' in a foreign country has no relevance to the determination of whether the same 'invention' would be obvious within the ambit of §103 since it is notoriously well known that the standards of patentability vary from country to country.").

[51] *See, e.g., THK Am.,* 917 F. Supp. at 571 (noting motions in limine regarding reference at trial to the issues of inequitable conduct and injunctive relief).

[52] 917 F. Supp. 563 (N.D. Ill. 1996).

for any other non-relevant references."[53] The ultimate decision may depend on other case-specific facts, such as whether the party moving to preclude intends to discuss injunctive relief.[54]

Regarding the issue of treble damages, courts have determined that informing a jury about the possibility of treble damages "would serve no useful function and its probable consequence would be harmful—an impermissible lowering of the amount of damages."[55] Accordingly, a court could appropriately grant a motion in limine to preclude mention of treble damages.

---

[53] *Id.* at 572.

[54] *See id.* at 571–72.

[55] Pollock & Riley, Inc. v. Pearl Brewing Co., 498 F.2d 1240, 1243 (5th Cir. 1974); *accord* Semke v. Enid Auto. Dealers Ass'n, 456 F.2d 1361, 1370 (10th Cir. 1972).

12

The Use of Special Masters, Court Appointed Expert Witnesses, and Technical Advisors to Aid the Court in Patent Litigation*

I. Introduction

Courts hearing highly complex and technical patent cases often find it helpful to employ a neutral expert to teach the court about the technology at issue.[1] In many patent cases, the paid experts that the parties put forward can play this role. But when the technology is particularly complex or the parties' experts confuse

---

*John L. Cooper, FACTL, Farella Braun & Martel LLP San Francisco, California.

[1] *See* Ellen E. Deason, *Court-Appointed Expert Witnesses: Scientific Positivism Meets Bias and Deference*, 77 Or. L. Rev. 59, 85 (1998) (noting that "patent cases ... are one context in which explaining complex concepts is a particularly important reason for appointing experts").

rather than clarify the issues, many courts turn to special masters, court-appointed expert witnesses, or technical advisors to assist them.

Case law, federal rules and principles of judicial restraint help define when courts may appoint special masters, court-appointed expert witnesses, and technical advisors; how such experts should be paid; and how each kind of expert may interact with the court and with parties.

II. Special Masters

The Supreme Court recognized long ago that courts have the inherent power to appoint special masters to assist them in resolving complex or technical matters. This inherent power is now codified in Federal Rule of Civil Procedure 53. However, Rule 53 does not limit the court's inherent power, and some courts have appointed special masters under their inherent powers in order to avoid the requirements of Rule 53.[2]

Rule 53 states that courts may appoint special masters to perform any duties "consented to by the parties." Absent consent, the special master may only "address pretrial and post-trial matters" that a judge cannot effectively or timely address, or hold "trial proceedings or recommend findings of fact" if the appointment is warranted by an "exceptional condition" or "the need to perform an accounting or resolve a difficult computation of damages."[3] The rule also states that the special master's compensation must come either from the parties or from a fund within the court's control.[4]

In patent cases, special masters may assist the court by tutoring "the fact finder—judge or jury—regarding technical issues

---

[2]Judges narrow scientific issues in dispute at pretrial conferences and pretrial hearings where potential technical experts may be subject to examination by the court. They also manage complex scientific issues through the appointment of scientific special masters. FED. JUDICIAL CTR., REFERENCE MANUAL ON SCIENTIFIC EVIDENCE 6 (3d ed. 2011) available at http:/www.au.af.mil/au/awc/awcgate/fic/manual_sic_evidence.pdf.

[3]FED. R. CIV. P. 53(a)(1)(A)–(C).

[4]FED. R. CIV. P. 53(g).

in litigation."[5] Specifically, special masters may be helpful in the claim construction process.[6]

Rule 53 requires the court to issue an order outlining the special master's duties and powers, and when, if ever, he may have ex parte communications with the court or a party. In general, though, the rule authorizes special masters to "regulate all proceedings," to conduct evidentiary hearings, and to "exercise the appointing court's power to compel, take, and record evidence."

The court's order appointing a special master in *Acer, Inc. v. Technology Properties, Ltd.* provides a recent example of how special masters may be used in patent cases. In that case, the court authorized the special master to control the timing of pretrial procedures, conduct pretrial conferences, establish disputed and undisputed material facts, and compile the list of witnesses necessary to testify at trial, among other things.[7] The court also indicated that it was considering appointing a technical advisor in addition to the special master.[8]

Rule 53 and the common practice of courts show that special masters typically play a highly visible role. They interact with parties, consider evidence, and behave in many respects like magistrate judges. However, regardless of whether the court appoints a special master under its inherent powers or under Rule 53, the court must be careful to structure the special master's duties "so as to not intrude on the judge's authority to adjudicate the merits of the case."[9] The Supreme Court has made clear that special masters may "aid judges in the performance of specific judicial duties," but they may not "displace the court."[10]

---

[5]FJC Reference Manual at 65 (citing *In re* Newman, 763 F.2d 407, 409 (Fed. Cir. 1985)).

[6]*See* Peter S. Menell et al., *Patent Claim Construction: A Modern Synthesis and Structured Framework*, 25 BERK. TECH. L.J. 713, 807–08 (2010) (noting approvingly that using special masters in claim construction may "alleviate[] some of the due process concerns inherent in the use of a technical advisor," but cautioning that it may distance the court from fully understanding the technology at issue).

[7]Acer, Inc. v. Tech. Properties, Ltd, Case No. 3:08-cv-00877 (N.D. Cal. Oct. 5, 2011) (order appointing special master) (Ware, J.).

[8]*Id.*

[9]FJC Reference Manual at 64 (citing La Buy v. Howes Leather Co., 352 U.S. 249, 256–59 (1957)).

[10]La Buy v. Howes Leather Co., 352 U.S. 249, 256 (1957) (quoting *Ex parte* Peterson, 253 U.S. 300, 312 (1920)).

III. Court-Appointed Experts Under Rule 706

Court-appointed experts under Federal Rule of Evidence 706 are another source of assistance for courts confronting complex and technical cases. The Federal Circuit has explicitly approved using Rule 706 experts in patent cases, although it cautioned that such appointments are appropriate "only in rare and compelling circumstances."[11]

Rule 706 provides that the court may appoint an expert witness either on its own or on a party's motion. The court must publicly define the expert's role either in writing or orally at a hearing, and the expert must be available for deposition and cross-examination by both parties.[12] The parties compensate the expert in proportions determined by the court.[13]

Like special masters, Rule 706 experts play highly visible roles and interact directly with the parties. Unlike special masters, however, it is assumed that Rule 706 experts will give testimony. The FJC Manual recommends that courts try to decide early on in a case through "pretrial procedure that enables a judge to anticipate problems in expert testimony"[14] whether a Rule 706 expert will be necessary. The Manual further recommends that courts allow the parties to generate lists of proposed experts, issue guidelines on how the expert will interact with the parties and the court, and enter an order with a detailed list of the expert's tasks.[15]

Monolithic Power is the leading patent case addressing the role of Rule 706 experts in patent cases. In *Monolithic Power,* the trial court identified the Rule 706 expert to the jury as "an independent witness retained by the parties jointly at the court's direction

---

[11]Monolithic Power Sys., Inc. v. 02 Micro Int'l Ltd., 558 F.3d 1341, 1348 (Fed. Cir. 2009); *see also* FJC Reference Manual at 61 (reporting that judges indicated that the need for Rule 706 appointments "will be infrequent and will be characterized by evidence that is particularly difficult to comprehend, or by a failure of the adversarial system to provide the information necessary to sort through the conflicting claims and interpretations").

[12]Fed. R. Evid. 706(b).

[13]Fed. R. Evid. 706(c).

[14]FJC Reference Manual at 61.

[15]*Id.* at 61–63.

to assist in explaining the technology at issue in this case."[16] The expert testified at trial on obviousness and the on-sale bar, and his testimony largely supported the defendant's position.[17] The Federal Circuit affirmed the court's appointment and use of the expert, finding "no abuse of discretion ... where the district court was confronted by what it viewed as an unusually complex case and what appeared to be starkly conflicting expert testimony."[18]

In a recent example of how expert witnesses may be used in patent cases, the court in *Oracle America, Inc. v. Google, Inc.* appointed a Rule 706 expert to "provide an independent professional analysis and view to inform the jury, in the event liability is found, on the issue of damages on the claims asserted in this action."[19] The court further ordered that the expert could attend the depositions of the parties' experts and ask questions, and the court outlined rules for communicating with the expert and appointed him a pro bono attorney.[20]

Although Rule 706 experts can be enormously helpful in complicated patent disputes, courts should appoint them only in rare circumstances. Academics have cautioned that such experts can be "enormously expensive" and typically are not appropriate for assisting the court in claim construction.[21] And although the Federal Circuit in *Monolithic Power* affirmed the court's Rule 706 expert appointment, it emphasized that Rule 706 "should be invoked only in rare and compelling circumstances."[22]

IV. Technical Advisors

Of the three types of experts discussed in this chapter, the role of technical advisor is the most amorphous. Unlike special masters and court-appointed experts, there's no rule that explic-

---

[16] *Monolithic Power*, 558 F.3d at 1346 (quoting Monolithic Power Sys., Inc. v. 02 Micro Int'l Ltd, No. C 04-2000 CW, Tr. Transc. at 96:21-24 (N.D. Cal. Apr. 7, 2007)).

[17] *Id.*

[18] *Id.* at 1348.

[19] Oracle America, Inc. v. Google, Inc., No. 3:10-cv-03561 (N.D. Cal. Sept. 9, 2011) (order regarding Rule 706 expert) (Alsup, J.).

[20] *Id.*

[21] *See* Menell et al., *supra* note 6, at 808.

[22] *Monolithic Power*, 558 F.3d at 1348.

itly authorizes courts to appoint technical advisors or provides guidance on what such advisors may and may not do. Yet despite this lack of formal authority, it is well-recognized that courts have the inherent power to appoint technical advisors in patent and other kinds of cases, although the Supreme Court has cautioned that "inherent powers must be exercised with restraint and discretion."[23]

The First Circuit issued perhaps the leading opinion on the proper role of technical advisors in *Reilly v. United States*. In this frequently cited medical malpractice case, the court noted that the appointment of technical advisors should be "hen's-teeth rare," and that such appointments are appropriate "only where the trial court is faced with problems of unusual difficulty, sophistication, and complexity, involving something well beyond the regular questions of fact and law with which judges must routinely grapple."[24]

The *Reilly* court went on to describe the role of a technical advisor as a "sounding board for the judge—helping the jurist to educate himself in the jargon and theory disclosed by the testimony and to think through the critical technical problems."[25] Since the technical advisor plays a behind-the-scenes role and is not a source of evidence, the court affirmed that there was "neither a right to cross-question him ... nor a purpose in doing so."[26] However, the court advised that in future cases, trial courts should identify technical advisors to the parties prior to appointing them, allow parties to object to the appointment based on bias or inexperience, provide a written "job description" for the advisor, and require the advisor to "file an affidavit attesting to his compliance with the job description" when his involvement in the case concludes.[27]

The leading case addressing the use of technical advisors in patent cases is *TechSearch LLC v. Intel Corp.*, in which the Federal Circuit approved the use of technical advisors to assist the court in *Markman* hearings.[28] However, the court issued a set of guidelines for district courts as "safeguards to prevent the technical advisor

---

[23]Chambers v. NASCO, Inc., 501 U.S. 32, 44 (1991).

[24]Reilly v. United States, 863 F.2d 149, 157 (1st Cir. 1988) (approving the use of a technical advisor to help the court understand the complex theory behind the plaintiff's projected future earnings, cost of medical care, etc.).

[25]*Id.* at 158.

[26]*Id.* at 159.

[27]*Id.* at 159–60.

[28]TechSearch LLC v. Intel Corp., 286 F.3d 1360 (Fed. Cir. 2002).

from introducing new evidence and to assure that the technical advisor does not influence the district court's review of the factual disputes."[29] The court's guidelines include:

- A "fair and open procedure for appointing a neutral technical advisor" that addresses "any allegations of bias, partiality or lack of qualifications."
- Clear limits on "the technical advisor's duties, presumably in a writing disclosed to all parties."
- A method to "guard against extra-record information."
- Courts should "make explicit, perhaps through a report or record, the nature and content of the technical advisor's tutelage concerning the technology."
- Courts should be "extremely sensitive" to the "risk that some of the judicial decision-making function will be delegated to the technical advisor" and must "minimize the potential for its occurrence."[30]

These guidelines leave courts with great discretion to shape the role a technical advisor will play in any particular case, but it's clear that technical advisors are generally much less visible than either special masters or Rule 706 experts. Rather, the proper role of a technical advisor is as a "tutor who aids the judge's understanding of the technology" including "explanation of the technical terminology used in the field, the underlying theory or science of the invention, or other technical aspects of the evidence being presented by the parties."[31]

Some academics raise concerns over the fact that technical advisors often work mostly behind the scenes, and they have suggested that all interactions between the court and the technical advisor should be recorded or transcribed.[32] Perhaps recognizing

---

[29] *Id.* at 1377. Note that because the court was applying Ninth Circuit law in reviewing the technical advisor appointment in this case, the guidelines are binding only on courts in that circuit. However, it's reasonable to assume that the Federal Circuit would require district courts in any circuit to establish similar safeguards.

[30] *Id.* at 1379.

[31] Menell et al., *supra* note 6, at 806; *see also* Joe S. Cecil & Thomas E. Willging, *Accepting* Daubert*'s Invitation: Defining a Role for Court-Appointed Experts in Assessing Scientific Validity*, 43 Emory L.J. 995, 1003–04 (stating that the proper role for technical advisors is to "give advice to the judge, not to give evidence and not to decide the case").

[32] *See* Menell et al., *supra* note 6, at 807.

that lack of transparency can be problematic, it seems that the best practice is to involve the parties in selecting the technical advisor and defining his role as much as possible.[33]

V. Conclusion

Patent cases often place significant demands on the court to understand highly complex and technical issues. Special masters, court-appointed experts, and technical advisors each play different roles in helping courts grapple with particularly complicated cases. The case law and rules authorizing the use of these experts make clear that courts should use them sparingly and as transparently as possible. The best practices discussed in this chapter will help courts deploy special masters, court-appointed experts, and technical advisors to their maximum effect but also ensure these experts stay within appropriate boundaries and do not entrench upon the court's constitutional duties.

[33] *See, e.g.*, Data Gen. Corp. v. IBM Corp., 93 F. Supp. 2d 89 (D. Mass. 2000) (including in the court's *Markman* order directions for the parties to cooperate in selecting a technical advisor; Xilinx, Inc. v. Altera Corp., 1997 WL 581426 (N.D. Cal. June 3, 1997) (ordering parties to meet and confer to select a technical advisor to assist in claim construction and to submit to the court proposed guidelines on the advisor's role).

13

Trial*

I. Introduction

Most, but not all, patent cases that go to trial are tried by juries. For example, cases involving Abbreviated New Drug Applications generally are not tried to a jury, and parties remain free to waive their right to a jury trial on those issues where such a right exists.

---

*George F. Pappas, Covington & Burling LLP, Washington, D.C. The assistance of Kevin B. Collins, Ranganath Sudarshan, and Scott C. Weidenfeller in preparing this material is greatly appreciated.

II. Pretrial Order

Pretrial orders can be more complicated in patent cases than in other civil cases because patent cases often involve many issues, claims, defenses, and counterclaims. For example, the defendant accused of infringing the plaintiffs' patent may also bring counterclaims alleging that the plaintiff infringes a different patent owned by the defendant. The defendant may also assert that the plaintiff has committed business torts by alleging infringement or informing the defendant's customers about the lawsuit and suggesting that the customers should stop buying the defendant's product. The defendant also may allege that the plaintiff has violated the antitrust laws by misusing its patent, such as by tying unpatented products with the patented product or engaging in licensing schemes that extend beyond the expiration date of the patent. In cases involving multiple patents, or complex defenses and counterclaims, the parties may not follow the typical order of presentation of evidence, and the pretrial order should specifically address this issue.

III. Selecting the Jury

Patent cases can involve unique potential bias concerns, including biases in favor of companies that are known as innovative, biases for or against well-known companies or against foreign businesses, and biases for or against small inventors. In addition, jurors may give undue deference to the PTO because they see it as an expert agency that issued an important document with important rights to the patentee. Jury questionnaires are important in patent cases to help ferret out such biases.

Another important consideration in selecting jurors in patent cases is the juror's scientific, technical, or financial expertise. Because patent cases often involve complicated technical and financial issues, individuals with some level of expertise in those fields may dominate the jury room without giving either party the opportunity to cross-examine their statements. Even if they do not exercise undue influence on other jurors, they may suffer more acutely than other jurors from "hindsight bias" and may have more difficulty casting their minds back to the time of the invention when evaluating obviousness, because of their experience with the same or similar technical matters. Thus, jury questionnaires often ask questions about the jurors' technical or financial expertise, and challenges based on those responses should be considered carefully.

IV. Use of Jury Notebooks

It can be beneficial to provide jurors with notebooks with key documents and exhibits to which the jurors can refer when appropriate.[1] Such notebooks may include the court's claim constructions, jury instructions, the patent, key excerpts from the file history of the patent, prior-art references used in the accused infringer's invalidity case, and key documents used in the patentee's infringement case, such as technical documents describing the accused infringing product. Selection of such documents is likely to be contentious. Care should be taken in the selection of documents included in such notebooks, however, to avoid overly emphasizing particular documents on the one hand, or overwhelming the jury with voluminous exhibits on the other.

Even courts that do not provide evidentiary notebooks to the jurors often provide them with blank notebooks for note taking, so that the jurors may attempt to keep track of the complex evidence presented.

V. Opening Statements and Burdens of Proof, Preliminary Jury Instructions

Preliminary jury instructions can be helpful in identifying which party bears the burden of proof and in explaining the applicable burden of proof to the jury. The preliminary jury instructions can be helpful in describing to the jury the exclusionary

---

[1] *See, e.g.*, PMG, Inc. v. Lockheed Martin Idaho Techs., Inc., No. CV-02-539-E-BLW, 2006 WL 1207609, at *3 (D. Idaho Apr. 27, 2006) (noting that the court had encouraged counsel to create jury notebooks); John Mezzalingua Assocs., Inc. v. Aries Int'l, Inc., No. 03-C-353-C, 2003 WL 23273967, at * 1 (W.D. Wis. Nov. 26, 2003) (noting that counsel were preparing jury notebooks "that will include a copy of the patent and other materials that will help the jurors follow the evidence and the arguments in the case").

right a patent provides, the parts of a patent, and the process of obtaining a patent from the PTO. The preliminary jury instructions may also describe the concept of prior art and how it can invalidate the patent claims. Many courts also provide the jurors with the construction of the claim terms at this stage of the case. Sample preliminary jury instructions can be found in the Uniform Jury Instructions for Patent Cases in the U.S. District Court for the District of Delaware, the Federal Circuit Bar Association Model Patent Jury Instructions, and the Model Patent Jury Instructions for the Northern District of California.[2]

In addition, the Federal Judicial Center's 2002 video, *An Introduction to the Patent System*, which the center is updating, provides background information that can be helpful to jurors. The video covers basic patent issues, the process of obtaining patents from the PTO, and patent infringement suits. The video is designed to be impartial and objective and to favor neither the patentee nor the accused infringer.[3]

Typically, the patentee will not assert that the accused infringer infringes all of the claims in the patent; rather, the patentee will select one or more of the claims in the patent to assert against the accused infringer.

The patentee's opening statement introduces the patent to the jury and identifies the claims at issue in the case. The patentee bears the burden of proving infringement by a preponderance of the evidence.[4] The patentee must show that each limitation of the asserted claim is present in the accused product or method, or that the accused product or method includes an equivalent to each limitation pursuant to the doctrine of equivalents.

In virtually every patent case, the accused infringer will assert as a defense to infringement that the asserted patent claims are invalid, usually because information already known in the field of the invention (called "prior art") describes the invention or makes the invention obvious to a person skilled in the field.[5] The accused

---

[2] *See infra* Chapter 11.

[3] The video is approximately 17 minutes in length, and it can be downloaded, along with an accompanying sample patent, from the Federal Judicial Center's website at http://www.fjc.gov/public/home.nsf/pages/557. Judges and court employees may also order a DVD copy of the video by contacting the Federal Judicial Center.

[4] *See, e.g.*, Cross Med. Prods., Inc. v. Medtronic Sofamor Danek, Inc., 424 F.3d 1293, 1310 (Fed. Cir. 2005).

[5] *See* 35 U.S.C. §§102, 103 (2000).

infringer may also argue that the claims are invalid because the patentee did not adequately describe or enable the claimed invention.[6] The accused infringer's opening statement will describe the grounds on which it asserts noninfringement and invalidity, and will briefly describe the pertinent prior art. In contrast to the burden of proof for infringement, the accused infringer bears the burden of proving the invalidity of the asserted claims of the patent by clear and convincing evidence because a patent is presumed valid once issued pursuant to 35 U.S.C. §282.[7]

The accused infringer may also allege that the patent is unenforceable because the patentee committed inequitable conduct in procuring the patent from the Patent and Trademark Office by, e.g., failing to disclose material information to the PTO with the specific intent to deceive, or by engaging in affirmative acts of egregious misconduct during prosecution.[8] Issues underlying the equitable determination of whether the patent is unenforceable because of the patentee's inequitable conduct in procuring the patent are for the judge, not the jury, to decide on a clear and convincing burden of proof.[9] Nevertheless, the judge can elect to have the issues tried to the jury; the jury can render an advisory verdict on the issues of materiality and intent, which underlie the inequitable conduct determination.[10] If these issues are presented to the jury, the opening statements or preliminary jury instructions should introduce the concepts of materiality and intent to the jury.[11]

Finally, accused infringers in patent infringement cases often bring antitrust and other tort claims as counterclaims. The jury must be informed about the elements of these claims, as well as the applicable burden of proof, which is typically a preponderance of the evidence. However, many of these claims may be preempted by the federal patent laws unless the patentee has engaged in "sham litigation."[12] Preliminary jury instructions or statements

---

[6] *See id.* §112.

[7] *See, e.g.*, Microsoft Corp. v. i4i Ltd. P'ship, 131 S. Ct. 2238, 2242 (2011).

[8] *See, e.g.*, Therasense, Inc. v. Becton, Dickinson & Co., 649 F.3d 1276 (Fed. Cir. 2011).

[9] *See* Duro-Last, Inc. v. Custom Seal, Inc., 321 F.3d 1098, 1110 (Fed. Cir. 2003).

[10] *See id.*

[11] Warner-Lambert Co. v. Teva Pharm. USA, Inc., 418 F.3d 1326, 1342–43 (Fed. Cir. 2005).

[12] *See, e.g.*, Globetrotter Software, Inc. v. Elan Computer Group, Inc., 362 F.3d 1367, 1376–77 (Fed. Cir. 2004).

by the parties regarding the sham litigation standard may also be beneficial to the jury.

VI. Presentation of the Evidence

Patent cases involve shifting burdens of proof that may complicate or change the order of presentation of evidence at trial. For example, because patents are presumed valid pursuant to 35 U.S.C. §282, the patentee need not offer any evidence that the patent is valid.[13] However, if the accused infringer makes out a prima facie case that the patent is obvious, the burden of production (but not the burden of persuasion) shifts to the patentee to show that one or more of the objective considerations of nonobviousness[14] apply to make the invention nonobvious.[15] In a case involving obviousness, the patentee may either offer evidence related to the objective considerations of nonobviousness as part of its initial presentation of evidence or wait until the accused infringer has made out its prima facie case of obviousness.

In complex patent cases, courts often sever certain issues from the patent issues.[16] Such bifurcation can simplify the presentation of evidence to the jury, separating the issues on which the patentee has the burden of proof from the issues on which the accused infringer has the burden of proof.

Courts also may encourage lawyers to use electronic technology and visual aids, such as slides summarizing key points, in their

[13] *See, e.g.*, Orthokinetics, Inc. v. Safety Travel Chairs, Inc., 806 F.2d 1565, 1570 (Fed. Cir. 1986); ABB Air Preheater, Inc. v. Regenerative Envtl. Equip. Co., 167 F.R.D. 668, 673 (D.N.J. 1996).

[14] Graham v. John Deere Co., 383 U.S. 1, 17–18 (1966). The objective considerations of nonobviousness include commercial success of products embodying the invention, a long-felt need for the invention, failure by others who attempted to make the invention, copying of the invention by others, unexpected results achieved by the invention, praise of the invention by others in the field, the taking of licenses under the patent, industry acceptance, and expressions of skepticism or disbelief by those in the field when the invention was made. *See* Brown & Williamson Tobacco Corp. v. Philip Morris, Inc., 229 F.3d 1120, 1129 (Fed. Cir. 2000); *In re* Rouffet, 149 F.3d 1350, 1355 (Fed. Cir. 1998).

[15] *See, e.g.*, Ashland Oil, Inc. v. Delta Resins & Refractories, Inc., 776 F.2d 281, 291–92 (Fed. Cir. 1985); ABB Air Preheater, 167 F.R.D. at 673.

[16] *See generally* Chapter 11.II.

presentations of evidence. Such visuals can help to make the complex issues involved in patent litigation more understandable to jurors.

A. *Infringement*

The patentee bears the burden of proving infringement, and the patentee usually will offer a witness to provide important background information about the field of the invention and to tell the story of the invention. The inventor can be the ideal witness in these areas, as he or she typically is skilled in the field covered by the patent and has unique credentials regarding the invention itself. Having the inventor speak about the patent and the invention can also humanize what could otherwise be seen as arcane technology. The inventor often will be called to testify regarding the nature of the field of technology prior to the invention, the invention itself, and, in certain cases, the products accused of infringement and the differences between the prior art and the claimed invention. The inventor can also describe the ideas underlying the invention and the advances he or she made over what was known.

Although to prove literal infringement a patentee "can employ any method of analysis that is probative of infringement,"[17] expert testimony is generally helpful and, in cases involving complex technology, may be necessary to satisfy the patentee's burden of proof.[18] The patentee can also prove infringement pursuant to the doctrine of equivalents, which is designed to prevent infringers from avoiding liability by making insubstantial changes to their products that fall outside the literal scope of the claims while remaining essentially identical to the claimed invention.[19] To prove infringement under the doctrine of equivalents, the patentee must provide "particularized testimony and linking argument" on

[17]Forest Labs., Inc. v. Abbott Labs., 239 F.3d 1305, 1312 (Fed. Cir. 2001). For a general review of pleading infringement, see *supra* Chapter 3.I.

[18]*See, e.g.*, Centricut, LLC v. Esab Group, Inc., 390 F.3d 1361, 1369–70 (Fed. Cir. 2004).

[19]*See, e.g.*, Graver Tank & Mfg. Co. v. Linde Air Prods. Co., 339 U.S. 605, 608 (1950).

a limitation-by-limitation basis showing how the accused infringing device or process is equivalent to the claimed invention.[20]

B. Validity

The accused infringer bears the burden of proving that the patent is invalid. Like the patentee's technical expert's testimony regarding infringement, the accused infringer's technical expert's testimony will set forth the accused infringer's invalidity allegations limitation-by-limitation, showing where each limitation of the claimed invention is found in the prior art.

Before reaching a determination that the patent is obvious and therefore invalid, a fact finder must collectively consider all evidence of obviousness and nonobviousness, including objective indicia of nonobviousness.[21]

C. Inequitable Conduct and Other Counterclaims

If the accused infringer has brought an allegation of inequitable conduct or other counterclaims, such as allegations that the patentee committed business torts or antitrust violations, the accused infringer will have one or more witnesses, often experts, testify about those matters. For example, an accused infringer alleging that the patentee committed inequitable conduct may call an expert witness to testify about the practices and procedures before the PTO and identify the patentee's omissions or misrepresentations to the PTO during the prosecution of the patent that were material to patentability. Similarly, the accused infringer may offer testimony regarding the appropriate market if the accused has brought antitrust counterclaims against the patentee. The patentee may also offer expert testimony to rebut the accused infringer's allegations.

---

[20] *See, e.g.*, Network Commerce, Inc. v. Microsoft Corp., 422 F.3d 1353, 1363 (Fed. Cir. 2005) (quoting Tex. Instruments, Inc. v. Cypress Semiconductor Corp., 90 F.3d 1558, 1567 (Fed. Cir. 1996)).

[21] *In re Cyclobenaprine Hydrochloride*, 676 F.3d 1063, 1078 (Fed. Cir. 2012). At all times, the burden of proof to establish invalidity by clear and convincing evidence remains on the party asserting invalidity. *Id.*

D. Damages

Finally, the patentee generally calls a damages expert to set forth the analysis underlying the damages to which it asserts it is entitled. Damages can be awarded based on either a lost profits or a reasonable royalty theory, and, as in any other case, the expert should explain how he or she applied the relevant factors to arrive at the amount sought by the patentee. Unlike many other cases, though, the damages analysis can be very complicated, as determining the profits lost as a result of infringement or the outcome of a hypothetical negotiation between the patentee and the infringer at the time infringement began can be very complicated. The damages expert typically will apply the multifactor analyses as set forth in *Panduit Corp. v. Stahlin Brothers Fibre Works, Inc.*[22] for lost profits and in *Georgia-Pacific Corp. v. United States Plywood Corp.*[23] for reasonable royalty.

To obtain damages for lost profits on sales the patentee would have made absent the infringement pursuant to *Panduit*, the patentee must prove: (1) that there is demand for the patented product, (2) the absence of acceptable noninfringing substitutes, (3) the patentee's manufacturing and marketing capability to exploit the demand, and (4) the amount of the profit the patentee would have made.[24] *Georgia-Pacific* sets forth a "comprehensive list of evidentiary facts relevant, in general, to the determination of the amount of a reasonable royalty for a patent license": (1) royalties received by the patentee for licenses to the patent–in–suit; (2) royalty rates paid by the licensee for licenses to comparable patents; (3) the nature and scope of the license, including exclusivity and restrictions on the license; (4) the patentee's policy either not to license or to place conditions on licenses; (5) the commercial relationship between the licensor and the licensee; (6) the effect of the patent on promoting "convoyed sales," or sales of other products not covered by the patent; (7) the durations of the patent and the license; (8) the commercial success of the patented product; (9) the advantages of the patent over the prior art; (10) the nature of the patented invention and the

---

[22]575 F.2d 1152 (6th Cir. 1978). *See also* Rooklidge, Gooding, Johnson and Yen, *Compensatory Damages Issues in Patent Judgment Cases: A Pocket Guide for Federal District Judges* (Federal Judicial Center 2011).

[23]318 F. Supp. 1116 (S.D.N.Y. 1970).

[24]*See Panduit*, 575 F.2d at 1156.

character of the accused infringing product; (11) the extent and value of the infringing use to the infringer; and (12) the customary royalty rates in the industry for analogous inventions.[25]

The accused infringer generally will offer expert testimony to rebut the patentee's damages case and to argue for a substantially lower damages award.[26]

VII. Closing Arguments

Special verdict forms are particularly important in patent cases because of the complex issues that the jury must resolve. The parties' arguments should closely track the special verdict form to be submitted to the jury. The forms are typically very detailed, setting forth the pertinent burdens of proof and often requiring the jury to set forth its verdicts on infringement and invalidity claim-by-claim.

VIII. Instructions to the Jury

Because patent cases offer complicated issues that can seem esoteric to jurors, extensive jury instructions are often necessary to describe, in plain English, the applicable patent law and issues in the case. The jury instructions should provide a brief background of the technology involved in the patent and explain what a patent is and the process of obtaining a patent. The instructions should also clarify the court's role in determining the meaning of the claims, and the relevant patent law of infringement, invalidity, and unenforceability, where appropriate. The instructions should set forth the relevant law of damages, explaining the law underlying the relevant damages theory or theories. In many cases, jury instructions will also provide a glossary of the technical or legal terms the jury will hear throughout the trial. In all instances, the jury instructions should clearly set forth the burdens of proof and identify the party that bears the burden of proof.

In many instances, it can be beneficial to break jury instructions into two sets of instructions. First, preliminary jury instruc-

---

[25] *See Georgia-Pacific*, 318 F. Supp. at 1120.

[26] *See also supra* Chapter 3.II.

tions can be read to the jury before the presentation of the evidence to inform the jurors about the basics of patents, the process of obtaining patents, claim construction, and the pertinent law of infringement, invalidity, damages, and other relevant areas. Final jury instructions, which set forth more detailed information about the burdens of proof and the particular patent law and damages doctrines involved in the case, can be read to the jury after the closing arguments to provide the jurors a more extensive basis for their deliberations. Many courts permit the jury to take the jury instructions into the jury room, where such instructions can be essential in helping the jury work through the complicated issues in patent cases. Other courts permit the jury to listen to a recording of the jury instructions as they were read by the court.

Several courts and bar associations have prepared excellent model jury instructions, including the U.S. District Court for the District of Delaware, the U.S. District Court for the Northern District of California, the Federal Circuit Bar Association, the American Intellectual Property Law Association, and the National Jury Instruction Project.[27]

---

[27]For the District of Delaware instructions, go to http://www.ded.uscourts.gov/jury/Patent%20Jury%20Instructions.pdf; for the Northern District of California in-structions, go to http://www.cand.uscourts.gov/CAND/FAQ.nsf/60126b66e42d004888256d4e007bce29/4b43c2137e17e03a88257393007bac13?OpenDocument; for the Federal Circuit Bar Association instructions (fee required), go to https://www.memberconnections.com/olc/pub/LVFC/events/LVFC2105558.html; for the AIPLA instructions, go to http://www.aipla.org/Content/ContentGroups/Publications1/Publications_available_for_viewing1/2008_03_27_AIPLA_Model_Jury_Instructions.pdf; for the National Jury Instructions Project's model instructions, go to http://www.nationaljuryinstructions.org/documents/NationalPatentJuryInstructions.pdf.

14

Post-trial Proceedings*

I. Motions for Judgment as a Matter of Law and New Trial

Standards for motions for judgment as a matter of law and a new trial are the same in patent cases as in other civil cases.

*Michael O. Warnecke, Perkins Coie LLP, Chicago, Illinois; updated by Brandy R. McMillion, Perkins Coie LLP, Chicago, Illinois.

II. Inequitable Conduct

Inequitable conduct refers generically to a breach of duty of candor and good faith to the U.S. Patent and Trademark Office. Applicants for patents are required to prosecute patent applications in the PTO with candor, good faith, and honesty.[1] Inequitable conduct includes affirmative misrepresentation of material fact, failure to disclose material information, and submission of false material information, coupled with an intent to deceive.[2] The established remedy for inequitable conduct is unenforceability of the patent, regardless of the patent's validity or infringement.

The determination of inequitable conduct is committed to the trial court's discretion.[3] The court's authority to render a patent unenforceable for inequitable conduct is founded in the equitable principle that "he who comes into equity must come with clean hands."[4] This judge-made doctrine has evolved from the doctrine of unclean hands to include not only acts of egregious misconduct, but also a broader scope of misconduct based on a mere nondisclosure of information to the PTO during patent prosecution. Because an issued patent is presumed valid, unenforceability based on inequitable conduct requires proof of intent to deceive and materiality by clear and convincing evidence.[5] As the doctrine has evolved, the standards of intent to deceive and materiality have fluctuated over time; and charging of inequitable conduct has become a common litigation tactic. Recognizing the expansion and often overuse of the inequitable conduct doctrine, the Federal Circuit has set forth tightened standards for finding both intent and materiality.[6]

To prevail on a claim on inequitable conduct, the accused infringer must prove that the patentee acted with specific intent to deceive the PTO.[7] It is not enough that the misrepresentation or omission amounts to gross negligence. The accused infringer

---

[1] Molins PLC v. Textron, 48 F.3d 1172, 1178 (Fed. Cir. 1995).

[2] *Id.*

[3] Hoffman-La Roche, Inc. v. Promega Corp., 323 F.3d 1354 (Fed. Cir. 2003).

[4] Dayco Prods., Inc. v. Total Containment, Inc., 329 F.3d 1358, 1364 (Fed. Cir. 2003).

[5] Kingsdown Med. Consultants, Ltd. v. Hollister, Inc., 863 F.2d 867, 872 (Fed. Cir. 1988).

[6] Therasense, Inc. v. Becton, Dickinson & Co., 649 F.3d 1276 (Fed. Cir. 2011).

[7] *Id.* at 1290.

bears the burden to prove by clear and convincing evidence that the applicant knew of a reference, knew it was material, and made a deliberate decision to withhold it.[8] Courts must separate the materiality requirement from intent.[9] Courts can no longer use a "sliding scale" when a weak showing of intent can be found as sufficient based on a strong showing of materiality and vice versa. Instead, courts must weigh the evidence of intent independent from materiality. Because direct evidence of deceptive intent is rare, courts can consider circumstantial and indirect evidence, so long as the single most reasonable inference from the evidence is the specific intent to deceive.[10] If multiple inferences can be drawn, specific intent cannot be found.[11] The party alleging inequitable conduct bears the burden of proof, and the patentee need not offer any "good faith explanation" unless the alleging party first meets its burden. However, the absence of a good faith explanation does not, by itself, prove the intent to deceive.[12]

As a general rule, the materiality required for a finding of inequitable conduct is "but-for materiality."[13] A reference is but-for material, when the PTO would not have allowed a claim had it known of the undisclosed reference.[14] Using the preponderance of the evidence standard, courts must therefore assess materiality of an undisclosed reference based on whether the PTO would have allowed a claim when giving the claim its broadest reasonable construction.[15] This determination will often go hand in hand with determining the validity of the claim. If a claim is properly invalidated based on a deliberately withheld reference, then that reference is necessarily material. While materiality is generally proved through the but-for analysis, there are exceptions for affirmative egregious misconduct in which inequitable conduct can be found—e.g., filing an unmistakably false affidavit.[16]

---

[8] *Id.*

[9] *Hoffman-LaRoche*, 323 F.3d at 1359.

[10] *Therasense*, 649 F.3d at 1290.

[11] *Id.* at 1291.

[12] *Id.*

[13] *Id.*

[14] This definition is very different from the PTO's Rule 56 definition of materiality. It is much more narrowly tailored, specifically to avoid patent litigators charging inequitable conduct in nearly every case as a litigation strategy. *Id.* at 1294–95.

[15] *Id.* at 1291.

[16] *Id.* at 1292.

There are several ways in which a trial court may handle the issue of inequitable conduct during a jury trial. Absent a clear showing of prejudice or failure to achieve a fair trial, the trial court's choice of procedure will not be disturbed.[17] First, the court may reserve the issue of inequitable conduct for itself. The Federal Circuit held that a trial court could also sever the issue of inequitable conduct and try it separately without a jury trial.[18] Specifically, the trial court can sever the issue of inequitable conduct so long as none of the other claims to be resolved in the case involve common issues.[19] Next, the court can submit special interrogatories to the jury on the facts of materiality and intent.[20] Finally, the court can instruct the jury to both find and weigh the facts of materiality and intent and also to decide the ultimate question of inequitable conduct.[21]

Inequitable conduct, as an equitable doctrine, hinges on basic fairness.[22] A finding of inequitable conduct in procuring a patent will render the entire patent unenforceable, not merely those claims directly affected by the misconduct.[23] Its application therefore should be limited to instances where the patentee's misconduct resulted in the unfair benefit of receiving an unwarranted claim.[24] Patentees cannot overcome their misconduct through reissued patents.[25] The same level of misconduct is required in both instances. The Federal Circuit has made clear that a reissue is not

---

[17]Hebert v. Lisle Corp., 99 F.3d 1109, 1114 (Fed. Cir. 1996).

[18]Agfa Corp. v. Creo Prods., Inc., 451 F.3d 1366 (Fed. Cir. 2006). *See also supra* Chapter 11.II.A.

[19]*See* Gardo Mfg., Inc. v. Herst Lighting Co., 820 F.2d 1209, 1213 (Fed. Cir. 1987) ("[T]he *conduct-of-the-applicant-in-the-PTO* issue raised in the non-jury trial and the separated infringement/validity issues are distinct and without commonality either as claims or in the relation to the underlying fact issues." (emphasis in original)).

[20]*Hebert*, 99 F.3d at 1114; Duro-Last, Inc. v. Custom Seal, Inc., 321 F.3d 1098, 1110 (Fed. Cir. 2003) ("A trial court has some discretion in choosing whether to submit special interrogatories to the jury regarding the underlying facts.").

[21]Juicy Whip v. Orange Bang, 292 F.3d 728, 737 (Fed. Cir. 2002).

[22]*Therasense*, 649 F.3d at 1292.

[23]*See* Lummus Indus., Inc. v. D.M. & E. Corp., 862 F.2d 267, 274 (Fed. Cir. 1988) ("The principle is well-settled that if inequitable conduct is established as to any claim, all claims of the patent are rendered unenforceable."); Consolidated Aluminum Corp. v. Foseco Int'l Ltd., 910 F.2d 804, 809 (Fed. Cir. 1990) (holding several related patents unenforceable because of inequitable conduct).

[24]*Therasense*, 649 F.3d at 1292.

[25]Hewlett-Packard Co. v. Bausch & Lomb, Inc., 882 F.2d 1556, 1563 (Fed. Cir. 1989).

available to obtain new claims and thereby rehabilitate a patent.[26] Continuation applications or divisional applications emanating from a parent application procured by inequitable conduct may also be deemed unenforceable. However, where the claims of a divisional application are subsequently separated from those of a parent application tainted by inequitable conduct, and the issued divisional claims have no relation to the omitted prior art, the divisional patent will not also be unenforceable because of inequitable conduct committed in the parent application.[27]

Other potential consequences of a finding of inequitable conduct may include an award of attorneys' fees under 35 U.S.C. §285 if the case is deemed to be exceptional by the court, sanctions against the attorney under Federal Rule of Civil Procedure 11, liability for unfair competition, and antitrust liability under Section 2 of the Sherman Act.[28]

III. Damages

A. *Supplemental Damages*

Supplemental damages can be awarded to compensate a plaintiff for any infringement occurring between the date of the jury's verdict and the date of the final judgment.[29] A failure to award such damages would grant an infringer a windfall by enabling it to infringe without compensating a plaintiff for the period of time between the jury's verdict and the final judgment.[30] A patentee is not fully compensated if a damages award does not include future sales.[31]

Although courts have broad discretion to weigh and balance multiple factors to determine an appropriate supplemental damage award, injunctions and damages must be tailored to

[26]*Id.* (reissue is unavailable to rescue patentee who committed inequitable conduct during original prosecution).

[27]Baxter Int'l, Inc. v. McGaw, Inc., 149 F.3d 1321 (Fed. Cir. 1998).

[28]15 U.S.C. §§1–7.

[29]Stryker Corp. v. Davol, Inc., 234 F.3d 1252, 1259 (Fed. Cir. 2000).

[30]Nat'l Instruments Corp. v. Mathworks, Inc., 2003 U.S. Dist. LEXIS 25863, 11–12 (E.D. Tex. June 23, 2003), *aff'd*, 164 Fed. App'x 997 (Fed. Cir. 2006).

[31]Finjan, Inc. v. Secure Computing Corp., 626 F.3d 1197, 1213 (Fed. Cir. 2010).

the circumstances and correlatively determined.[32] Even where a jury fails to aware post-trial damages, the court must assess them under 35 U.S.C. §284. "When damages are not found by a jury, the court *shall* assess them."[33] The court can apply the royalty rate determined by the jury to assess post-verdict sales.[34] The court can also extrapolate a royalty rate from the jury's verdict.[35] Post-verdict supplemental damages can also be measured by the infringer's profits.[36]

B. Prejudgment Interest

Section 284 of title 35 of the U.S. Code provides for prejudgment interest. Prejudgment interest is to be awarded on patent infringement damages measured both by lost profits and by reasonable royalty absent some justification for denying such relief.[37] Prejudgment interest is interest on a monetary judgment against an infringer awarded to a prevailing party measured from the date of the infringement to the date of the judgment. It is designed to compensate for the delay a patentee experiences in obtaining money it would have received sooner if no infringement had occurred.[38] Where no statute specifically authorizes an award of prejudgment interest, such an award lies within the discretion of the court as part of its equitable powers.[39]

In exercising its discretion, the trial court must be guided by the purpose of prejudgment interest, which is to ensure that the patent owner is placed in as good a position as it would have been

---

[32]*Id.*; *see also* SRI Int'l, Inc. v. Advanced Tech. Labs., Inc., 127 F.3d 1462, 1468–1469 (Fed. Cir. 1997).

[33]*Finjan*, 626 F.3d at 1212 (citing 35 U.S.C. §284) (emphasis in the original).

[34]Stryker Corp. v. Davol, Inc., 75 F. Supp. 2d 746, 747 (W.D. Mich. 1999) (awarding supplemental damages based on the jury's determination of a reasonable royalty rate of 20 percent of infringing sales over a one-month period between verdict and injunction).

[35]Oscar Mayer Foods Corp. v. ConAgra, Inc., 869 F. Supp. 656, 668 (W.D. Wis. 1994) (awarding supplemental damages at the jury-determined royalty rate applied to a post-verdict revenue).

[36]Padco, Inc. v. Newell Cos., 13 USPQ2d 1607, 1616 (E.D. Wis. 1988); Kori Corp. v. Wilco Marsh Buggies and Draglines, Inc., 761 F.2d 649 (Fed. Cir. 1985).

[37]Gen. Motors Corp. v. Devex Corp., 461 U.S. 648 (1983).

[38]Beatrice Foods Co. v. New England Printing & Lith. Co., 923 F.2d 1567 (Fed. Cir. 1991).

[39]United States v. Imperial Food Imports, 834 F.2d 1013 (Fed. Cir. 1987).

had the infringer entered into a reasonable royalty agreement when the infringement began.[40] The rationale for awarding interest to successful plaintiffs is not particular to patent law; prejudgment interest, like all monetary interest, is simply compensation for the use or forbearance of money owed.[41]

The interest rate applied is within the discretion of the trial court and will not be disturbed unless the court abused its discretion.[42] In view of that, the specific rate of prejudgment interest and whether it should be compounded or uncompounded are matters left to the trial court. Thus, courts have awarded simple interest or interest compounded on a variable rate over different time periods, and have based the award on the prime rate, rates above prime, the state statutory rate, or Treasury bill rates. A court may also limit prejudgment interest, or deny it altogether, in certain circumstances.[43] However, a court's justification for limiting prejudgment interest must have some relationship to its award.[44]

Prejudgment interest is compensatory and cannot be applied to the punitive portion of a damage award.[45] Accordingly, prejudgment interest itself cannot be trebled, nor can there be prejudgment interest on the increased portion of treble damages.[46]

C. *Enhancing Damages—35 U.S.C. §284*

Under 35 U.S.C. §284, the trial court is required to award damages adequate to compensate for any infringement and is authorized, in its discretion, to treble the compensatory damages. It is for the court to determine whether and to what extent

[40]Electro Sci. Indus. v. Gen. Scanning, Inc., 247 F.3d 1341, 1354 (Fed. Cir. 2001).

[41]Transmatic, Inc. v. Gulton Indus., Inc., 180 F.3d 1343, 1347 (Fed. Cir. 1999).

[42]Crystal Semiconductor Corp. v. Tritech Microelectronics Int'l, Inc., 246 F.3d 1336, 1346 (Fed. Cir. 2001).

[43]*Devex Corp.*, 461 U.S. at 656–57 (holding that it may be appropriate to limit prejudgment interest where the patent owner has been responsible for undue delay in prosecuting the lawsuit).

[44]Group One, Ltd. v. Hallmark Cards, Inc., 407 F.3d 1297, 1308 (Fed. Cir. 2005).

[45]*Beatrice Foods*, 923 F.2d 1567.

[46]Lam, Inc. v. Johns-Manville Corp., 718 F.2d 1056 (Fed. Cir. 1983).

to increase the damages award, considering the totality of the circumstances.[47]

Enhancement of damages under 35 U.S.C. §284 involves two steps: first, the fact finder must determine that the infringer engaged in culpable conduct, and second, the court must exercise its discretion to determine whether and to what extent to enhance the damages.[48] In exercising its discretion, the trial court may consider the evidence of the infringer's culpability in light of the factors set forth in *Read Corp. v. Portec, Inc.*,[49] summarized as follows: (1) whether the infringer deliberately copied the ideas or design of another; (2) whether the infringer, when it knew of the other's patent protection, investigated the scope of the patent and formed a good-faith belief that the patent was invalid or that it was not infringed; (3) the infringer's behavior as a party to the litigation; (4) the infringer's size and financial condition; (5) the closeness of the case; (6) the duration of the infringer's misconduct; (7) any remedial action by the infringer; (8) the infringer's motivation for harm; and (9) whether the infringer attempted to conceal its misconduct.[50] The court has discretion to identify and balance the most relevant factors so as to effectuate the punitive and deterrent purposes of enhanced damages and to fashion a just remedy.[51]

Willful infringement is a prerequisite to an award of enhanced damages.[52] To find willfulness, the patentee has to prove that (i) the alleged infringer was aware of the patent, (ii) acted despite an objectively high likelihood that its actions infringed a valid patent; and (iii) that this objective high risk was either known or so obvious that it should have been known.[53] However, because of the trial court's broad discretion, a finding of willful infringement authorizes but does not mandate an award of increased damages.[54] The paramount determination is the egregiousness of the defendant's

---

[47]Jurgens v. CBK, Ltd., 80 F.3d 1556, 1570 (Fed. Cir. 1996).

[48]*Id.*

[49]970 F.2d 816, 827 (Fed. Cir. 1992).

[50]Johns Hopkins Univ. v. CellPro, Inc., 152 F.3d 1342, 1352 (Fed. Cir. 1998).

[51]SRI Int'l, Inc. v. Advanced Tech. Labs., Inc., 127 F.3d 1462, 1468–1469 (Fed. Cir. 1997).

[52]i4i LP v. Microsoft Corp, 598 F.3d 831, 858 (Fed. Cir. 2010); *In re* Seagate Tech. LLC, 497 F.3d 1360 (Fed. Cir. 2007).

[53]*Id.*

[54]Harris Corp. v. Ericsson, Inc., 417 F.3d 1241, 1259 (Fed. Cir. 2005).

conduct based on all the facts and circumstances.[55] However, it is worth noting that litigation misconduct alone is not grounds for enhanced damages.[56]

Increased damages also may be awarded to a party because of the opposing party's bad faith.[57]

D. Attorneys' Fees—35 U.S.C. §285

Under 35 U.S.C. §285, the trial court is charged with the determination of whether a party's conduct is exceptional and whether attorneys' fees should be awarded. ("The court in exceptional cases may award reasonable attorney fees to the prevailing party.") First, the trial court must determine whether a case is exceptional, which is a factual determination reviewed for clear error. Second, the court must determine whether attorneys' fees are appropriate, a determination reviewed for abuse of discretion.[58] Federal Circuit law governs the court's determination as to whether a case is "exceptional" under Section 285.

The purpose of Section 285 is twofold: (1) to permit an award of fees where it would be grossly unjust that the winner be left to bear the burden of its own counsel, something prevailing litigants normally bear; and (2) to deter parties from bringing bad-faith litigation.[59]

Any claim to attorneys' fees must be processed in compliance with Federal Rule of Civil Procedure 54(d)(2).[60] Under Rule 54(d)(2), the motion for attorneys' fees must: (1) be filed no later than 14 days after entry of judgment; (2) specify the judgment and the statute, rule, or other grounds entitling the moving party to the award; and (3) state the amount or provide a fair estimate of the amount sought.

---

[55]Cybor Corp. v. FAS Techs., 138 F.3d 1448, 1461 (Fed. Cir. 1998); *see also In re* Seagate Tech. LLC, 497 F.3d 1360 (Fed. Cir. 2007).

[56]*i4i*, 598 F.3d at 859.

[57]King Instruments Corp. v. Perego, 65 F.3d 941, 947 (Fed. Cir. 1995).

[58]Phonometrics, Inc. v. Westin Hotel Co., 350 F.3d 1242 (Fed. Cir. 2003).

[59]Mathis v. Spears, 857 F.2d 749, 753–54 (Fed. Cir. 1988) (holding that attorneys' fees under Section 285 are available deterrents to blatant, blind, willful infringement of valid patents).

[60]IPXL Holdings, LLC v. Amazon.com, Inc., 430 F.3d 1377, 1386 (Fed. Cir. 2005).

The trial court has broad discretion in determining whether to award attorneys' fees.[61] The court can weigh intangible as well as tangible factors when determining an award, including: the degree of culpability of the infringer; the closeness of the question; litigation behavior; and any other factors whereby fee shifting may serve as an instrument of justice.[62] Whether a case is exceptional depends on findings of fact. Situations where the prevailing party may prove the existence of an exceptional case include the following: fraud or inequitable conduct in procuring the patent; litigation misconduct; vexatious, unjustified, or otherwise bad faith litigation; conduct that violates Federal Rule of Civil Procedure 11; a frivolous suit or willful infringement; or like infractions.[63]

While a finding of willful infringement is legally sufficient to meet the criterion of an "exceptional case," the trial court in its discretion does not have to award attorneys' fees.[64] However, the general rule is that the trial court must normally explain why it decides that a case is not exceptional under 35 U.S.C. §285 when a factual finding of willful infringement has been established, and, if exceptional, why it decides not to award attorneys' fees.[65]

Absent misconduct by the patentee in the litigation or in securing the patent, a trial court may only sanction the patentee if the litigation is both brought in subjective bad faith and is objectively baseless.[66] There is a presumption that the assertion of infringement of a duly granted patent is made in good faith.[67] Thus, the underlying improper conduct and the characterization of the case as exceptional must be established by clear and convincing evidence.[68]

---

[61] nCube Corp. v. SeaChange Int'l, Inc., 436 F.3d 1317, 1325 (Fed. Cir. 2006).

[62] Juicy Whip, Inc. v. Orange Bang, Inc., 382 F.3d 1367, 1373 (Fed. Cir. 2004).

[63] Epcon Gas Sys., Inc. v. Bauer Compressors, Inc., 279 F.3d 1022, 1034 (Fed. Cir. 2002).

[64] Modine Mfg. Co. v. Allen Group, Inc., 917 F.2d 538 (Fed. Cir. 1990).

[65] Transclean Corp. v. Bridgewood Servs., 290 F.3d 1364, 1379 (Fed. Cir. 2002).

[66] Prof'l Real Estate Investors v. Columbia Pictures Indus., 508 U.S. 49, 60–61 (1993); Serio-US Indus. v. Plastic Recovery Techs. Corp., 459 F.3d 1311, 1321–22 (Fed. Cir. 2006).

[67] Springs Willow Fashions, LP v. Novo Indus., LP, 323 F.3d 989, 999 (Fed. Cir. 2003).

[68] Brooks Furniture Mfg. v. Dutailier Int'l, Inc., 393 F.3d 1378, 1382 (Fed. Cir. 2005).

IV. Injunctions

A. *Permanent Injunctions*

Pursuant to 35 U.S.C. §283, the court is empowered to "grant injunctions in accordance with the principles of equity to prevent the violation of any right secured by patent, on such terms as the court deems reasonable." The same standards are applied in hearing and granting injunctive relief in patent cases as are applied in other federal cases.[69] The decision to grant or deny permanent injunctive relief is an act of equitable discretion by the court, reviewable on appeal for abuse of discretion.[70]

Permanent injunctions should not issue automatically following a finding of infringement. Upon the finding that a valid patent is infringed, patent holders must demonstrate, through four equitable factors, the fairness of a permanent injunction on a case-by-case basis.[71] In *eBay, Inc. v. MercExchange LLC*, the Supreme Court overturned the Federal Circuit's "general rule" that a patentee is presumptively entitled to a permanent injunction upon a finding of infringement at trial.[72] The Court stated that in determining whether to grant a permanent injunction, rather than applying an "automatic" injunction rule, courts should adhere to "well-established principles of equity."[73] In particular, a plaintiff seeking such an injunction must demonstrate that: (1) irreparable injury is likely to occur to plaintiff absent an injunction; (2) remedies available at law, such as monetary damages, would be insufficient to compensate for the injury; (3) the balance of the hardships that would respectively be suffered by the plaintiff and the defendant militates toward granting the injunction; and (4) the public interest would not be disserved by a permanent injunction.[74] Prior to the *eBay* ruling, patent holders enjoyed an almost automatic

[69]Atlas Powder Co. v. Ireco Chems., 773 F.2d 1230, 1233 (Fed. Cir. 1985).
[70]eBay, Inc. v. MercExchange LLC, 126 S. Ct. 1837, 1839 (2006).
[71]*Id.* at 1837.
[72]*Id.*
[73]*Id.* at 1839.
[74]*Id.*

right to injunctive relief upon the finding that a valid patent was infringed.[75]

Despite *eBay* and its progeny, the Federal Circuit has made clear that injunctions are still the norm in competitor cases. While *eBay* abolished the general rule of an automatic right to injunction, it does not swing the pendulum in the opposite direction. Although a patentee's right to exclude alone cannot justify an injunction, it should not be ignored in determining whether a permanent injunction should issue in the patent context, especially as it relates to competitors.[76] Courts will still have to undergo the four factor test, but these factors will be evaluated based on factual circumstances such as; (i) the fact that other infringers may be in the marketplace does not negate irreparable harm; (ii) the fact that an infringer's harm affects only a portion of a patentee's business says nothing about whether harm can be rectified; (iii) the fact that money damages can often not account for lost business opportunities, price erosion and lost market share; and (iv) the fact that a party cannot escape an injunction simply because it is smaller than the patentee or because its primary product is an infringing one.[77]

Injunctions should follow the dictates of Federal Rule of Civil Procedure 65(d), which states that "every order granting an injunction and every restraining order shall set forth the reasons for its issuance, shall be specific in terms, [and] shall describe in reasonable detail... the act or acts sought to be restrained." An injunctive order runs afoul of Rule 65 when it does not use specific terms or describe in reasonable detail the acts sought to be restrained, and when it does not limit its prohibition to the manufacture, use, or sale of the specific infringing devices, or to those no more than colorably different from the infringing devices.[78] Thus, although a trial court is given broad discretion in shaping equitable decrees, injunctive relief should be narrowly tailored to fit the specific legal violations at hand.[79]

---

[75] *See, e.g.*, Fuji Photo Film Co. v. Jazz Photo Corp., 394 F.3d 1368, 1380 (Fed. Cir. 2005) ("Generally an injunction will issue when infringement has been adjudged, absent a sound reason for denying it.").

[76] Robert Bosch v. Pylon Mfg. Corp., 659 F.3d 1142, 1149 (Fed. Cir. 2011).

[77] *Id.*

[78] Oakley, Inc. v. Sunglass Hut Int'l, 316 F.3d 1331, 1346 (Fed. Cir. 2003).

[79] Gemveto Jewelry Co. v. Jeff Cooper, Inc., 800 F.2d 256, 259 (Fed. Cir. 1986).

B. Contempt

Once a court issues a permanent injunction, courts are often faced with evaluating violations of the injunction orders based on continued infringement with new products. For example, after a finding of infringement, infringers will often develop "design-arounds" or "redesigns" which are variations on the infringing product that they believe do not infringe. The Federal Circuit has streamlined the inquiry for evaluating whether these new products continue to infringe the patent.[80] Determination of whether contempt proceedings are properly initiated is within the broad discretion of the trial court.[81] However, what is required for a district court to hold a contempt proceeding is a detailed accusation of the alleged continued infringement and the facts supporting the claim. To determine whether the injunction itself has been violated, courts should employ a "more than colorable difference" standard.[82] The party seeking to enforce the injunction must prove by clear and convincing evidence: (i) that the newly accused product is not more than colorably different from the product found to infringe; and (ii) that the newly accused product actually infringes.[83]

A product is colorably different if, when focusing on the aspects of the accused product that were previously found to infringe, the modified features of the new product are significantly different.[84] The significances of the differences will most always be dependent on the nature of the products at issue.

When a court finds that there are no more than colorable differences, it must still find that the newly accused product infringes. Therefore, the court must evaluate the newly accused product on a limitation by limitation basis, using any prior claim construction it had preformed.[85] If the patentee proves by clear and convincing evidence that the newly accused product meets the claim limitations, a contempt finding is warranted.

---

[80]Tivo, Inc. v. Echostar Corp., 646 F.3d 869 (Fed. Cir. 2011).
[81]*Id.* at 881.
[82]*Id.*
[83]*Id.* at 882.
[84]*Id.*
[85]*Id.* at 883.

15

Special Considerations in Hatch-Waxman Litigation*

*Noah Leibowitz of Simpson, Thacher & Bartlett, LLP, New York, New York, prepared this chapter with the assistance of Katherine A. Helm of the same firm.

I. Introduction

The Drug Price Competition and Patent Term Restoration Act of 1984, commonly referred to as the Hatch-Waxman Act ("Hatch-Waxman") provides a special regime by which generic drug manufacturers may more quickly enter the market with generic versions of popular, brand name pharmaceuticals by challenging their patents. This chapter provides a brief overview of the Hatch-Waxman statutory and regulatory structure and identifies some unique issues that arise in these cases.

II. The Basic Framework of Hatch-Waxman Litigation

The intent of Hatch-Waxman is to accelerate the Food and Drug Administration's ("FDA") approval of generic versions of previously-approved pharmaceuticals,[1] while balancing the incentives for continued investment in new and innovative drug products.[2] This is accomplished by permitting generic drug manufacturers to file Abbreviated New Drug Applications ("ANDAs"), relying on the clinical safety and efficacy data originally provided by the brand-name manufacturer for its approved product. So long as the generic manufacturer demonstrates that its version is "bioequivalent" to the approved brand-name drug, it is not required to conduct the extensive and expensive clinical testing required for approval of the branded drug.

An ANDA applicant must also include a certification regarding the patent rights of the brand-name company, certifying either:

[1]Hatch-Waxman applies only to drugs regulated under the Federal Food, Drug and Cosmetic Act. 21 U.S.C. §301 *et seq.* These drugs are generally chemically-synthesized small molecules and do not include larger, more complex biologic molecules such as vaccines, antibodies and other protein-based biologics. The Biologics Price Competition and Innovation Act, enacted in 2010 as part of the Patient Protection and Affordable Care Act, addresses such biologics, but the issues unique to patent litigation over biosimilars are beyond the scope of this chapter.

[2]149 Cong. Rec. S15582, S15584 (Nov. 25, 2003) (remarks of Sen. Kennedy, Medicare Prescription Drug, Improvement, and Modernization Act of 2003).

(i) that patent information on the brand-name drug has not been filed;
(ii) that the listed patent or patents have expired;
(iii) that it will not seek to market its generic version before all listed patents have expired; or
(iv) that the listed patent or patents are invalid or will not be infringed by the manufacture, use or sale of the generic drug for which the ANDA is submitted.[3]

Patent litigation typically ensues when an ANDA applicant, wishing to come on the market before expiration of the patents for the approved drug or its use, files a certification that the patents are invalid or would not be infringed by the manufacture, use or sale of the generic equivalent.[4] This is known as a "Paragraph IV" certification and its filing constitutes a constructive act of infringement. An ANDA applicant making a Paragraph IV certification must send to the patent holder "a detailed statement of the factual and legal basis" for its opinion that the patent is invalid or will not be infringed.[5] This notifies the brand-name company of the generic's ANDA filing and provides an opportunity for the patent holder to initiate patent litigation before the generic product is approved for marketing.

If the patent holder files an infringement suit against the ANDA applicant within 45 days of receiving a Paragraph IV notice, the ANDA's approval by the FDA is automatically stayed for up to 30 months (unless prior to that time the suit is resolved or the patent expires).[6] As the Federal Circuit explained in *Teva Pharms USA, Inc. v. Novartis Pharms Corp.*,[7] the 30-month stay "provides a safety net and an incentive to patentees who would otherwise not be inclined to bring a suit against the generic because at the time the ANDA is filed, the patentee has not suffered any economic loss. Where no commercial activity has yet taken place, a

---

[3]Brand-name companies are required to list the patents that they assert cover the approved drug, or methods of using the drug, in the FDA publication entitled "Approved Drug Products With Therapeutic Equivalence Evaluations," commonly known as the Orange Book. *See* 21 U.S.C. §355(j)(2)(A)(vii)(I-IV).

[4]*See* 21 U.S.C. §355(j)(2)(A)(vii)(IV).

[5]21 U.S.C. §355(j)(2)(B)(iv)(II).

[6]21 U.S.C. §355(j)(5)(B)(iii).

[7]482 F.3d 1330, 1343, n.8 (Fed. Cir. 2007).

patentee becomes susceptible to having its patent found invalid or not infringed."[8]

As an incentive, the first applicant to file an ANDA with a Paragraph IV certification against a particular patent is entitled to 180 days of exclusivity from any other generic competition. The only competition during that exclusivity period would come from the brand name product itself and any authorized generic (licensed under the relevant patent and given permission by the brand name pharmaceutical company to rely on its FDA approval, without the need for an ANDA). Being the "first-to-file" an ANDA on a blockbuster drug can have very substantial value and provides a powerful incentive to generic companies to file ANDAs with respect to successful pharmaceutical products, as evidenced by the frequency of Paragraph IV challenges to listed patents and the volume of patent litigation that results.

III. Subject Matter Jurisdiction in Hatch-Waxman Cases

Hatch-Waxman created subject matter jurisdiction where none existed before. Prior to adoption of the statute, an infringement action could not have been filed against a generic drug company unless it had manufactured, sold or used its generic version of the patented product in a way that infringed the exclusive rights of the patent holder. Typically, that could not occur until the generic company had conducted the extensive work necessary to secure FDA approval and then launched its generic product, risking liability for substantial damages, if the patent holder successfully enforced its patent rights. By providing that simply filing an ANDA with a Paragraph IV certification is a constructive act of infringement, the Hatch-Waxman Act eliminated this requirement and established jurisdiction to adjudicate these patent challenges. It also codified that the prerequisite research and

---

[8]A district court has discretion to shorten or extend the 30-month stay if "either party to the action fail[s] to reasonably cooperate in expediting the action." *Id. See* Allergan, Inc. v. Alcon Labs, Inc., 324 F.3d 1322, 1337 n.5 (Fed. Cir. 2003) (Schall, J., concurring) (noting that Congress gave district courts the ability to control the timing and extent of the stay).

development needed for the ANDA filing itself is exempt from infringement.[9]

Amendments to Hatch-Waxman now allow ANDA applicants, as opposed to patent holders, to initiate litigation under certain circumstances as well. The Medicare Prescription Drug, Improvement and Modernization Act of 2003 (the "MMA") created two new causes of action: (1) if the brand-name company does not file an infringement suit within the 45 day period, an ANDA applicant may file a declaratory judgment action seeking a ruling that any Orange Book-listed but "unasserted" patent is invalid or would not be infringed by the generic drug product; and (2) an ANDA applicant may bring a claim to de-list a patent from the Orange Book if it is being wrongfully asserted.[10]

The Federal Circuit has read the Hatch-Waxman declaratory judgment jurisdiction provisions broadly enough to permit actions by ANDA applicants seeking judgments of non-infringement even where the patentee could not have brought an infringement action to enforce the patents.[11]

---

[9]35 U.S.C. §§271(e)(2) and (e)(1). As a jurisdictional matter, Section 271(e)(2) has been construed to provide a method of use patent owner the right to bring an action based upon a generic manufacturer's ANDA filing even if the ANDA does not seek approval for the particular use claimed in the patent. *See* AstraZeneca Pharms LP v. Apotex Corp., 2012 WL 400306, *5 (Fed. Cir. Feb. 9, 2012) (the requirements for jurisdiction in the district courts are met once a patent owner alleges infringement by the filing of an ANDA under Section 271(e)(2)).

[10]The former action is referred to as a "civil action to obtain patent certainty," whereby the ANDA applicant has statutory jurisdiction to obtain a judgment on listed but unasserted patents. *See* 21 U.S.C. §355(j)(5)(C) and 35 U.S.C. §271(e)(5); *see also Teva Pharms USA, Inc.*, 482 F.3d at 1344 (there is a case or controversy sufficient for courts to hear these cases "merely because the patents at issue have been listed"). The latter cause of action for de-listing a patent may only be raised as a counterclaim to an infringement suit and the sole remedy is to compel the patent holder to correct or remove an improper Orange Book listing. *See* 21 U.S.C. §355(j)(5)(C)(ii)(I) (denoting an improper listing as one where "the patent does not claim either—[aa] the drug for which the application was approved; or [bb] an approved method of using the drug").

[11]*See* Caraco Pharm. Labs., Ltd. v. Forest Labs., Inc., 527 F.3d 1278, 1291–94 (Fed. Cir. 2008) (finding subject matter jurisdiction where, despite patentee's covenant not to sue, the generic manufacturer was deprived of the ability to market its drug absent a judicial finding that the listed patent was invalid or not infringed); *see also* Teva Pharm. USA, Inc. v. Eisai Co.., 620 F.3d 1341, 1346–48 (Fed.Cir.2010) (same). Separately, the Supreme Court recently held that 21 U.S.C. §355(j)(5)(C)(ii)(I) authorizes a generic manufacturer to force correction of a use code that inaccurately describes the brand's patent as cover-

IV. Special Case Management Issues Arising in Hatch-Waxman Cases

A. *Timing and Order of Disclosure and Evidence*

One important factor in establishing the schedule for a Hatch-Waxman case is the impact of the 30-month stay. While in some cases the statutory stay period may provide ample time in which to resolve the matter, at least through trial, in other cases more time may be required. The parties may also have their own reasons, unrelated to the demands of the litigation, to wish to lengthen the schedule and to extend the stay. And given that most Hatch-Waxman cases involve bench trials, and the District Court itself may need additional time in which to prepare a written decision based upon a lengthy and complex trial record, the stay can be, and under appropriate circumstances, is extended by stipulation.

Certain characteristics of Hatch-Waxman cases can provide efficiency opportunities. For example, the ANDA applicant is obligated to provide the brand-name company with "a detailed statement of the factual and legal basis for the opinion of the applicant that the patent is invalid or will not be infringed" as part of its Paragraph IV certification.[12] Thus, even before the litigation commences, the ANDA filer will have prepared its main invalidity and non-infringement arguments and shared them with the patent holder. District courts may accordingly elect to expedite initial disclosure and discovery deadlines given the ANDA applicant's statutory filings. Indeed, some districts have implemented local patent rules that require an ANDA defendant to provide its invalidity and non-infringement contentions before requiring the plaintiff patent holder to provide its infringement contentions.[13]

The number of issues to resolve in an ANDA case may also be fewer than in a typical patent infringement action. For exam-

---

ing a particular method of using the drug in question by bringing a counterclaim against the brand manufacturer in a patent infringement suit. *See* Caraco Pharm. Labs., Ltd. v. Novo Nordisk A/S, No. 10–844, 2012 WL 1288732 (U.S. Apr. 17, 2012) (holding the counterclaim provision permits a challenge by a generic manufacturer to a patent listing when the listed patent claims at least one approved method of using the drug).

[12] *See* 21 U.S.C. §355(j)(2)(B)(iv)(II).

[13] *See, e.g.*, Local Patent Rule 3.6 for the District of New Jersey.

ple, in an action with respect to a patented pharmaceutical compound (as opposed to a specific formulation or method of use), the ANDA filer that has already told the FDA it wishes to produce a bioequivalent version of the same compound, typically does not contest infringement, challenging validity and, perhaps, enforceability instead. Since infringement occurs with the filing of the ANDA, and in the absence of any commercial sales of the infringing product, damages may not be an issue either.

The limited number of issues litigated in many ANDA cases may also affect the scope of necessary discovery and typically places a heavier discovery burden on the patent holder than on the ANDA filer. For example, in cases where infringement is not contested, the ANDA defendant may have little substantive factual discovery to provide beyond the ANDA filing itself. The absence of a damages claim can also have a substantial effect on the scope of discovery. By contrast, the plaintiff patent holder may have significant discovery obligations relating to the drug discovery and development process and, if the patent holder asserts commercial success as a response to obviousness, financial and marketing materials as well. The speed and sequence of discovery ordered by district courts in Hatch-Waxman cases should reflect the specific discovery considerations in each case.[14]

B. Trial

At trial, the presentation of evidence, in particular the order of proof, in an ANDA case may differ from the typical patent case.[15] For example, in cases where infringement is not contested, the only issues to be resolved (e.g., invalidity and unenforceability) may be those on which the defendant has the burden of proof, prompting the normal order of proof in a civil case to be reversed, with the defendant proceeding first. District courts have the discretion to tailor the presentation of evidence to best address the issues that arise in each Hatch-Waxman case. The fact

---

[14]District courts also should be mindful of the Federal Circuit Advisory Council's recent Model Order regarding e-discovery in patent cases. The Model Order seeks to streamline e-discovery and endorses cost-shifting in patent cases where there is a disproportionate amount of discovery required from one party. The Model Order is available at http://www.cafc.uscourts.gov/images/stories/the-court/Ediscovery_Model_Order.pdf.

[15]*See generally,* Chapter 15.

that, as discussed immediately below, most ANDA cases are tried to the bench, rather than a jury, allows for greater flexibility in devising an efficient order of trial presentation.

C. Bench Trial vs. Jury Trial

One of the starkest distinctions between Hatch-Waxman and other patent litigation is that most Hatch-Waxman cases are tried by the court rather than by a jury. In the typical Hatch-Waxman case, where the allegedly infringing drug product has not been commercialized, the patentee is statutorily limited to claims for prospective declaratory and injunctive relief.[16] Since the relief sought is strictly equitable, the Federal Circuit has held that the Seventh Amendment does not provide any right to a jury trial in a Hatch-Waxman case, even as to any counterclaims of patent invalidity and noninfringement asserted by an ANDA applicant.[17]

The exception arises in a case where the generic launches its product "at risk," either because no 30-month stay applies or because the stay has expired before resolution.[18] In such a case, either party can demand a jury trial, because the available remedy is no longer solely equitable.[19]

While at-risk launches were once rare, they are becoming more common among certain generic companies. Some courts

---

[16] *See* 35 U.S.C. §271(e)(4).

[17] *See, e.g., In re* Apotex, Inc. 49 Fed. App'x 902, 903 (Fed. Cir. 2002) ("[U]nder the unusual circumstances of this case, involving only possible future infringement, and in which there can be no damages because no infringing products have been marketed, ... the underlying controversy is entirely equitable, [and] there can be no right to a jury trial."); *In re* Technology Licensing Corp., 423 F.3d 1286, 1291 (Fed. Cir. 2005) ("if the patentee seeks only equitable relief, the accused infringer has no right to a jury trial").

[18] Sanofi–Synthelabo v. Apotex, 470 F.3d 1368, 1383 (Fed. Cir. 2006) (characterizing an at-risk launch as a "calculated risk to launch [a generic] product pre-judgment."). *See* 35 U.S.C. §271(e)(4)(C) (providing for the award of damages "only if there has been commercial manufacture, use, offer to sell, or sale within the United States or importation into the United States of an approved drug").

[19] *See, e.g.,* Sepracor Inc. v. Dey L.P., Case No. 06-113-JJF, 2010 WL 2802611, *3. (D. Del. July 15, 2010) (denying ANDA defendant's request for bifurcation of damages and granting patentee's motion to file an amended complaint adding a jury demand following defendant's at-risk launch because "the claims are no longer exclusively equitable in nature ... a jury trial is appropriate on the issues of patent infringement, validity and damages").

have required ANDA defendants to provide advance notice to patent holders before launching at-risk while litigation is pending, but other courts have held that no such notice is required.[20] In addition to introducing potential damage issues and a jury trial, at-risk launches also often present the issue of a motion for temporary and preliminary injunctive relief.[21]

District courts have significant discretion in deciding how to try mixed claims, with and without a jury, in the course of Hatch-Waxman litigation. For example, when the action involves multiple ANDA defendants and only some have launched at–risk, the court may bifurcate the action into separate trials of discrete issues or claims in the interest of fairness and efficiency.[22] Alternatively, a court could utilize its power under Fed. R. Civ. P. 39(c) to try common issues before a single jury that renders a verdict only as to the defendants who launched at–risk and is advisory as to the remaining defendants.[23]

Factors of convenience, economy, expedition and prejudice are paramount in deciding whether to bifurcate claims or issues,

---

[20] *Compare* The Research Found. of State Univ. of New York v. Mylan Pharms., Inc., 723 F. Supp. 2d 638, 645 (D. Del. 2010) (generic agreed not to launch its generic product before a stipulated date after the court was advised the generic was contemplating an at-risk launch) *with* Novartis Corp. v. Teva Pharms. USA, Inc., Case Nos. 04-4473, 06-1130-HAA, 2007 WL 1695689, 30 (D.N.J. June 11, 2007) (noting that "Teva launched its products without first notifying the Court, or providing Novartis sufficient notice to obtain a TRO prior to the launch. Indeed, Teva was under no obligation to provide such notice.").

[21] *See, e.g.*, Sciele Pharma, Inc. v. Lupin Ltd., Case No. 09-0037, 2011 WL 6097741 (D. Del. Dec. 6, 2011) (granting a preliminary injunction after ANDA defendant launched at-risk a generic version of Plaintiff's Fortamet® drug); Sanofi-Synthelabo v. Apotex Inc., 488 F. Supp. 2d 317, 350 (S.D.N.Y. 2006) (granting Sanofi's motion for a preliminary injunction after an at-risk launch of Sanofi's Plavex® drug by Apotex); King Pharms., Inc. v. Corepharma, LLC, Case No. 10-1878, 2010 WL 1850200 (D.N.J. May 7, 2010) (entering a temporary restraining order against one generic manufacturer who attempted an at-risk launch of a generic metaxalone product and entering a preliminary injunction against a second generic manufacturer that launched at–risk); *But see* Altana Pharma AG v. Teva Pharms USA, Inc., 532 F. Supp. 2d 666, 684 (D.N.J. 2007) (denying a motion for preliminary injunction and permitting at-risk launch where plaintiffs failed to establish likelihood of success on the merits).

[22] *See, e.g.*, Kos Pharms, Inc. v. Barr Labs, Inc., 218 F.R.D. 387, 390 (S.D.N.Y. 2003), citing Fed. R. Civ. P. 42(b).

[23] *See, e.g.*, Althan Pharma AG v. Teva Pharmaceuticals USA, Inc., Case Nos. 04-2355, 05-1966, 05-3920, 06-3672, 08-2877(JLL), 2009 WL 1929327, *2 (D.N.J. July 1, 2009) (opting for a jury in a fact-finding capacity as to the defendants who launched at–risk and in an advisory capacity as to the remaining defendants).

while preserving a party's Seventh Amendment right to a jury trial.[24]

V. Substantive Patent Issues Arising in Hatch-Waxman Litigation

A. *Validity*

Since infringement is often admitted in ANDA cases, the litigation focuses on defenses of invalidity, and in some cases, unenforceability due to inequitable conduct.

In addition to validity arguments based on obviousness[25] or anticipation, some recent Hatch-Waxman cases have raised the doctrine of inherent anticipation. Under 35 U.S.C. §102, an inventor is not entitled to a patent if the invention sought to be patented is not novel over, and is thus anticipated by, what came before. An invention may be inherently anticipated, even though the prior art does not expressly disclose the claimed invention, if the invention is necessarily present in the prior art. It is not enough that the prior art would possibly or even probably produce the claimed invention; the invention must flow as a natural consequence from the prior art.[26] In Hatch-Waxman case law the doctrine has been held to include later recognition of the prior art's inherent characteristics. For example, in *Schering Corp. v.*

---

[24]Fed. R. Civ. P. 42(b); *see also,* Pfizer, Inc. v. Novopharm Ltd., Case No. 00 C 1475, 2000 WL 1847604, *1 (N.D. Ill. Dec. 14, 2000) (noting that while the Federal Circuit has advised courts in patent cases to carefully consider bifurcation, the decision to order separate trials is committed to the broad discretion of the trial court).

[25]For a comprehensive recent discussion of the obviousness analysis in the context of an ANDA case, *see In re* Cyclobenzaprine Hydrochloride Extended-Release Capsule Patent Litig., 2012 WL 1320225 (Fed. Cir. Apr. 16, 2012) (holding that the fact finder must consider all evidence of obviousness and nonobviousness "collectively" before reaching a determination and reversing application of a burden-shifting framework to consider whether the patentee's objective indicia of non-obviousness were sufficient to rebut the prima facie case of obviousness based on the prior art).

[26]*See* Continental Can Co. v. Monsanto Co., 948 F.2d 1264, 1269 (Fed. Cir. 1991); *see also In re* Woodruff, 919 F.2d 1575, 1578 (Fed. Cir. 1990) ("[M]erely discovering and claiming a new benefit of an old process cannot render the process again patentable.")

Geneva Pharmaceuticals, Inc.,[27] a patent that claimed an antihistamine drug and described its administration to patients was found to inherently anticipate later claims to a metabolite that formed in the bodies of patients treated with the original drug, even though the metabolite was not disclosed in the prior art patent and its existence was not previously appreciated.[28] As the patents on basic drug compounds begin to expire, Hatch-Waxman patent challenges are increasingly being mounted against patents that cover improvements upon the core element of the primary drug. These so-called "second-generation" patents include those claiming: sustained-release versions, combination or new formulations, new methods of use (i.e., new indications or patient populations), new dosing regimens and new methods of manufacture. Second-generation patents are often challenged on the basis of their distinction over the invention claimed in the primary, "first-generation" patent. These challenges can take the form of traditional anticipation or obviousness attacks, or under the doctrine of obviousness-type double patenting. The latter doctrine prohibits a patentee from obtaining a second patent containing claims directed to obvious variants of inventions that were disclosed and claimed in an earlier, commonly-owned patent.[29] While this doctrine is not a mainstay of patent litigation generally, it arises more often in Hatch-Waxman litigation.[30]

---

[27] 339 F.3d 1373 (Fed. Cir. 2003).

[28] *See also* Abbott Labs. v. Baxter Pharm. Prods., Inc., 471 F.3d 1363 (Fed. Cir. 2006) (claims directed to a formulation comprising the drug sevoflurane and water were inherently anticipated by a prior water-saturated sevoflurane composition, even though that composition did not display the same stability as the improved formulation); King Pharmaceuticals, Inc. v. Eon Labs, Inc., 616 F.3d 1267, 1276 (Fed. Cir. 2010) (holding invalid claims to increase the bioavailability of the drug metaxalone by taking it with food because the prior art disclosed taking metaxalone with food which inherently increases the drug's bioavailability); *In re* Omeprazole Patent Litig., 483 F.3d 1364, 1373 (Fed. Cir. 2007) (holding invalid for inherent anticipation a method for stabilizing a drug that formed a separating layer in situ where the formation was a natural result flowing from a known combination of ingredients).

[29] *See, e.g.*, Perricone v. Medicis Pharm. Corp., 432 F.3d 1368 (Fed. Cir. 2005) (claims directed to method of treating damaged or aged skin were held invalid for double patenting over earlier claims to a method for treating a sunburn because sunburn was deemed a type of skin damage).

[30] The doctrine of obviousness-type double patenting has recently been interpreted to permit a comparison of the later patent's claims with the unclaimed disclosure in an earlier patent. *See, e.g.*, Sun Pharm. Indus., Ltd. v. Eli Lilly & Co., 611 F.3d 1381 (Fed. Cir. 2010) (later-claimed method of using compound to

B. Infringement

Because the filing of an ANDA is itself considered a constructive act of infringement under Section 271(e)(2), the issue of proving infringement may not play as large a role in Hatch-Waxman cases as in other patent actions.

Further, in many cases, the primary evidence of infringement will come from the ANDA itself. In its ANDA, the generic manufacturer will have demonstrated "bioequivalence" based on data showing that the rate and extent of absorption of the active ingredient in the generic does not bear significant differences from that of the branded product.[31] Whether the ANDA data alone are sufficient to prove infringement will depend on the type of patent claims being asserted, and how closely the asserted patent claims align with the data set forth in the ANDA. While patents with basic compound claims to the active pharmaceutical ingredient may be infringed by any alternate formulation or method of treatment containing the compound, second-generation patents on new formulations or methods of treatment may be infringed only by the particular formulation or treatment specifically claimed. In the former cases infringement is typically not contested.

Additional complexities arise in proving infringement of method of treatment claims (e.g., administering a drug formulation to a patient with a specific condition). For example, patentees may have to prove conduct by numerous parties—i.e., inducement by the ANDA applicant's proposed label instructing physicians that a drug is indicated for a particular, patented use.[32]

---

treat cancer not patentably distinct over earlier patent that disclosed but did not claim compound's anticancer activity); *see also* Pfizer, Inc. v. Teva Pharms. USA, Inc., 518 F.3d 1353, 1363 (Fed. Cir. 2008) (holding invalid for obviousness-type double patenting patent claims to a method of using a compound where the use was described but not claimed in the specification of an earlier patent claiming the compound); Geneva Pharms., Inc. v. GlaxoSmithKline PLC, 349 F.3d 1373, 1385–86 (Fed. Cir. 2003) (same) ("A claim to a method of using a composition is not patentably distinct from an earlier claim to the identical composition in a patent disclosing the identical use.").

[31] 21 U.S.C. §355(j)(8)(B).

[32] *See, e.g.,* Global-Tech Appliances, Inc. v. SEB S.A., 131 S. Ct. 2060, 2068 (2011) ("induced infringement under Section 271(b) requires knowledge that the induced acts constitute patent infringement"); DSU Med. Corp. v. JMS Co., 471 F.3d 1293, 1305–06 (Fed. Cir. 2006) (inducement "requires evidence of culpable conduct, directed to encouraging another's infringement.").

VI. Settlements in Hatch-Waxman Litigation

Finally, it should be noted that the settlement of Hatch-Waxman litigation poses unique challenges, because such settlements have come under increased scrutiny by the antitrust regulatory authorities, especially the FTC, and have resulted in antitrust claims by both public and private plaintiffs.[33] In addition, the MMA provisions of Hatch-Waxman require that certain agreements between the patentee and the ANDA applicant be filed by the parties with the FTC and Department of Justice ("DOJ") within 10 days of execution.[34] These filings are typically not made public on an individual basis, but the FTC's year-end reports provide a summary of the agreements. As a result of this review, the FTC has taken enforcement action against certain pharmaceutical companies it contends have entered into what it calls "pay-for-delay" or "reverse payment" agreements.

---

[33] *See, e.g.*, Schering-Plough Corp. v. F.T.C., 402 F.3d 1056, 1074 (11th Cir. 2005) (reversing the FTC's decision that the settlement between Schering and Upsher-Smith violated Section 5 of the FTC Act and deeming the settlement "a natural by-product of the Hatch-Waxman process"); Carpenters Health and Welfare Fund v. Bayer AG, 604 F.3d 98, 105 (2d Cir. 2010) (holding branded-generic settlement acceptable as being within the exclusionary zone of the patent and noting the divide on this issue between the FTC and many courts that have rejected such antitrust challenges as a matter of law).

[34] The agreements that must be filed include "Generic-Brand Agreements" and "Generic-Generic Agreements" as characterized in the Pharmaceutical Agreement Filing Requirements, *available at* http://www.ftc.gov/os/2004/01/040106pharmrules.pdf. *See* May 9, 2011 letter from FTC, *available at* http://www.ftc.gov/opa/2011/05/sanofi.shtm, broadening the types of agreements, including as to stays, that must be filed in Hatch Waxman cases.

16

The Appeal*

---

*Robert Long, Covington & Burling LLP, Washington, D.C. The author wishes to thank Ranganath Sudarshan for his assistance in preparing this chapter revision and Ford F. Farabow, Jr., Finnegan, Henderson, Farabow, Garrett & Dunner, LLP, Washington, D.C., who prepared the original version of this chapter.

I. Federal Circuit Jurisdiction

A. Cases "Arising Under the Patent Laws"

The U.S. Court of Appeals for the Federal Circuit has exclusive jurisdiction on any appeal from a U.S. district court that had jurisdiction, in whole or in part, based on 28 U.S.C. §1338, except for cases that arise under the Copyright or Trademark Acts or deal with exclusive rights in mask works, and no other claims under Section 1338(a) exist.[1] The district courts have original jurisdiction over any civil action arising under any act of Congress relating to patents, plant variety protection, copyrights, and trademarks; such jurisdiction is exclusive of the state courts in patent, plant variety protection, and copyright cases.[2] The Federal Circuit will apply its own law, and not regional circuit law, in determining its jurisdiction over any appeal.[3]

The Federal Circuit's jurisdiction is not limited to actions brought under title 35 of the U.S. Code, but includes actions that

---

[1]28 U.S.C. §1295(a)(1) (2000); Phillips v. AWH Corp., 363 F.3d 1207, 1211 (Fed. Cir. 2004).

[2]28 U.S.C. §1338(a) (2000); Pixton v. B&B Plastics, Inc., 291 F.3d 1324, 1326 (Fed. Cir. 2002).

[3]Woodard v. Sage Prods., Inc., 818 F.2d 841, 844 (Fed. Cir. 1987) (en banc).

implicate or raise substantial questions under title 35.[4] Examples of substantial questions under title 35 include infringement;[5] whether the director of the Patent and Trademark Office violated the Administrative Procedure Act in applying Patent Cooperation Treaty rules and regulations;[6] vesting title to the U.S. government for inventions made in government labs;[7] mandamus claims related to attorneys' authority to practice before the PTO;[8] and claims under 16 U.S.C. §831r for reasonable compensation for patent infringement.[9]

1. *Implication of Federal Patent Law*

The Supreme Court defined the boundaries of the exclusive jurisdiction provided to the federal district courts under Section 1338(a) by construing the "arising under" language to be the same as the "arising under" language of the general federal-question jurisdiction provision of 28 U.S.C. §1331.[10] Section 1338(a) jurisdiction "extend[s] only to those cases in which a well-pleaded complaint establishes either that federal patent law creates the cause of action or that the plaintiff's right to relief necessarily depends on resolution of a substantial question of federal patent law, in that patent law is a necessary element of one of the well-pleaded claims."[11] If a substantial question of patent law is necessary to determine a required element of a state-law cause of action, such as an unfair competition claim asserted against a patentee, then under Section 1338(a), the case arises under the patent laws and

[4]Univ. of W. Va., Bd. of Trustees v. VanVoorhies, 278 F.3d 1288, 1295 (Fed. Cir. 2002) (action involving breach-of-assignment agreement properly transferred from the regional circuit to the Federal Circuit because the dispute focused on whether specific applications were continuation-in-part (CIP) applications, which raised a question of substantive patent law).

[5]U.S. Valves, Inc. v. Dray, 212 F.3d 1368, 1372 (Fed. Cir. 2000).

[6]Helfgott & Karas, P.C. v. Dickenson, 209 F.3d 1328, 1334 (Fed. Cir. 2000); claims based on 42 U.S.C. §5908.

[7]Cedars-Sinai Med. Ctr. v. Watkins, 11 F.3d 1573, 1577–80 (Fed. Cir. 1993).

[8]Wyden v. Comm'r of Patents & Trademarks, 807 F.2d 934, 936–37 (Fed. Cir. 1986) (en banc).

[9]Alco Standard Corp. v. Tenn. Valley Auth., 808 F.2d 1490, 1493–94 (Fed. Cir. 1986).

[10]Christianson v. Colt Indus. Operating Corp., 486 U.S. 800, 808–09 (1988).

[11]*Id.*

federal jurisdiction is exclusive of the state courts.[12] However, as discussed in subsection I.A.2, below, a defendant's counterclaim alleging patent infringement does not create arising-under jurisdiction because it is not part of the plaintiff's well-pleaded complaint.[13]

If the federal patent law does not create the cause of action, subject-matter jurisdiction can still lie if "plaintiff's right to relief necessarily depends on resolution of a substantial question of federal patent law."[14] Thus, one must address what constitutes a "substantial question" of patent law.

The mere presence of a patent as relevant evidence to a claim does not by itself present a substantial issue of patent law.[15] Causes of action that have been deemed to raise a substantial question of patent law sufficient to satisfy the jurisdiction requirements of Section 1338(a), are those that address (1) infringement; (2) patent validity; (3) patent enforceability; (4) inventorship issues; (5) attorneys' fees under 35 U.S.C. §285; or (6) revival of unintentionally abandoned patent applications.[16]

2. *Patent Law Defense Does Not "Arise Under"*

Under the well-pleaded-complaint test for jurisdiction, the fact that a federal patent law defense might be implicated by a state-law cause of action is not conclusive of whether the action arises under the patent laws for purposes of jurisdiction under

---

[12]Hunter Douglas, Inc. v. Harmonic Design, Inc., 153 F.3d 1318, 1329 (Fed. Cir. 1998), *overruled in part on other grounds*, Midwest Indus., Inc. v. Karavan Trailers, Inc., 175 F.3d 1356, 1358–59 (Fed. Cir. 1999) (en banc).

[13]Holmes Group, Inc. v. Vornado Air Circulation Sys., Inc., 535 U.S. 826, 829–30 (2002).

[14]*Christianson*, 486 U.S. at 808–09.

[15]Bonzel v. Pfizer, 439 F.3d 1358, 1363 (Fed. Cir. 2006) (affirming dismissal for lack of subject-matter jurisdiction when breach of patent license action did not arise under the patent laws).

[16]Hunter Douglas, Inc. v. Harmonic Design, Inc., 153 F.3d 1318, 1330 (Fed. Cir. 1998) (see cases cited therein), *overruled in part on other grounds*, Midwest Indus., Inc. v. Karavan Trailers, Inc., 175 F.3d 1356, 1358–59 (Fed. Cir. 1999) (en banc). *See also* Apotex, Inc. v. Thompson, 347 F.3d 1335, 1344 (Fed. Cir. 2003) (ruling that court had subject-matter jurisdiction over generic-drug manufacturer's claim against the FDA for not delisting patents from the Orange Book because generic's complaint included a claim against a pioneer drug manufacturer to delist its patents and that claim presented a claim under the patent laws despite fact that the court had previously ruled that the patent laws provided no private cause of action for delisting a patent from the Orange Book).

Sections 1338(a) and 1295(a)(1). Rather, under the well-pleaded-complaint rule, arising under jurisdiction is determined from the plaintiff's statement of his or her own claim "unaided by anything alleged in anticipation or avoidance of defenses which it is thought the defendant may interpose."[17] State courts are not precluded from consideration of evidence regarding patent validity or infringement as they may relate to a state-court action so long as the "case" is not one arising under the patent laws.[18] Similarly, the fact that factual findings relating to a state-law claim may implicate potential prospective federal patent law determinations in future actions does not make the cause of action arise under the patent laws.[19]

3. *Patent Claim Is Part of Original Complaint*

Pursuant to 28 U.S.C. §1295(a)(1), the Federal Circuit has jurisdiction over an appeal where the district court's jurisdiction was "in part" based on 28 U.S.C. §1338. Accordingly, where a patent claim is joined with a state-law claim or other federal nonpatent claim in the complaint, the Federal Circuit will have jurisdiction over the entire appeal of the final judgment if the patent claims are adjudicated on the merits or dismissed with prejudice.[20]

4. *Patent Claim Added by Amendment*

The Supreme Court has not yet decided whether an infringement claim added by an amendment to a complaint suffices to give the Federal Circuit jurisdiction.[21] Justice Stevens, in his concurring opinion in *Holmes*,[22] has nonetheless stated that because appellate jurisdiction is based on the circumstances existing at the time the notice of appeal is filed, amendments to a complaint that

---

[17] *Christianson*, 486 U.S. at 808–09.

[18] Pratt v. Paris Gaslight & Coke Co., 168 U.S. 255, 259, 261 (1897).

[19] Becher v. Contoure Labs., Inc., 279 U.S. 388, 391–92 (1929).

[20] Atari, Inc. v. JS&A Group, Inc., 747 F.2d 1422, 1429–30 (Fed. Cir. 1984) (en banc), *overruled on other grounds by* Nobelpharma AB v. Implant Innovations, Inc., 141 F.3d 1059, 1068 (Fed. Cir. 1998) (en banc); Amini Innovation Corp. v. Anthony California, Inc., 439 F.3d 1365, 1368 (Fed. Cir. 2006).

[21] Holmes Group, Inc. v. Vornado Air Circulation Sys., Inc., 535 U.S. 826, 829 n.1 (2002).

[22] *Id.*

add patent infringement claims are included in the Federal Circuit's jurisdiction.[23]

The Federal Circuit has itself stated in another context that the determination of its appellate jurisdiction should be "viewed pragmatically at the time of the appeal."[24] The Federal Circuit has held that infringement claims added by an amended complaint created Section 1338(a) arising under jurisdiction; the Federal Circuit has jurisdiction over such an appeal when the patent claim was not frivolous or asserted as a tactical maneuver attempting to manipulate appellate jurisdiction of the state-law claims.

5. *Effect of Dismissal*

When a patent claim is dismissed without prejudice from the underlying suit but state-law causes of action remain, the case no longer arises under the patent laws and any appeal must go to the regional circuit.[25] If, however, the district court dismisses the patent claims with prejudice, then the arising under jurisdiction remains in effect and any appeal of that decision or final judgment of the remaining claims goes to the Federal Circuit, because the dismissal with prejudice constitutes an adjudication on the merits.[26]

6. *Mootness*

An Article XI case or controversy must exist at all stages of appellate review.[27] "[A] case becomes moot if, through the action of the party seeking review, the immediate controversy is terminated."[28]

---

[23] *Id.* at 835 (Stevens, J., *concurring in part*); *see also* Christianson v. Colt Indus. Operating Corp., 486 U.S. 800, 823–24 (1988) (Stevens, J., concurring).

[24] *Atari,* 747 F.2d at 1436 (en banc), *overruled on other grounds by Nobelpharma,* 141 F.3d at 1068 (en banc). *See also* Eaton Corp. v. Appliance Valves Corp., 790 F.2d 874, 876 n.3 (Fed. Cir. 1986).

[25] Nilssen v. Motorola, Inc., 203 F.3d 782, 784–85 (Fed. Cir. 2000).

[26] Zenith Elecs. Corp. v. Exzec, Inc., 182 F.3d 1340, 1346 (Fed. Cir. 1999).

[27] Aqua Marine Supply v. AIM Machining, Inc., 247 F.3d 1216, 1219 (Fed. Cir. 2001).

[28] *Id.* at 1220.

B. *Jurisdiction Over Other Claims Brought With Patent Claim*

1. *Supplemental Jurisdiction—28 U.S.C. §1367*

Pursuant to 28 U.S.C. §1367(a), "in any civil action over which the district courts have original jurisdiction, the district courts shall have supplemental jurisdiction over all other claims that are so related to claims in the action within such original jurisdiction that they form part of the same case or controversy under Article III of the United States Constitution," including "claims that involve the joinder or intervention of additional parties." Under this statute, a district court may exercise supplemental jurisdiction over a state-law claim if the court can exercise original jurisdiction over some other federal claim also contained within the lawsuit that is related to the state-law claim.[29] Thus, for example, the Federal Circuit held that a district court that had original jurisdiction based on patent law claims also had supplemental jurisdiction over state-law claims for breach of contract and misappropriation of trade secrets that "form[ed] part of the same case or controversy."[30]

The exercise of supplemental jurisdiction under 28 U.S.C. §1367(a) is not compulsory. District courts have the discretion to refuse to exercise supplemental jurisdiction under Section 1367(c) if (1) the claim raises a novel or complex issue of state law; (2) the claim substantially predominates over the claim or claims over which the district court had original jurisdiction; (3) the district court has dismissed all claims over which it has original jurisdiction; or (4) there are other compelling reasons for declining jurisdiction.

When a district court exercises its discretion to remand to state court after declining to exercise supplemental jurisdiction, the Federal Circuit has jurisdiction to review the remand decision.[31] Notably, the Federal Circuit's appellate review of such a remand order is not limited by 28 U.S.C. §1447(d), which provides that "[a]n order remanding a case to the State court from which it was removed is not reviewable on appeal or otherwise."[32]

---

[29]Mars, Inc. v. Kabushiki-Kaisha Nippon Conlux, 24 F.3d 1368, 1374 (Fed. Cir. 1994).

[30]Crater Corp. v. Lucent Techs., Inc., 255 F.3d 1361, 1369–70 (Fed. Cir. 2001).

[31]Carlsbad Tech., Inc. v. HIF Bio, Inc., 129 S. Ct. 1862, 1867 (2009).

[32]*Id.*

2. *Supplemental Jurisdiction Over Foreign Patent Claims*

Traditionally, district courts lack subject-matter jurisdiction to hear infringement claims based on acts committed in foreign countries that are alleged to infringe foreign patents.[33] However, in some cases, the doctrine of supplemental jurisdiction may provide a basis to hear such claims when asserted in a suit that raises claims of infringement of a U.S. patent. Whether a district court will exercise supplemental jurisdiction over an infringement claim involving a foreign patent will depend on whether the acts of infringement of the foreign patent are sufficiently related to the acts of infringement of the U.S. patent at issue in the suit. If the acts of foreign infringement are based on an accused product or process different from the product or process accused of infringing the U.S. patent, supplemental jurisdiction likely will not be proper.[34]

In affirming a denial of a preliminary injunction seeking to enjoin the patentee from pursuing an infringement action in Great Britain based on British patents alleged to correspond to U.S. patents, the Federal Circuit also suggested that considerations of international comity, the "Act of State" doctrine, and principles of abstention might preclude a district court from exercising supplemental jurisdiction pursuant to 28 U.S.C. §1367(c).[35]

3. *Unfair Competition Claims—28 U.S.C. §1338(b)*

Reliance on the supplemental jurisdiction provision of 28 U.S.C. §1367 is not necessary when unfair competition claims that relate to a claim of patent infringement are asserted. Section 1338(b) expressly provides that "[t]he district courts shall have original jurisdiction of any civil action asserting a claim of unfair competition *when joined with a substantial and related claim* under the copyright, *patent,* plant variety protection or trademark laws" (emphasis added). Congress permitted joinder of a state unfair competition claim with a federal patent infringement claim under Section 1338(b) in order to avoid "piecemeal litigation."[36]

---

[33] *Mars,* 24 F.3d at 1373 (ruling that "a claim of infringement of a foreign patent does not constitute a claim of unfair competition within the meaning of section 1338(b)").

[34] *Id.* at 1374.

[35] Stein Assocs. v. Heat & Control, Inc., 748 F.2d 653, 658 (Fed. Cir. 1984).

[36] *Mars,* 24 F.3d at 1372.

4. Patent Infringement Counterclaims

A defendant's counterclaim alleging patent infringement does not create arising under jurisdiction in the district court (and therefore no appellate jurisdiction for the Federal Circuit) because it is not part of the plaintiff's well-pleaded complaint.[37] Where only such claims remain in a case, or no patent claim was ever asserted in the original complaint, the Federal Circuit would have to transfer the appeal to the appropriate regional circuit.[38]

5. Patent Declaratory Judgment Claims

The Federal Circuit looks only to the well-pleaded complaint to determine subject-matter jurisdiction in the court below.[39] If an accused infringer's complaint asserts a declaratory judgment claim of noninfringement, invalidity, or unenforceability of a patent, such actions are considered ones seeking coercive relief under the patent laws that will confer appellate jurisdiction on the Federal Circuit.[40]

The Federal Circuit applies the well-pleaded complaint rule "not to the declaratory judgment complaint, but to the hypothetical action that the declaratory judgment defendant would otherwise have brought directly against the declaratory judgment plaintiff."[41] After constructing such a hypothetical complaint, the Federal Circuit has "to determine both under which federal

---

[37]Holmes Group, Inc. v. Vornado Air Circulation Sys., Inc., 535 U.S. 826, 829–30 (2002).

[38]*Id. Holmes* creates the possibility that a patent infringement counterclaim could be adjudicated in a state court proceeding. *Cf.* Green v. Hendrickson Publishers, Inc., 770 N.E.2d 784, 793, 63 USPQ2d 1852, 1858 (Ind. 2002) (following *Holmes* to allow a claim for copyright infringement to stay in state court when it was asserted as a counterclaim to plaintiffs' claim for breach of contract relating to a copyright license).

[39]*Holmes*, 535 U.S. at 829–30.

[40]*See, e.g.*, Golan v. Pingel Enter., Inc., 310 F.3d 1360, 1366–67 (Fed. Cir. 2002) (holding complaint sought declarations of patent noninfringement that arose, in part, under 28 U.S.C. §1338); Unitherm Food Sys., Inc. v. Swift-Eckrich, Inc., 375 F.3d 1341, 1348 (Fed. Cir. 2004) (exercising jurisdiction over appeal of accused infringer's antitrust claim and state-law claims for tortious interference where accused infringer also brought a claim for a declaratory judgment of invalidity and unenforceability).

[41]Cedars-Sinai Med. Ctr. v. Watkins, 11 F.3d 1573, 1578 (Fed. Cir. 1993).

statute(s) the hypothetical cause of action would have 'aris[en],' and whether those federal statute(s) 'relat[e] to' patents."[42]

The presence of a declaratory judgment claim dismissed without prejudice for lack of subject-matter jurisdiction should not support arising under jurisdiction for an appeal of any other claims asserted with the declaratory judgment claim.[43] However, if an accused infringer appeals the dismissal of its declaratory judgment claims for lack of subject-matter jurisdiction, that appeal will lie in the Federal Circuit.[44]

6. *No Jurisdiction Over Ownership or Licensing Disputes*

The Federal Circuit does not have exclusive jurisdiction over patent-related actions that may arise in state court or in federal court based on diversity jurisdiction, e.g., actions for breach of licensing agreements.[45] Conversely, the fact that the accused infringer sets up a defense of license that would require an analysis of state contract law will not defeat subject-matter jurisdiction when the complaint alleges patent infringement.[46]

7. *Transfer of Appeals to Regional Circuit*

If the Federal Circuit decides it lacks subject-matter jurisdiction over an appeal, the court can transfer the appeal to the regional circuit, which could exercise jurisdiction over the appeal pursuant to 28 U.S.C. §1631.

---

[42]*Id.* The Federal Circuit affirmed the dismissal of plaintiffs' declaratory judgment complaint for lack of subject-matter jurisdiction, and one not arising under § 1338(a), because declaratory judgment defendant's well-pleaded complaint would have been one to recover money due under a contract to transfer ownership of a patent, a matter of state law, and declaratory judgment plaintiffs' patent claims only related to possible defenses to that state-law action. Speedco, Inc. v. Estes, 853 F.2d 909, 912–13 (Fed. Cir. 1988).

[43]*See* Hunter Douglas, Inc. v. Harmonic Design, Inc., 153 F.3d 1318, 1328 (Fed. Cir. 1998).

[44]Gen-Probe, Inc. v. Vysis, Inc., 359 F.3d 1376, 1379–82 (Fed. Cir. 2004).

[45]*In re* Oximetrix, Inc., 748 F.2d 637, 641–42 (Fed. Cir. 1984); for a determination of patent ownership, *see* Beghin-Say, Int'l, Inc. v. Ole-Bendt Rasmussen, 733 F.2d 1568, 1571–72 (Fed. Cir. 1984).

[46]Pixton v. B&B Plastics, Inc., 291 F.3d 1324, 1327 (Fed. Cir. 2002).

C. *Finality Requirement*

1. *Final Decision Rule*

The "final decision" requirement of 28 U.S.C. §1295(a)(1) is coextensive with the final decision requirement of 28 U.S.C. §1291, governing appeals to other federal courts of appeal.[47]

2. *Final but for an Accounting—28 U.S.C. §1292(c)(2)*

Under 28 U.S.C. §1292(c)(2), the Federal Circuit has jurisdiction to review a patent infringement judgment that is final except for an accounting of damages.[48] "Accounting" as used in 28 U.S.C. §1292(c)(2) refers only to infringement damages pursuant to 35 U.S.C. §284.[49]

3. *Final but for an Award of Attorneys' Fees or Costs*

Ordinarily an infringement judgment will not lack finality simply because the district court has not yet calculated the amount of attorneys' fees it will award.[50] However, if the parties are specifically appealing only the issue of the award of attorneys' fees, then an order that awards fees but does not determine the amount of those fees is a nonfinal order.[51]

4. *Rule 54(b) Certification*

When an appeal is certified pursuant to Federal Rule of Civil Procedure 54(b), the Federal Circuit reviews the finality of the judgment de novo in order to ensure that it has jurisdiction to hear the appeal.[52]

---

[47]Johannsen v. Pay Less Drug Stores Nw., Inc., 918 F.2d 160, 161 n.1 (Fed. Cir. 1990).

[48]*Id.* at 162.

[49]Special Devices, Inc. v. OEA, Inc., 269 F.3d 1340, 1343 n.2 (Fed. Cir. 2001).

[50]*Johannsen*, 918 F.2d at 164.

[51]*Special Devices*, 269 F.3d at 1345–46.

[52]Ultra-Precision Mfg. Ltd. v. Ford Motor Co., 338 F.3d 1353, 1356 (Fed. Cir. 2003).

5. *Injunctions and Stay Orders*

The Federal Circuit has exclusive jurisdiction to review interlocutory orders granting, continuing, modifying, refusing, or dissolving injunctions, or refusing to dissolve or modify injunctions in cases arising under the patent laws pursuant to 28 U.S.C. §§1292(a)(1) and (c)(1), except where direct review may be had in the Supreme Court.[53] When an interlocutory order effectively denies injunctive relief (e.g., the dismissal of an infringement counterclaim that sought an injunction), the Federal Circuit generally will not exercise its subject-matter jurisdiction unless the party seeking appeal shows that serious or irreparable harm will result if the appeal is not immediately heard.[54]

If the district court's jurisdiction over a claim for patent infringement was based in part on 28 U.S.C. §1338(a), the Federal Circuit will have jurisdiction under Section 1292(c)(1) to hear an appeal of a preliminary injunction entered on nonpatent issues, such as copyright infringement.[55] An interlocutory order that ordinarily would not be appealable may be given discretionary appellate review when it is ancillary to other matters that are appealable when it would promote judicial economy and advance the interest of justice.[56]

Stay orders are generally not final for purposes of 28 U.S.C. §1295.[57]

6. *Certified Questions*

Section 1292(c)(1), title 28 of the U.S. Code, gives the Federal Circuit jurisdiction to hear appeals of interlocutory orders, in a case arising under the patent laws, that satisfy the conditions of Section 1292(b). Section 1292(b) permits appellate review of certain interlocutory orders that present a controlling question of law subject to a substantial difference of opinion, and whose resolution would materially advance the ultimate termination of the

---

[53]Cross Med. Prods., Inc. v. Medtronic Sofamor Danek, Inc., 424 F.3d 1293, 1301 (Fed. Cir. 2005).

[54]Woodard v. Sage Prods., Inc., 818 F.2d 841, 842 (Fed. Cir. 1987) (en banc).

[55]Atari, Inc. v. JS&A Group, Inc., 747 F.2d 1422, 1429–30 (Fed. Cir. 1984) (en banc).

[56]Katz v. Lear Siegler, Inc., 909 F.2d 1459, 1461 (Fed. Cir. 1990).

[57]Nystrom v. Trex Co., Inc., 339 F.3d 1347, 1351 (Fed. Cir. 2003).

dispute, upon compliance with certain procedural requirements, including a certification by the district court.

Even if the district court certifies the appeal in accordance with the requirements of Section 1292(b), the decision by the Federal Circuit to accept such an appeal is entirely discretionary.[58] "[S]uch appeals are rarely granted."[59] When an order is certified under Section 1292(b), the Federal Circuit may review the entire order, not just the specific questions certified by the district court.[60]

Procedurally, a party seeking an interlocutory appeal in the Federal Circuit under Sections 1292(b) and (c)(1) must file in the Federal Circuit a "petition for permission to appeal" within the 10-day time limit of Section 1292(b). Under Federal Rule of Appellate Procedure 5(d)(2), "notice of appeal" is not required. The specific requirements for the content of the petition are set forth in Appellate Rule 5(b)(1).

In general, the Federal Circuit does not exercise general supervisory authority over district court judges. Accordingly, the Federal Circuit may not issue writs of mandamus on the basis of inherent supervisory authority of administrative matters of the district court, as the regional circuit court of appeals may do.[61] The Federal Circuit will only entertain petitions for writs of mandamus in patent cases in which "the patent jurisprudence of this court plays a significant role."[62]

II. Standards of Review

Questions of law reviewed de novo by the Federal Circuit include claim construction,[63] prosecution history estoppel,[64]

---

[58] *Ultra-Precision,* 338 F.3d at 1357–58.

[59] *Nystrom,* 339 F.3d at 1351.

[60] Senza-Gel Corp. v. Seiffhart, 803 F.2d 661, 668 (Fed. Cir. 1986).

[61] *In re* Oximetrix, Inc., 748 F.2d 637, 643 (Fed. Cir. 1984).

[62] *In re* Innotron Diagnostics, 800 F.2d 1077, 1083–84 (Fed. Cir. 1986).

[63] Cybor Corp. v. FAS Techs., Inc., 138 F.3d 1448, 1456 (Fed. Cir. 1998) (en banc).

[64] Honeywell Int'l, Inc. v. Hamilton Sunstrand Corp., 370 F.3d 1131, 1139 (Fed. Cir. 2004) (en banc).

obviousness,[65] enablement,[66] indefiniteness,[67] inventorship,[68] priority,[69] conception,[70] reduction to practice,[71] the availability of lost profits,[72] and Noerr-Pennington immunity.[73]

Questions of fact reviewed under the clearly erroneous rule (for a bench trial) or under the substantial evidence test (for issues in a jury trial) include infringement,[74] utility,[75] anticipation,[76] best mode,[77] written description,[78] materiality and intent,[79] patent misuse,[80] the amount of reasonable royalty damages,[81] the amount of lost profits,[82] willfulness,[83] and an exceptional case determination.[84]

In the case of obviousness, the district court's fact findings underlying the obviousness conclusion are reviewed for clear error (or substantial evidence in a jury trial).[85] The same is true for the fact findings underlying other legal determinations, such

---

[65]Riverwood Int'l Corp. v. Mead Corp., 212 F.3d 1365, 1366 (Fed. Cir. 2000).

[66]Invitrogen Corp. v. Clontech Labs, Inc., 429 F.3d 1052, 1070 (Fed. Cir. 2005).

[67]IPXL Holdings, LLC v. Amazon.com, Inc., 430 F.3d 1377, 1380 (Fed. Cir. 2005).

[68]Board of Educ. v. Am. Bioscience, Inc., 333 F.3d 1330, 1337 (Fed. Cir. 2003).

[69]Innovative Scuba Concepts, Inc. v. Feder Indus., Inc., 26 F.3d 1112, 1115 (Fed. Cir. 1994).

[70]*Invitrogen Corp.*, 429 F.3d at 1063.

[71]Fujikawa v. Wattanasin, 93 F.3d 1559, 1564 (Fed. Cir. 1996).

[72]Micro Chem., Inc. v. Lextron, Inc., 318 F.3d 1119, 1122 (Fed. Cir. 2003).

[73]Nobelpharma AB v. Implant Innovations, Inc., 141 F.3d 1059, 1068 (Fed. Cir. 1998) (en banc).

[74]Golden Blount, Inc. v. Robert H. Peterson Co., 438 F.3d 1354, 1359 (Fed. Cir. 2006).

[75]Brooktree Corp. v. Advanced Micro Devices, Inc., 977 F.2d 1555, 1571 (Fed. Cir. 1992).

[76]Sentry Prot. Prods., Inc. v. Eagle Mfg. Co., 400 F.3d 910, 914 (Fed. Cir. 2005).

[77]Minco, Inc. v. Combustion Eng'g, Inc., 95 F.3d 1109, 1115 (Fed. Cir. 1996).

[78]Koito Mfg. Co. v. Turn-Key-Tech, LLC, 381 F.3d 1142, 1149 (Fed. Cir. 2004).

[79]Purdue Pharma L.P. v. Endo Pharms., Inc., 438 F.3d 1123, 1129 (Fed. Cir. 2006).

[80]Windsurfing Int'l, Inc. v. AMF, Inc., 782 F.2d 995, 1001–02 (Fed. Cir. 1986).

[81]Unisplay S.A. v. Am. Elec. Sign Co., 69 F.3d 512, 517 (Fed. Cir. 1995).

[82]Vulcan Eng'g Co. v. Fata Aluminum, Inc., 278 F.3d 1366, 1376 (Fed. Cir. 2002).

[83]*Golden Blount*, 438 F.3d at 1359–60.

[84]Cybor Corp. v. FAS Techs., Inc., 138 F.3d 1448, 1459 (Fed. Cir. 1998) (en banc).

[85]*Vulcan Eng'g*, 278 F.3d at 1372.

as enablement,[86] and priority, conception, and reduction-to-practice determinations.[87]

The Federal Circuit uses an abuse-of-discretion standard to review an inequitable conduct determination,[88] the methodology used to calculate lost profits[89] and reasonable royalties,[90] an award of attorneys' fees,[91] and the grant or denial of an injunction.[92]

III. Governing Law

The Federal Circuit has held that, for all substantive issues of patent law that are within its exclusive jurisdiction, it will apply its own law as binding authority.[93] However, the Federal Circuit applies regional circuit law to procedural issues so long as they do not (1) pertain to patent law; (2) bear an essential relationship to matters committed to its exclusive control by statute; or (3) clearly implicate the jurisprudential responsibilities of the Federal Circuit in a field within its exclusive jurisdiction.[94]

The Federal Circuit has adopted the precedents of the U.S. Court of Customs and Patent Appeals and the U.S. Court of Claims as binding precedents on the court.[95]

---

[86]Plant Genetic Sys., N.V. v. DeKalb Genetics Corp., 315 F.3d 1335, 1339 (Fed. Cir. 2003).

[87]Hitzeman v. Rutter, 243 F.3d 1345, 1353 (Fed. Cir. 2001).

[88]*Purdue Pharma,* 438 F.3d at 1129.

[89]Micro Chem., Inc. v. Lextron, Inc., 318 F.3d 1119, 1122 (Fed. Cir. 2003).

[90]SmithKline Diagnostics, Inc. v. Helena Labs. Corp., 926 F.2d 1161, 1164 (Fed. Cir. 1991).

[91]Cybor Corp. v. FAS Techs., Inc., 138 F.3d 1448, 1459 (Fed. Cir. 1998) (en banc).

[92]Oakley, Inc. v. Sunglass Hut Int'l, 316 F.3d 1331, 1339 (Fed. Cir. 2003).

[93]Golan v. Pingel Enter., Inc., 310 F.3d 1360, 1368 (Fed. Cir. 2002).

[94]Int'l Nutrition Co. v. Horphag Research Ltd., 257 F.3d 1324, 1328 (Fed. Cir. 2001).

[95]South Corp. v. United States, 690 F.2d 1368, 1369–70 (Fed. Cir. 1982) (en banc).

IV. Remand

A change in the claim construction at the appellate level generally necessitates a remand to the district court to resolve any new factual issues raised by the new claim construction.[96] Nonetheless, if the evidence submitted by the patentee during trial was insufficient to prove infringement under the proper claim construction, and the patentee had notice of the claim construction being advocated by the alleged infringer, then reversal, not remand, is warranted.[97]

---

[96]Electra Scientific Indus., Inc. v. Dynamic Details, Inc., 307 F.3d 1343, 1350 (Fed. Cir. 2002).

[97]CVI/Beta Ventures, Inc. v. Tura LP, 112 F.3d 1146, 1161–62 (Fed. Cir. 1997).

17

Trial of a Patent Case in Canada*

*The Hon. Roger T. Hughes, Justice of the Federal Court of Canada, Ottawa, Ontario and revised and updated in 2012 by Ronald E. Dimock, FACTL, of Dimock Stratton LLP of Toronto.

I. Overview

Patent litigation in the Canadian courts has many of the same attributes of such litigation in the United States and as in other jurisdictions having Anglo-American heritage such as Great Britain, Australia and New Zealand. The complex interaction of science and law has created a special category of practice and jurisprudence grafted onto the more general practice and jurisprudence of the courts arising in complex civil litigation. A specialized bar has developed, knowledgeable in this area, and, given the usually high stakes in money and the marketplace, that bar is known to press at the limits of procedure and jurisprudence, requiring constant vigilance from the courts and creating difficulties for lawyers who, while often highly skilled, may not have previously encountered this particular area of the law.

Among the more prominent differences between U.S. and Canadian practices are:

- Most patent litigation is conducted in the Federal Court of Canada, which has no juries; all trials are by a judge alone.
- There is no forum shopping. The trial will be conducted by one of the 30 or so judges of the Federal Court regardless of where the proceedings were started or the parties reside.
- There is no *Markman* hearing; patent claims are construed as part of the trial itself.
- Motions for summary judgment are rarely used and are rarely successful.
- There is no deposition practice; discovery of an adverse party is akin to the United States Rule 30(b)(vi) deposition of a corporate representative.
- Normally a lawsuit is bifurcated so that the issues of extent of infringement and monetary relief are deferred to a reference after the initial trial on the issues of infringement and validity.
- There are no expert depositions prior to trial; experts may be cross-examined at trial on all issues within their exertise and beyond what is in their evidence in chief.
- A whole area of patent litigation exists under the *Patented Medicines (Notice of Compliance) Regulations*,[1] which are imper-

[1]SOR/93-133. Unofficial version available online at http://laws.justice.gc.ca/en/ShowFullDoc/cs/SOR-93-133///en.

fectly modeled after the United States *Hatch-Waxman Act*.[2] These proceedings ("NOC proceedings") are discussed below in more detail, but they occupy a huge amount of the Federal Court's calendar in dealing with patent litigation. These proceedings are conducted by way of an application; evidence is by affidavit and out of court cross-examination. A decision must be given within two years from the date the proceedings are instituted.

II The Canadian Patent System

The Canadian Patent system today is similar to that of the United States and Europe. Effective October 1, 1989, significant changes were made to the Canadian Patent Act[3] so that care must be taken in distinguishing patents issuing from applications filed in the Canadian Patent Office before that date ("Old" Act patents) and those issuing from applications filed in the Canadian Patent Office after that date ("New" Act patents).

An "Old" Act patent has a term of 17 years from the date it was granted (it may have taken several years between the time the application was filed and the patent was granted). An early date of invention prior to the filing of an application may be established in evidence where "obviousness" is challenged; the patent is to be construed as of the date of its grant, and remedies can be awarded only after the grant of the patent. A "New" Act patent has a term of 20 years from the date that the application was filed in the Canadian Patent Office. The application is made public 18 months after the filing of the application in Canada (or if an earlier application was filed elsewhere upon which priority is claimed, then from that earlier date or at an even earlier date if the patent applicant so instructs the Patent Office). The patent is construed as of its publication date, and damages by way of reasonable compensation can be awarded in certain circumstances, going back to the date of publication.

---

[2]Drug Price Competition and Patent Term Restoration Act of 1984, Pub. L. No. 98-417, 98 Stat. 1585 (1984) (codified as amended 21 U.S.C. §355 (1994)).

[3]R.S.C. 1985, c. P-4. Unofficial version available online at http://laws.justice.gc.ca/en/ShowFullDoc/cs/P-4///en.

A patent cannot be enforced until it is granted. Only Canadian patents can be enforced in Canada. Foreign patents, for instance United States patents, have no validity or effect in Canada and cannot be enforced in Canadian courts.

III. The Canadian Court System

Patents may be enforced in the Federal Court or in a superior court of any one of the 10 provinces or three territories of Canada.

Provincial and territorial superior courts have jurisdiction over patent matters if there is a sufficient connection between the proceedings and the province or territory. The Federal Court has jurisdiction in respect of the whole of Canada and has jurisdiction in respect of activity taking place anywhere in the country.

Provincial and territorial courts do, on rare occasions, hear patent trials. These courts can give all the usual remedies if infringement is found. If a defense of invalidity is raised, those courts may determine the matter, but the determination is binding only on the parties. The Federal Court may give all the usual remedies for infringement. Where a defense or counterclaim as to invalidity is raised in the Federal Court, a finding of invalidity will result in an expungement of the patent or claims held to be invalid. Thus a judgment of invalidity in the Federal Court is in rem and affects not only the parties but the patent itself.

IV. Anatomy of a Patent Case for Novices

The "Anatomy" found in Chapter 1 can, in many respects serve equally well for Canadian purposes. The structure of a patent, disclosure, drawings, and claims are essentially the same. The approach to how the patent (and in particular the claims) is understood is different, however, particularly in the use of language to define certain concepts. The results nevertheless are often the same.

In both Canada and the United States, the claims of a patent define the monopoly. A patent may have many claims, some very broadly drafted, others more narrowly; some may be directed to a device; and others directed to use of the device; yet others may be directed to how to make the device.

The patent and its claims are usually drafted by specialists qualified as "patent agents" whose task is to secure as broad of a monopoly within the claims as possible, while keeping the claim valid. The Patent Act requires that a claim set out "distinctly and in explicit terms" the invention for which a monopoly is sought.[4] Thus, a claim is a monopoly, described in the inventor's own language, assisted by patent agents. If the monopoly is described in terms that do not encompass the whole invention, the rest is considered to be public property. If the monopoly described goes beyond the invention as disclosed in the patent so as to include something old, or useless or beyond what was invented and described, the claim is invalid and cannot be enforced, even if only part of it goes too far. For this reason, most patents have many claims, each describing the invention in different ways and in broader or narrower language.

To distinguish how Canadian courts interpret claims differently than United States courts, the following are the more important differences:

- Canadian courts look to the patent alone in the context of the common general knowledge in the relevant art in seeking the proper meaning of the claims. United States courts also look at the "file wrapper," which is the history of discussions between the U.S. Patent & Trademark Office and the inventor or, more likely, the inventor's patent agent. While various attempts have been made to put both Canadian and foreign "file wrappers" before a Canadian court as an aide to interpretation of the claims, Canadian courts at the highest level have resisted doing so.[5] Other extrinsic evidence, such as an inventor's note, is also inadmissible for claim construction.
- United States courts use words like "doctrine of equivalents" to deal with interpretation of a claim in a way such that a strictly literal interpretation can be avoided in order to deal with alleged infringement and validity issues. While Canadian courts may occasionally use a word such as "equivalents" the common language used is "essential" and "non-essential" elements of a claim. Essential elements

---

[4]R.S.C. 1985, c. P-4, s. 27(4).

[5]Free World Trust v. Électro Santé Inc., 2000 SCC 66, [2000] 2 S.C.R. 1024 at paras. 63–66.

must be strictly adhered to while some variance is permitted when considering non-essential elements. For a finding of infringement, all essential elements of the claim must be embodied in the alleged infringing activity. If an essential element is missing or varied there is no infringement.
- Since the October 1, 1989 amendments to the Patent Act, a patent owner or any other interested person can seek to have a patent "re-examined" by the Patent Office, usually because some piece(s) of prior art has come to light which may require amendment to the claims. Re-examination is rarely sought by a third party because that person, once re-examination is requested, has no official role in continued dialogue with the Patent Office; only the patent owner and the owners' patent agent have that right. If validity is challenged in the court by a third party, then, of course, the third party has all the usual rights of a party litigant in bringing evidence, challenging the evidence of others, and arguing its case.

The principles of claim construction as approached by the Canadian courts in most cases are as follows:[6]

- Claim construction is for the judge alone to decide, as a question of law, and evidence, even expert evidence, is not admissible in this respect except for limited exceptions where it is necessary to explain the meaning of technical words or expressions.
- The claim is to be construed through the eyes of a "person skilled in the art to which the patent pertains" as of the date of publication of the application ("New" Act patents) or the date of its grant ("Old" Act patents).
- The "person skilled in the art" is considered to be reasonably well read in the field and reasonably competent to carry on a task in that field.
- The court is to consider a claim in light of what is disclosed in the rest of the patent, that is, the descriptions and drawings if any, but should not limit itself just to specific examples given if the patent, reasonably read, extends more broadly than the specific examples; and

---

[6]Free World Trust v. Électro Santé Inc., 2000 SCC 66, [2000] 2 S.C.R. 1024; Whirlpool Corp. v. Camco, Inc., 2000 SCC 67, [2000] 2 S.C.R. 1067.

- The claim is to be read "purposively" with a view to determining that it should be read so as to cover what the inventor has fairly disclosed in the patent as being the invention.

Canadian courts will not determine claim construction in advance of the trial. It is an integral part of the trial process. Construction is given as part of the Reasons for Judgment. In this way, Canadian courts are acting in the same way as, for instance, the courts of Great Britain, Australia, and New Zealand.

V. Pleadings

A. *Statement of Claim*

An action for patent infringement or for a declaration as to invalidity and for non-infringement is usually brought in the Federal Court. Only the Federal Court can make a declaration as to invalidity binding on the patent itself.

The Statement of Claim follows the usual rules of draftsmanship as in any other civil action. Usually it is quite detailed and should set out:

- *The parties.* The owner of the patent must be a party to the litigation. A licensee, exclusive or not, has the right to sue for damages. Foreign and domestic defendants can be named. Defendants may include all those who infringe directly by making, using or selling the invention of the patent as well as those who so induce and influence others to infringe.
- *The infringement.* The infringement must be specified with reference to the pertinent claims of the patent. A person who makes, imports, uses or sells to others an infringing product or practices an infringing process or imports into Canada a product made abroad that would, if practiced in Canada, infringe is an infringer. A person who induces infringement by knowingly selling essential components to another who commits an infringement is (by jurisprudence) an infringer. The area of inducement is evolving on a case-by-case basis. A good pleading should specify what claims are infringed and set out a comparative table showing on the one hand the elements of the claim and on

the other hand what the defendant(s) are alleged to have done. Such pleading, however, is not always done in the first instance, provoking motions by the defendant for particulars or pre-trial orders requiring a pleading like this to be set aside.

- *The relief sought.* Often a claim just for "damages or profits" is made leaving the exact amount, particularly in the case of ongoing infringement, to be determined later. The word of an accounting of profits made by the infringer is discretionary and if so granted, the plaintiff may eventually choose between the taking of damages or profits. Damages can take the form of a reasonable royalty and lost profits as would be the case in the United States. An injunction is usually sought, as well as delivery up of any infringing material owned or controlled by the defendant. While punitive or exemplary damages may be claimed, they are rarely if ever granted except for outrageous conduct by a defendant in the course of the litigation, such as breach of an injunction. Pre- and post-judgment interest is claimed in respect of any monetary award. There is no multiplying of damages for willful infringement. Pre-judgment interest is usually awarded at the level of 1 percent above the prevailing prime bank lending rate not compounded at the time judgment is rendered. Post-judgment interest is governed by the Interest Act[7] and is fixed at 5 percent not compounded. Costs are claimed.

B. *Defense (and Counterclaim)*

A defendant in the United States will have 40 days. or 60 days with the consent of the plaintiff to deliver its defense. A defendant may enter a general denial as to infringement but normally, before trial, particulars as to non-infringement must be given.

It is usual to challenge the validity of the patent, in which case the defense must be very specific. Often a defense is coupled with a counterclaim in which a declaration as to invalidity is requested in the prayer for relief. If successful in a Federal Court action, the patent, or claims at issue, will be expunged from the Patent Of-

[7]R.S.C. 1985, c. I-15. Unofficial version available online at: http://laws.justice.gc.ca/en/ShowFullDoc/cs/I-15///en.

fice record. More recently, defenses and counterclaims as to anti-competitive activity under the Competition Act[8] have been raised relating to the making, in public, of false or misleading statements by the patentee about the scope of the patent or infringement by the defendant. Much more prevalent in the United States, these claims are just coming into the litigation arena in Canada.

Challenges to the validity of a patent, or specific claims, can be made on a number of grounds. These should be well particularized in the pleading and can include:

- obviousness
- lack of novelty
- insufficient disclosure
- lack of utility
- claims broader than the invention disclosed
- ambiguity
- sound prediction

Canada does not specifically have a doctrine of "inequitable conduct," which is well developed in the United States. Section 53 of the Canadian Patent Act states that a patent applicant shall not put misleading information in the petition for a patent filed with the application, but this is a very brief document and is rarely in issue. The balance of Section 53 says that a patentee shall not put more or less than is required in the patent for the purpose of misleading, however willful intent is an element of this offence. Rarely has a Section 53 allegation proved to be successful. It can be said colloquially that "what happens in the Patent Office stays in the Patent Office."

Costs will be claimed by a defendant/counterclaimant.

VI. Interlocutory Motions Respecting Pleadings

Motions attacking the soundness of the pleadings may be made, usually before a party enters its own pleading. Rarely is a well-drafted pleading struck out or, if struck out, leave to file an amended pleading is given.

---

[8]R.S.C. 1985, c. C-34. Unofficial version available online at: http://laws.justice.gc.ca/en/ShowFullDoc/cs/C-34///en.

Motions to transfer jurisdiction are unknown in the Federal Court as it is one single court.

Motions requiring particulars of pleadings are not uncommon. In such instances, the moving party bears the burden, except in obvious cases, of showing that it cannot respond to or otherwise deal with a pleading unless further and better particulars are given.

A foreign plaintiff without significant assets in Canada may be required to post security for costs. Sometimes cash is posted with the court, but more frequently a bond or letter of credit is provided. Costs in Canada are based on what the United States attorneys call the "English Rule" and can be significant. Thus, a requirement to post security for costs can entail a significant amount of money. Often security is posted in stages as the litigation progresses. An action to impeach a patent, similar to the DJ action in the United States, brought in a separate lawsuit and not as a counterclaim to an infringement action, also requires the posting of security for costs at the start of the lawsuit.

VII. Preliminary Injunctions

A patentee may make a motion for an injunction to restrain a defendant from certain allegedly infringing activity before trial. Such a motion is usually brought very early in the proceedings. The requirements for a preliminary injunction are similar to those in the United States.

It is an essential requirement to the granting of an injunction that the plaintiff give an undertaking backed up by security, if the plaintiff has limited means, to make good on any damages suffered by the defendant by the injunction should the defendant win at trial.

Preliminary injunctions are rarely granted in patent actions. More often the court will provide for an early trial date and case management. A defendant usually keeps a strict accounting as to its relevant activities.

VIII. Case Management

The Federal Court and most provincial and territorial superior courts provide for case management of complex civil litigation such as patent cases. This may be ordered: as a result of a request by one or all of the parties, because the action has been pending for a period of months without apparent activity, or as a result of a motion for an injunction that has been granted or denied and case management ordered.

Case management is usually conducted by a prothonotary of the Federal Court or a master of the provincial/territorial courts. The purpose of case management is: to move the case along, define the issues, resolve what can be resolved, and deal efficiently with procedural motions and like matters as they arise. There is no formal template or agenda for case management. Meetings with counsel in person or by teleconference occur on a periodic basis. Generally all procedural motions are heard by the case manager and the process for setting a motion down for hearing and the paperwork requirements are somewhat relaxed. The Federal Court does offer complimentary mediation and other ADR services to encourage the parties to settle.

Early in the case management process a tentative trial date can be set and the venue for the trial established. The Federal Court, if either side seeks an orderly process to trial, will strive to have the trial take place within two years of the start of the lawsuit. For Federal Court proceedings, the venue can be any of the major cities in Canada where the court has, or has access to, court facilities. Factors such as the location of the parties, location of counsel and convenience for witnesses are taken into account when fixing a venue. Toronto, Montreal, Ottawa, Calgary, and Vancouver are among the most common venues.

IX. Severing of Issues

It is common in patent cases that issues relating to the quantum of any award as to damages or profits be severed for determination at a later date if the patent is found to be valid and infringed. This still means that a plaintiff must show that it is entitled to an award of damages or profits; it is only the quantification that is deferred.

Severing can be done in one of two ways. The trial can be severed, which means that the trial judge must subsequently hear the matter as to quantification. On the other hand, the quantification may be referred to a "Referee" who may be for instance a prothonotary, who hears the parties and evidence as to quantification and prepares a report which is given to the trial judge for approval or other action.

Sometimes other issues, for instance anti-competitive claims, may be severed. However, issues of infringement and validity are almost always heard together.

X. Discovery

Discovery in patent cases in Canada is conducted in the same way as discovery in any other complex civil action in the chosen court. In most jurisdictions, for instance the Federal Court, discovery may be taken for an assignor of a property right at issue, even if the assignor is not a party.[9] In practice this means that the inventor(s) named in the patent can be examined for discovery, but the discovery transcript or portions thereof cannot be introduced into evidence at trial unless the inventor appears as a witness or special leave is granted.

This discovery is said to be "informational only." Some provincial superior courts permit pre-trial examination of experts who have delivered a report to a party for use at trial. The Federal Court does not.

From a United States attorney's point of view, the Canadian discovery system is quite different. It begins with a disclosure of documents limited to those documents that a party intends to use at trial to support its case or rebut its opponent's case. A more general disclosure can be sought before or during oral discovery. Oral discovery is conducted by asking questions of a single representative of the opposite party usually chosen by the party being examined. That person must provide answers or undertake to

[9] *E.g.*, Federal Courts Rules, R. 237(4).

give answers to all relevant questions whether or not the answer is within their personal knowledge. The answer is binding on the party. There is no right, except in exceptional cases, to examine any other person. Usually, discovery occurs in two or three sessions so that answers undertaken or ordered to be answered can be given at the later session. It should be noted, however, that there is an implied undertaking, not existing in the United States with respect to depositions, that information obtained through discovery cannot be used outside the specific Canadian lawsuit without leave of the court or consent of the other party. The case manager usually hears motions as to whether answers or better answers need to be provided. The answers given may, on a basis as selected by the party doing the questioning, be introduced as evidence at trial against the party who was examined. Sedona principles have been adopted in Canada for e-discovery.

XI. Pre-Trial Issues

The judge assigned to hear the trial, usually several weeks before the trial is scheduled to begin, will hold a pre-trial conference to discuss matters including:

- The number of experts each party intends to call as witnesses. The Federal Court has a limit of five experts per party, while some provincial superior courts have a limit of three per party. Courts may allow a greater number in special circumstances;
- Confidentiality of documents, evidence and argument. The normal rule is that there is no confidentiality, but the courts will take into consideration things such as trade secrets and proprietary information;
- Settling and defining of issues;
- Factual admissions and agreement as to documents to be put in evidence;
- Interpretation of evidence that is not in the French or English language;
- Provision of "real time" transcription of evidence and daily transcripts;
- Taking evidence out of the jurisdiction by way of commission or otherwise; and
- Disclosure of witnesses.

XII. The Trial

A patent trial takes place before a judge sitting alone. There are no jury trials in patent matters in Canada.

The trial begins with opening statements usually made by each party although in the Federal Court and some other courts, the defendant may defer an opening statement until it is time for the defendant to present its evidence.

The plaintiff leads with evidence first. Factual witnesses are called and examined and cross-examined orally. There is no requirement to disclose the identity of factual witnesses before they are called but most judges at pre-trial conferences will insist on such disclosure. Expert witnesses who have submitted a report or affidavit setting out in detail their evidence, findings, opinions and conclusions may be called to give evidence orally. The report (affidavit) must have been given to the other party several weeks in advance but is not read or considered by the court until it is actually put to the expert and identified and confirmed by the witness on the stand or unless the party has undertaken earlier to the court that such evidence will be tendered at trial. New Federal Court Rules include a Code of Conduct for expert witnesses to follow in preparing expert reports and testifying at trial and include provisions for having some expert testimoney, if appropriate, be given by way of a panel of experts. The expert can be asked in chief as to what is in the report so as to amplify and explain. While this exercise is intended to be brief and to let the report speak for itself, the tendency of counsel is to ask protracted questions in chief to enable the expert to advocate the court on the very technical matters. Oral cross-examination follows. Cross-examination is not limited to the report or examination in chief but may extend to any matter relevant to the issues before the court. Selected portions of the discovery may be put in evidence by the party conducting discovery. Agreed facts and documents are usually put in evidence at the beginning of a party's case.

The defendant puts in its evidence in the same manner as the plaintiff. If there is a counterclaim by the defendant, it puts in its evidence in chief in that regard.

The plaintiff replies with further evidence, and the defendant by counterclaim can reply on those issues.

Oral argument by counsel for the parties follows. Usually, each counsel prepares a written memorandum outlining the facts, issues, and legal argument which it will address. A limit of 30 pages is typical, but may be extended by the court. The memorandum is in paragraph form with points stated concisely. It does not follow the narrative form used in some United States courts. Legal authorities are cited and counsel may agree to submit a common book of authorities. Often the court will allow an interval of a few days between the end of the hearing of the evidence and presentation of argument so as to allow counsel to prepare their legal memoranda and compose their final arguments.

There is no particular limit imposed on the time for oral argument; however, the trial judge will usually, during the course of the trial, fix limits of a day or so for each party.

After hearing argument the court will almost always reserve the matter with judgment to follow at a later date.

XIII. Judgment and Post-Trial Matters

There is no fixed time within which a judge is required to deliver a judgment. It is very much an individual matter; however, a period between two to six months after argument is finished is considered to be normal. In the Federal Court, the judge often prepares the Judgment himself or herself if it is straightforward. Where the Judgment is complex, a draft may be given to counsel for comment. Often, the question of costs is reserved to be spoken to after judgment is given on the other matters. Canada has adopted what United States attorneys call the "English Rule" on costs which means that normally a winning party is allowed to recover from the losing party reasonable disbursements, including expenses for experts, together with lawyers' fees on a scale that permits recovery of usually a third to a half of actual legal costs. On occasion, increased costs to a substantial indemnity level can be awarded, but this is when a party has acted improperly in the conduct of the litigation itself.

Judgment will be delivered with detailed Reasons provided by the judge. If it is clear that the court has decided that an injunction is appropriate, that injunction must be obeyed immediately, even if only the Reasons for Judgment or a draft Judgment is provided. Instructions are given almost as a matter of course after a finding of infringement. On rare occasions, if irreparable harm is proven, the Federal Court of Appeal will stay an injunction until the appeal is heard and decided on an expedited basis.

Where a matter has been reserved for later consideration, the parties should apply for directions from the trial judge as how to proceed.

It is rare that any motion in respect of the Judgment or Reasons is brought. However if the Judgment is unclear, clarification may be sought. If some matter has been inadvertently overlooked, the court may be asked to consider and determine that matter. The usual remedy is appeal.

XIV. Appeals

An appeal from a final decision of a trial judge of the Federal Court exists as of right to the Federal Court of Appeal. Similarly, a final decision in a complex civil matter such as a patent trial in the superior court of a province or territory exists as of right to the appellate court of that province or territory. Appeals from a trial decision are usually heard within one year. Appeals from these appellate courts may be brought to the Supreme Court of Canada by way of a motion for leave (like a United States certiorari petition). The Supreme Court has discretion as to whether or not to accept the case. Usually it does not, but generally one patent case a year has been the recent record of that Court.

An appeal is taken upon the record consisting of the evidence before the trial judge. Rarely if ever does an appellate court admit further evidence. The Court of Appeal can allow or dismiss an appeal and can, if it considers it to be appropriate, modify the Judgment of the trial judge. Costs are usually awarded to the winning party on the appeal and, if the lower court is reversed, in the lower court as well, on the "English Rule."

XV. NOC Proceedings

A unique form of patent proceedings involving patents for medicines or use of a medicine was established in 1993 by the

Patented Medicines (Notice of Compliance) Regulations,[10] often referred to as NOC proceedings. These NOC Regulations were imperfectly modeled after the United States Hatch-Waxman Act[11] and are intended to deal with situations where generic drug companies are seeking approval to market copies of patented drugs in Canada by simply referencing much of the safety and efficacy data already submitted by the innovator company to the Canadian health authorities.

In general the NOC Regulations allow an innovator company that owns or is licensed to use a patent to list that patent on a list maintained by the Minister of Health in respect to the drug in question. The patent must bear some relationship to the drug approved by the Minister for sale by the innovator.

A generic who wishes to copy the innovator's drug and simply reference much of the data submitted by the innovator must send a letter, called a Notice of Allegation, to the innovator in respect to all listed patents. This letter must state, in great detail, why a listed patent is not infringed or is invalid, or that the generic has a license or will wait until the patent expires. On receipt of such Notice, the innovator may launch proceedings in the Federal Court by way of a Notice of Application, taking issue with any or all matters raised in the Notice of Allegation and requesting that the Minister not issue any approval to the generic to market its drug in Canada. Once the application is filed, a 24-month freeze is put on the generic's application.

The generic cannot amend its Notice of Allegation, but it can submit a new one. If it does, the innovator can file a new application and get a new 24-month freeze.

All NOC proceedings are now case managed, since a final decision of the Federal Court has to be given within 24 months from the date the application was filed. The parties can agree to extend that time but seldom do.

Evidence is provided by affidavit, cross-examination may be taken, and a transcript provided to the court. Only five experts per party are allowed without leave of the Court.

---

[10]SOR/93-133.

[11]Drug Price Competition and Patent Term Restoration Act of 1984, Pub. L. No. 98-417, 98 Stat. 1585 (1984) (codified as amended 21 U.S.C. §355 (1994)).

The matter is set down for a hearing that proceeds on the basis of a record of the affidavit evidence and cross-examination and written argument of the parties. Counsel argues the matter in court usually for two to four days in all. A Judgment with Reasons for Judgment before the end of the 24–month deadline is delivered. If the generic prevails, it usually receives permission to market its drug from the Minister that same day, which, as a practical matter, means that the Federal Court of Appeal will not hear an appeal since the matter sought to be prohibited has already occurred and an appeal is moot. If the generic loses, the Court of Appeal will hear the matter if it is appealed.

Table of Cases

References are to chapter and footnote number (e.g., ***5:*** 12, 13; ***10:*** 6 *refers to footnotes 12 and 13 in Chapter 5 and footnote 6 in Chapter 10). Alphabetization is letter-by-letter (e.g., "Newman" precedes "New Railhead Mfg.").*

B

C

H

I

J

K

L

M

P

U

V

W

X

Z

Index

*References are to chapters and section numbers (e.g., **5:** II.B.4; **17:** V.B refers to section II.B.4 in Chapter 5 and to section V.B in Chapter 17).*

D

J